A
COMMUNITY
of
INQUIRY

Conversations Between
Classical American Philosophy
and American Literature

PATRICK K. DOOLEY

The Kent State University Press
Kent, Ohio

© 2008 by The Kent State University Press, Kent, Ohio 44242
ALL RIGHTS RESERVED
Library of Congress Catalog Card Number 2007044974
ISBN 978-0-87338-915-0
Manufactured in the United States of America

LIBRARY OF CONGRESS CATALOGING-IN-PUBLICATION DATA
Dooley, Patrick Kiaran.
    A community of inquiry : conversations between classical American philosophy
and American literature / Patrick K. Dooley.
    p.   cm.
    Includes bibliographical references and index.
    ISBN 978-0-87338-915-0 (pbk.. : alk. paper) ∞
    1. Philosophy in literaature. 2. American literature—19th century—History and
criticism. 3. American literature—20th century—History and criticism. 4. Literature—
Philosophy. 5. Philosophy, American—19th century. 6. Philosophy, American—20th
century. I. Title.
    PS217.P45D66 2008
    810.9'384—dc22   2007044974

British Library Cataloging-in-Publication data are available.

12 11 10 09 08   5 4 3 2 1

A COMMUNITY *of* INQUIRY

To Gregory, Hester, Rupert, and Edith

Contents

Foreword

by Louis J. Budd and Peter H. Hare

One size fits all only in cut-rate baseball caps. When generalizing about literary critics—more specifically, my coworkers in departments of English—I'm nagged by a doubt. Actually, the most effortlessly effective metaphysician I've talked with regularly is tenured in such a department. He's as comfortable with Melville's *The Confidence-Man* as if it were a comic book. He's comfortable enough with Mark Twain's late fantasies not to be intimidated into showing that Twain coordinated the abstractions that he fired off so colorfully. Twain, he concedes in writing, would as a philosopher make a good third baseman. As for Huck Finn, he marvels at the intricate profundities with which critics almost drown a near-illiterate river rat. He interprets Wallace Stevens without cribbing from the secondary commentary that his colleagues thresh for the survey course. After I had pressed him several times as to why he had not majored in philosophy rather than belles lettres, he confessed to being tempted as a sophomore. However, judging that he would have to master Greek first, he did not want to detour for that. So my generalizing doesn't account for him. Fortunately he has an amiable sense of humor and won't grow Swiftian over my presuming to grade anybody as deficient metaphysically. Therefore, I'll harass two sizable blocs in departments of English who will benefit (as will their enrollees) from boning up on the fundamentals of philosophy, past and present.

The aesthetically committed form the most cohesive bloc. Though their profession trains them almost too well in shooting down clichés, they keep flying the banner of "art for art's sake." Not quite so rigorous as to achieve circular reasoning, they settle for definitions of "art" or "beauty" that attract sparse constituencies beyond the definer. Full disclosure requires admitting that as an undergraduate I considered myself to be majoring in philosophy until I took the course in aesthetics. It left me feeling like a blowball of a dandelion that the Walkyries had buzzed. (Germanic names dominated the textbook.) Admittedly, the aesthetic bloc favors poetry over fiction, drama, or other genres, and the psycho-emotional complexities of how the brain responds to language deployed by a genius can baffle the nimblest of metaphysicians. But the devotees or simply the purveyors of the novel could amplify their approach without stomping on the ineffable.

My wobbly stint as chair of a department confirms that. A colleague who was courteous to students, fluent in an accessible vocabulary, and as mentally alert as humans need to be asked me to block a course in the Department of Religion from assigning the classic twentieth-century American novelists—Hemingway, Fitzgerald, Faulkner, etc. Too many undergraduates were electing that course over the matching one in our department. The catalog showed that the competing course treated novels not solely as problems in aesthetic formalism but also as highly personalized displays of ethical options. Perhaps less urgently today (so I'm told), undergraduates, like the rest of us, keep asking, "How shall I live eventually?" or, more prosaically, "How should I get through the day?"

Patrick Dooley warns against narrowing philosophical discussion of literature down to practical ethics. That's sound advice. The classic, enduring novel embodies the author's rounded, innerly complex mental-emotional universe. Certainly, its epistemology emerges explicitly or by graspable implication. But (*pace* Dooley) experience has convinced me that some of my professional peers would benefit if they knew better the main campaigns of the debate, ancient and current, about ethics. For instance, they use rarified standards for judging characters—such as the tutor in Henry James's short story "The Pupil." They would benefit (as I did) from Dooley's analysis of a "supererogatory" or "heroic" ethics. I'm still grateful that I took a course in ethics. Parts of the textbook—Wilbur M. Urban's *Fundamentals of Ethics: An Introduction to Moral Philosophy* (1930)—have stayed with me. Though I confess to doubts about Urban's hortatory conclusion that "moral progress" is a "fact."

I don't presume to draw a map for anybody willing to desert the "art for art's sake" tower. Some major texts in philosophy outrun my mind, which follows Hume more easily than Hegel, Rorty more easily than Wittgenstein. Most aesthetes will think more broadly after fairly considering Simon Blackburn's luminous *Being Good: An Introduction to Ethics* (2001). Dooley himself cites Martha C. Nussbaum's *Love and Knowledge: Essays on Philosophy and Literature* (1990), which—using Henry James for its chief exhibits—demonstrates how ethics as a discipline can add a political-social dimension to the house of fiction.

However, the bloc in departments of English that stands in most need of informed philosophy is that of the fast-break metaphysicians who declaim sweepingly about personality, culture, history, or society. At least four subsets stand out, especially the heralds of "new" revelations at the cutting edge. Though they surely know elementary history, they ignore the long-running exchanges between the partisans of newness and tradition. Nevertheless, the theories sweeping out all minds that have reasoned before about their subject flash by more and more quickly. Post-colonialism, for instance, is already passé (except for a tenured rear guard).

The subset that has (re)discovered relativism—sometimes (re)packaged as social constructivism or else, militantly, as diversity—lecture us as triumphantly as if they had invented the first video game. Ignoring even the contemporaries who could enlighten them, they typically stay innocent about how Bernard Williams combines depth of learning with alertness to historical contingency and current experience. Nor have they read, probably, Thomas Nagel's reminder: "The familiar point that relativism is self-refuting remains valid in spite of its familiarity" (*The Last Word,* 15). My respect for the esprit behind the subsets championing originality concedes that Ralph Waldo Emerson was helpful when preaching that the reverend sages were once just young persons in libraries. But he did imagine them in libraries, not Starbucks. Meyer Abrams, undazzled by metacritical flights above the pull of fact as well as erudition, decided that their pilots were not "serious." He would agree with a Polish saying from the 1920s: Nobody is so avant-garde as to bring the soup spoon up to his ear.

The third subset, somewhat amorphous, has discovered the black hole of subjectivity without help from Plato on down, even Bishop Berkeley. Certifying their discovery as postmodern, they need not pause for empiricist or realist or naturalist or positivist roadblocks. They can sweep on to connecting with their innate identity, most attractive as the "true" self yearning to run free. No need to comprehend those pragmatist philosophers who suggest that the self is formed socially through interaction with stubborn experience. No need to slog through George Herbert Mead's analyses of how self-imaging develops.

The fourth, final subset, enviable for its shortcut to universality, has decided that all preceding generalizations naively—even cloddishly—believed that language is directly referential, that most users of words accept them as mirrors of reality. With unintended humor, this approach proclaims that both speech and writing convey merely some groping toward meaning, which flickers in the interstices. Rather than researching counterarguments, I prefer to enjoy listening to this subset agree that the school of Derrida, say, has precisely proved the case against literalism. Now, of course, I have segued into elementary logic rather than what literary specialists could learn from knowing at least the basic arguments among epistemologists about referentiality.

Deftly mediating between mental worlds, Dooley counsels that philosophers can learn from the personalized experiences created through belles lettres. Wallace Stevens reminds us all: "In a village of the indigines, / One would have still to discover. Among the dogs and dung, / One would continue to contend with one's ideas" ("The Glass of Water"). I could quote likewise from G. M. Hopkins, W. B. Yeats, and Robert Frost. For many of us fiction can still more effectively project abstract ideas through pulsating human shapes. Overall I've been agitating for my departmental peers to add metaphysical breadth, perspective, and finesse to their pronouncements. They could start by visiting more often *Philosophy and Literature,* which does include two of our own superstars—Marjorie Perloff and Frederick Crews—on its board of editors. Elsewhere, Crews urges his colleagues to learn from the rigorous historical discipline of empiricism. Sufficiently educated humanists don't have to huddle in Plato's cave, and the weather outside can invigorate them.

Admittedly, I've explored merely the shallows of the teeming sea of philosophy while wearing water wings. Emboldened by reading Dooley, my colleagues and I should swim farther, dive deeper.

Louis J. Budd

The scale of American culture during the "conversation" between philosophy and literature that Patrick Dooley so vividly describes in this book was radically different from what it is today. How small our "cultural matrix" was in the late nineteenth and early twentieth centuries was first brought home to me in 1960 when I interviewed Wilmon Sheldon in his Yale office. Knowing that Sheldon had been an undergraduate and graduate student at Harvard in the 1890s, receiving his doctorate under Josiah Royce in 1899, I peppered him with questions about which philosophers he was personally acquainted with. "Did you know James Edwin Creighton?" "Do you recall much about Arthur O. Lovejoy?" "Do you remember any conversations with William Pepperell Montague?" After regaling me with anecdotes about philosopher after philosopher, he began to show signs of exasperation. "Hare! Why are you so surprised that I knew all these people? What you don't understand is that, when I became APA president, I knew personally *every* member of the Association. In fact, I got drunk with every member!"

Sheldon's fondness for liquor and conversation was legendary. On his retirement, an old friend wrote him, "I could never match your unrivalled Socratic ability to enjoy the spirit of alcohol while discoursing shrewdly and humorously about life and nature." And a younger friend observed, "Like Socrates, you can spend a happy evening and see most philosophers my age under the table."

In that period even philosophers less liquidly gregarious than Sheldon had little difficulty being friends with every philosopher in America. Abraham Edel recalled that, as late as the beginning of the 1930s, "We sat at a common table for the [APA] dinner—all of us—and [Alfred North] Whitehead read his presidential address." Today that would be physically impossible. By some estimates, there are now more than 10,000 people trying to make a living teaching philosophy.

In terms of publications also, in literature and philosophy, the cultural world of Stephen Crane, Jack London, and William James was tiny compared to what it is today. There were only a handful of general periodicals such as *The Atlantic Monthly* and *The Nation,* and every seriously literate person was expected to be able to discuss their contents. Although novels were an important part of the American scene, there were not so many published that everyone couldn't share familiarity with them all. In philosophy, even a modestly ambitious scholar would have been disgraced at an APA "smoker" if conversation revealed his ignorance of *any* volume published in the previous year. In 1913, heaven help anyone who could not explain what aspects of William Ernest Hocking's *The Meaning of God in Human Experience* were owed to the influence of Josiah Royce and what were owed to his study with James.

Not only was the scale of the cultural world Dooley discusses different, there were not the sharp divisions among science, literature, mathematics, art, and philosophy that we have come to take for granted in our day. James in *The Principles of Psychology* (1890) thinks nothing of quoting from Virgil's *Aeneid* in Latin. He also quotes at length Jane Austen's description of Miss Bates in *Emma,* appeals to Robert Browning's poetry when expounding the nature of space-relations, cites the novelist Samuel Butler in explaining how necessary truths are related to experience, and draws on Mozart, Shakespeare, Dante, Dumas, Goethe, Coleridge, and William Dean Howells on a wide range of topics. William James weaves together experimental psychology and references to novels, plays, symphonies, and poems. What was marketed by his publisher, Holt, as a textbook in psychology, in some respects had more in common with Herman Melville's *Moby-Dick* than with conventional textbooks. James's masterpiece was no more just a book of scientific psychology than *Moby-Dick* was only a fictional narrative of the sea. Melville mingled marine biology, geography, theology, metaphysics, lexicography, ethnic studies, cultural anthropology, Shakespeare, and oceanography with the high drama of a whaling voyage.

I like to quip, only half in jest, that *The Principles* was William James's attempt—in competition with his brother Henry—to write the great American novel. In *The Principles* and *Moby-Dick,* James and Melville both tell "The Story of the Human Condition"—neither book in a recognizable genre. Through Ishmael Melville tries to make sense of a bizarre cast of characters who find themselves imprisoned on a ship whose sole purpose is the mad one of killing a mysterious white whale. James narrates the intellectual journey of a huge cast of psychologists/philosophers imprisoned in the mad task of understanding the mystery of human consciousness. James cherishes each of these psychologists/philosophers as a *character* as well as an intellect. He cherishes also their styles of expressing themselves. All are given ample opportunity to deliver soliloquies—some pedantic, some pompous, some glib, some lyrical, some petty, some heroic, etc. On board the *Pequod* we find all the human flotsam and jetsam of the nineteenth-century nautical world. On board *The Principles* we find all the human flotsam and jetsam of the nineteenth-century world of psychology/philosophy.

Just as freely, James's lifelong friend and collaborator in founding pragmatism Charles Sanders Peirce crossed boundaries. Often, on a sheet of paper filled with his mathematical calculations can be found a line or two of poetry. Josiah Royce, the close friend of Peirce and James, published a novel, *The Feud of Oakfield Creek,* after he joined the *philosophy* and *psychology* faculty at Harvard in 1882. George Santayana, a philosophy student of James and Royce, crossed boundaries of discipline and genre even more radically than his teachers by producing a volume of poetry before publishing any philosophy books. He was awarded a Pulitzer Prize in literature.

I applaud the novel ways in which Dooley brings to life the interchanges between philosophy and literature in America during this period. Although numerous literary scholars have published in this field, Dooley is, to my knowledge, the first professional philosopher to make a major contribution. As a philosopher thoroughly trained in the American tradition, Dooley is able to highlight features of the conversation hitherto neglected by those with literary training—notably the epistemological and metaphysical aspects. However, Joan Richardson's recently published *A Natural History of Pragmatism: The Fact of Feeling from Jonathan Edwards to Gertrude Stein* may be a harbinger of a wave of studies by literary scholars and historians that give serious attention to problems of knowledge and reality. Dooley and Richardson represent, I hope, the beginning of a trend.

It is also my hope that this work—and the historical work outside the American tradition by Martha Nussbaum as well as those who publish in *Philosophy and Literature*—will encourage conversation between *current* literature and *current* philosophy. But I fear this is wishful thinking. If there is to be a revival of the energetic and culturewide conversation of 1890–1920 between philosophy and literature, center stage will be taken by TV, movies, and the Internet. In that earlier period, novels by such writers as Willa Cather and the poetry of Walt Whitman dominated popular culture as well as high culture.

Let me offer an illustration from my personal experience. In 1999 William Irwin (who a few years before studied Jean-Paul Sartre's novels, plays, and philosophy with me) inaugurated a book series in "Philosophy and Popular Culture." His first edited volume in the series was *Seinfeld and Philosophy: A Book about Everything and Nothing*. That volume has sold 250,000 copies and is still selling briskly. Later books in the series such as *The Sopranos and Philosophy: I Kill Therefore I Am* (for which I was persuaded to contribute an essay) have not done so handsomely, but the series as a whole has had sales in the millions. Irwin's book series, a mass culture phenomenon as well as reading assigned in college courses, is squarely in the middle of today's most lively conversation between philosophy and literature.

Here is another autobiographical illustration of how conversation in mass culture often trumps traditional academic scholarship. Last year I received a frantic e-mail from an entertainment reporter for a Canadian newspaper. The reporter was in Los Angeles attending a press conference held by David Milch (of *Hill Street Blues, NYPD Blue,* and *Deadwood*) to announce his new HBO drama series, *John from Cincinnati*. The 200 reporters in attendance were flummoxed by Milch's unwillingness to answer their specific questions. Instead, he rambled on about how the philosopher/psychologist William James had always served as his life guide. Milch offered a detailed exposition of James's philosophy and quoted James at length from memory. This reporter and many of his colleagues were incredulous. Did Milch really know and care that much about a philosopher/psychologist who has been dead for nearly a century? Disgorging his notes in e-mail, the Canadian reporter demanded that I, as current president of the William James Society, tell him whether Milch's exposition was accurate and whether the quotation from memory was word perfect. Thirty minutes later I assured him that the exposition was faithful and the quotation contained only inconsequential inaccuracies. The quotation was from "Is Life Worth Living?": "If this life be not a real fight, in which something is eternally gained for the universe by success, it is no better than a game of theatricals from which one may withdraw at will. But it *feels* like a real fight." I had checked the quotation in the critical edition of *The Will to Believe* published by Harvard University Press. After a hasty e-mail thank you, I didn't hear from the reporter for a couple of days—when he wrote to tell me that before his article had been published his editor, after consulting a copy of James's essay, had corrected my version of the quotation. Miffed, I e-mailed the reporter to ask him to tell his editor: "Obviously, you consulted a corrupted edition of the essay. What I sent your reporter was a careful transcription from the authoritative critical edition published by Harvard University Press." No apologies were forthcoming.

My point in telling this anecdote is that mass culture often trumps academic scholarship. I'm sure that Patrick Dooley joins me in hoping that in the near future conversation between philosophy and literature comes to flourish in *both* mass and high culture.

PETER H. HARE

Acknowledgments

This has been a longer-term project than I ever dreamt. As I note below, part of my participation in a National Endowment for the Humanities Summer Seminar in 1978 was a short presentation on William Dean Howells's *The Rise of Silas Lapham* and developments in nineteenth-century moral philosophy. Stuart Levine, director of the Summer Seminar, suggested I expand my presentation and submit it to *American Studies*. That article became my first foray into the literature/philosophy interface. Levine's suggestion set the pattern: virtually all the chapters in my book were similarly conference presentations which were subsequently expanded into journal articles. St. Bonaventure University has been very supportive with funds that made possible travel and time at several major libraries and also underwrote my participation in more than one hundred regional, national, and international conferences.

I am pleased to acknowledge years of friendship and support from the members of the Bonaventure philosophy department and, for their extra-mile assistance, deans of arts and sciences Jim White and Steve Stahl, academic vice-presidents John Watson and Ed Eckert, and president Bob Wickenheiser.

Beyond Bonaventure, Louis Budd and Peter Hare have been a steady source of encouragement, helpful suggestions, and informed critique. In addition, they were kind enough to engage in a written conversation that further spreads the good news that there is much to be gained by reading literature and philosophy in tandem, and so I thank them for the foreword they have provided. I was a visiting professor of English and philosophy at the United States Air Force Academy from 1996 to 1999. My office at the Academy was in the English department, where I found a congenial home and gained three valuable allies: Jim Meredith, Verner Mitchell, and Don Anderson.

No one could ask for a more patient, persistent, and prompt helper than Theresa Shaffer, who cheerfully brought me armloads of books and stacks of articles via interlibrary loan. Thanks to my sociology colleague and grammar guru, Kathy Zawicki, for her careful editing of earlier drafts of these essays. Finally I am grateful for those who make it worthwhile, our four children to whom this book is dedicated and my dear wife, Nora, for her unstinting love and encouragement.

Introduction

This work is concerned with connections between American philosophy and American literature. Its overriding thesis is that a cluster of elements normally identified as the signature components of classical American philosophy, most famously articulated by the pragmatist William James, is prominent in influential works of the American literary realists and naturalists. Other classical American philosophers, given less emphasis, are also examined in relation to turn-of the-(last)-century literary works. Finally, working from the other direction, several novels dramatizing the contested and shifting borderline between moral and heroic actions are used to critique representative nineteenth-century (nonpragmatic) American philosophers influenced by the Scottish common sense school and selected twentieth-century philosophers.

A general introduction will survey the philosophical climate in America from 1890 to 1920 and briefly explain six commonly shared commitments of the classical American philosophers (including the first-generation pragmatists C. S. Peirce, William James, and John Dewey, and the next generation of thinkers—Josiah Royce, George Herbert Mead, and George Santayana). Following the introduction, eighteen essays are grouped into four sections. Though most of the essays explore philosophical facets in literature, the conversation between American philosophy and American literature became such a richly diverse discussion on a plurality of levels and on a variety of issues that readers may want to pick and choose chapters based on their interests in specific authors, literary topics, or philosophical questions. Accordingly, the chapters are structured as self-contained essays. Nonetheless, each section features a group of essays on related themes. Indeed, some themes—notably religious experiences pragmatically interpreted and moral issues dealing with actions above and beyond the call of duty—flow through several sections.

STEPHEN CRANE: METAPHYSICAL, EPISTEMOLOGICAL, AND ETHICAL PLURALISM

The five essays in this section examine the works of Stephen Crane with an eye to perennial philosophical problems. What emerges is a striking restatement of the central tenets of the classical American pragmatists from the perspective of a very perceptive and gifted writer whose inimitable stylistic and descriptive ability offers his readers concrete, experience-funded, and vivid dramatizations of humans grappling with theoretical dilemmas and confronting existentially significant choices. Examining Crane's thought with an eye to matters philosophical reveals that he espouses views on nearly every aspect of philosophy: metaphysical commitments regarding the structure of experienced reality, epistemological stances on the nature of truth and the limitations of human knowledge, a philosophical anthropology that celebrates human freedom and the significance of individual and joint actions in an indifferent world, a social philosophy tolerant of a variety of ways of being human and being virtuous, and an ethics that offers an insightful topology on the contested and uncertain borderlines between required and optional moral actions and between heroic and foolish conduct. Furthermore, readers approaching the essays as a group should note that the sequence of topics is as traditional as the order of books in Aristotle's *Organon:* foundational inquiries about knowledge and reality give way to ethical and social philosophy, culminating in a comprehensive account of the human situation in an indifferent universe.

WILLIAM DEAN HOWELLS AND HAROLD FREDERIC: ETHICAL AND RELIGIOUS PRAGMATISM

In the three essays in this section, Howells and Frederic offer exegesis of and commentary upon developments in American philosophy during the 1890s. These novelists are paired because of the warm personal relationship between them, and because both offered criticisms of the views of their philosophical contemporaries.

Harold Frederic was strongly influenced by William Dean Howells's prescriptions regarding realistic fiction, and Howells thought highly of Frederic's work. They exchanged letters, reviewed each other's work, and met briefly in 1890.[1] With reference to *The Rise of Silas Lapham,* Frederic wrote to Howells on May 5, 1885:

At a private dinner here last evening, confined to some dozen professional men of whom I was the only American, the talk turned upon "The Rise of Silas Lapham", and the expressions of delight in it, and of admiration for it were so cordial and warm that I yield to the temptation to write to you about them. The guests were mostly men of distinction—artists, writers, scientists and so on—and were certainly all men of fine discernment in literature. They talked a long time, upon many subjects, but upon nothing else was there nearly so much unanimity expressed or feeling shown, as upon the proposition that in choice shading of character, in deftness of analysis of motives and feelings, and in the quality of life in dialogue, the work marked a distinct advance step in fiction.

They were not able to understand as well as I do, I think, how much more there is in the story—to realize that it means the scrutiny of a master turned for almost the first time upon what is the most distinctive phase of American folk-life, but their praise was good to hear, all the same. (1977, 58)

On *The Damnation of Theron Ware,* Howells commented:

I will tell you of some novels I have been recently reading, and like very much. I like "The Damnation of Theron Ware." I think that a very well imagined book. It treats of middle New York State life at the present day, such as Mr. Frederic had treated before, in "Seth's Brother's Wife," and in "The Lawton Girl." I was particularly interested in the book, for when you get to the end, although you have carried a hazy notion in your mind of the sort of man Ware was, you fully realize, for the first time, that the author has never for a moment represented him anywhere to you as a good or honest man, or as anything but a very selfish man. (1897, 23–24)

In addition to having high regard for each other's works, Howells and Frederic are not just aware of developments in American philosophy, they also take the next step in offering astute critique and commentary via their fiction. The first two essays examine, in detail, how *The Rise of Silas Lapham* treats the emergence of a business ethic in late nineteenth-century America and how, in light of developments in early or later ethical thought, the same actions (by Lapham and Rogers) can be either required matters of duty or optional deeds of heroism. The third essay examines Frederic's exploration of the risk and reward of reducing religious belief to its pragmatic utility.

William James, Theodore Roosevelt, Jack London, and Frank Norris: Heroism and the Strenuous Mood

The essays in this section discuss personality formation and character change from psychological, ethical, and political perspectives. "Habit" was easily the most influential chapter of William James's most popular work, *The Principles of Psychology*. The third essay in this section shows how Jack London's short story of character building and conversion, "South of the Slot," embodies James's synopsis of his own theory: "Sow an action, and you reap a habit; sow a habit and you reap a character; sow a character and you reap a destiny."[2]

The character transformation that turn-of-the-(last)-century American intellectuals thought particularly important for America's national destiny was for their fellow citizens to trade lives of ease and comfort for the risks, dangers, and hardiness of the strenuous life. Still, since not all forms of strenuousness are morally beneficial and socially sound, a debate emerged over higher and lower forms of strenuousness and over the personality traits of saints and strongmen. The debaters in the first two essays are James and Theodore Roosevelt,[3] and then James and Jack London. The fourth essay examines Frank Norris's careful diagnosis of the differences between muscular and moral heroism, and genuine courage and bogus bravery.

Willa Cather, John Steinbeck, and Norman Maclean: Temperament, Memory, Community, and Work

The six essays in the final section explore philosophical themes in Willa Cather, a writer barely contemporaneous with the high point of classical American philosophy, and two others—John Steinbeck and Norman Maclean—who were members of the next generation.

Willa Cather was managing editor of *McClure's* when it published (six months after his death) William James's celebrated "The Moral Equivalent of War." In addition, she was a regular participant in Viola Roseboro's discussion group, which worked through James's *The Principles of Psychology* and *The Varieties of Religious Experience*.[4] (Roseboro and Cather were both editors at *McClure's*.)

Several aspects of the works of both James and Royce disclose important philosophical themes in Steinbeck. In *The Grapes of Wrath*, Steinbeck offers an indirect but instantly recognizable tribute to the first philosopher.

Recall that during the first day of the Joads' western errand, Grampa has a stroke. That night he dies, and his body is buried with a note in a Mason jar wrapped in a quilt. The note says, "This here is William James Joad, dyed of a stroke, old, old man. His fokes bured him because they got no money to pay for funerls" (Steinbeck 1939, 194). With regard to the second philosopher, I show how neatly Steinbeck's skillful narration and Royce's abstract theorizing about community-building dovetail.

As for Maclean, I explore how Royce, Dewey, and Mead offer insightful cues to Maclean's treatment of work, friendship, and community. Above all, this final group of essays demonstrates that the pervasive and seminal impact of classical American philosophy continued to strongly influence early and mid-twentieth-century American writers.

RECENT DEVELOPMENTS IN THE ANCIENT ENMITY BETWEEN PHILOSOPHY AND LITERATURE

In the tenth and last book of the *Republic,* Plato's Socrates recounts that "there has been from old a quarrel between philosophy and poetry" and claims that he has sound reasons for exiling poets from his ideal city. In the nearly 2,500 years since then, philosophers and poets have, in the words of Karl Marx, "stood in constant opposition to one another, carried on an uninterrupted, now hidden, now open fight" (1848, 9). Of course, in his *Communist Manifesto* Marx was referring to the bourgeois and proletariat as the rival partners, but there is little doubt that the intellectual warfare between philosophy and literature has been intense, nasty, and damaging, too. Marx continues his analysis by explaining that after each clash between the contending pairs, the battle was resumed, albeit between reconstituted versions of the previous groups. Analogously, philosophy and literature have undergone numerous self- and other redefinitions that have redrawn the disputed areas and reformulated the contested issues. So, for example, while paradigmatic representatives at the ends of the spectrum have preserved a clear dichotomy separating technical and literal philosophical analyses from allegorical and metaphorical literary treatments, the controversial middle ground continues to spawn confusion. When there are only differences of degree between texts that *argue* and accounts that *show*, both sides have wondered where and how to renegotiate the borderlines of demarcation. For example, are Plato's dialogues philosophy or literature? What about Nietzsche's *Thus Spake Zarathrustra,* which is both argumentative and dramatic? What of the Nobel Prize for literature? The 1929 award went to the French philosopher Henri Bergson; two years after John Steinbeck was the winner, the Swedish Academy named Jean-Paul Sartre its 1964 laureate—he refused the prize. In short, a radical questioning of the bases for the ancient quarrel has regularly produced calls, from both sides, to stand down.

While many of these truces have been short lived, an important armistice was declared in 1976 with the launching of *Philosophy and Literature.* Since its inception, this scholarly journal has increasingly won more and more converts to the view that the ancient quarrel and the subsequent banning of imaginative writing from the pursuit of truth and the quest for a good life and a good society were unnecessary and harmful to both parties. Martha Nussbaum is the best-known and most persistent apologist for the view that philosophy and literature should see themselves as complementary and rein-forcing inquiries at work in the same territory. Indeed, Nussbaum's "Conse-quences and Character in Sophocles' *Philoctetes*" was featured in *Philosophy and Literature's* inaugural issue. (In addition to contributing nearly two dozen articles and reviews, she was one of the journal's associate editors from 1976 to 1983 and continues to serves on it editorial advisory board.)

In her influential and well-received book *Love's Knowledge: Essays on Phi-losophy and Literature,* Nussbaum's thesis is that Plato's account of the ancient quarrel has been badly misdiagnosed. Arguing that Plato's exclusion of the tragic and lyric poets was *not,* as seems to have been generally believed, based upon the claim that the techniques, methods, and styles of poetry disqualify it from the search for wisdom, Nussbaum shows that Plato and Aristotle (along with Aristophanes and Sophocles) have to be listened to, for all four are pondering elemental questions: "For the Greeks of the fifth and early fourth centuries B.C., there were not two separate sets of questions in the area of human choice and action, aesthetic questions and moral-philosophical questions, to be studied and written about by mutually detached colleagues in different departments. Instead, dramatic poetry and what we now call philosophical inquiry in ethics were both typically framed by, seen as ways of pursuing, a single and general question: namely, how human beings should live" (1990, 15). Nussbaum goes on to explain that Plato objected to the con-clusion of the Greek dramatists. The short version of their disagreement has to do with each one's overall account of human life: while the tragic and epic poets believe that our lives are scripted and thereby fated (making the only appropriate responses for a playgoer fear and pity), Plato and Aristotle hold that we have sufficient freedom to support personal responsibility and to sustain human dignity. Witness Socrates as he steadfastly and calmly argues in the *Apology,* even in the throes of overpowering forces and faced with rapidly diminishing options, that while his body can be destroyed, his soul cannot be harmed.

Count the essays in this conversation between philosophy and literature as votes on the side of seeing the practitioners of these disciplines as allies. My premise, then, is both/and (instead of either/or), and I am pleased to join the *Philosophy and Literature* campaign, with these differences: Nussbaum's articles and books (and earlier, Peter Jones's essays and his 1975 volume, *Philosophy and the Novel*) and the editors of *Philosophy and Literature* have concentrated on analyses dealing with a good society and a moral life. While not neglecting these important and perennial queries, I have also listened to the conversations that literature and philosophy have had on fundamental epistemological and metaphysical questions. Additionally, recent investigations on the philosophy/literature overlap have stressed ancient Greek philosophers and dramatists, along with English novels and novelists (save a handful of essays on Twain's *The Adventures of Huck Finn*). Nussbaum, for example, is especially keen on Greek philosophers and tragedians, Charles Dickens, and Henry James. My interests are American philosophy, especially classical American pragmatism, and American literature, particularly the realists and naturalists—writers and works generally ignored despite the fact that they offer fertile resources wherein the methods and findings of literature and philosophy powerfully illuminate each other.

Notes

1. For more on their relationship, see my "William Dean Howells and Harold Frederic: A Two-Way Literary Influence."

2. This summary in James's own hand in his personal copy of *Psychology: A Briefer Course* is revealed by his first biographer, Ralph Barton Perry (1948, 196).

3. Though now Theodore Roosevelt is almost exclusively identified as our thirtieth president, in his own day he was also regarded as an influential historian and respected literary essayist.

4. For more on the Cather-James connection via Viola Roseboro, see Skaggs (2002).

WORKS CITED

Dooley, Patrick K. 2006. "William Dean Howells and Harold Frederic: A Two-Way Literary Influence." *The Howellsian* 9 (1): Spring, 3–9.

Frederic, Harold. 1977. *The Correspondence of Harold Frederic.* Edited by George Fortenberry, Stanton Garner, and Robert Woodward. Fort Worth: Texas Christian University Press.

Howells, William Dean. 1897. "My Favorite Novelist and His Best Book." *Munsey's Magazine,* March, 23–24.

Marx, Karl. 1848. *The Communist Manifesto.* New York: International Publishers, 1948.

Nussbaum, Martha C. 1990. "The Ancient Quarrel." In *Love's Knowledge: Essays on Philosophy and Literature.* New York: Oxford University Press, 3–53.

Perry, Ralph Barton. 1948. *The Thought and Character of William James: Briefer Version.* Cambridge, MA: Harvard University Press.

Skaggs, Merrill Maguire. 2002. "*Death Comes for the Archbishop:* Willa Cather's Varieties of Religious Experience." In *Willa Cather and the Culture of Belief,* edited by John J. Murphy, 101–22. Provo, UT: Brigham Young University Press.

Steinbeck, John. 1939. *The Grapes of Wrath.* New York: Penguin Books, 1992.

A COMMUNITY *of* INQUIRY

The Philosophical Climate in Turn-of-the-(Last)-Century America

My area of philosophical specialization is the classical American pragmatists, especially William James. In the early 1970s, while I was reading the unpublished papers of James at Harvard in conjunction with revising my doctoral dissertation for publication, my wife insisted we travel to Concord and Salem to visit the shrines of Thoreau, Emerson, Alcott, and Hawthorne. She was the student of American literature, not I. This shrine visiting had little immediate impact on me, for I continued to view James as a philosopher; his Americanness was, to me, a peripheral and incidental matter. Later, when I completed a series of articles on conscience and civil disobedience in Thoreau and Emerson, the American cultural setting moved a bit closer to the center of my concerns.

In 1978 I participated in a National Endowment for the Humanities Summer Seminar for College Teachers at the University of Kansas. That seminar, "Literature and Culture in Nineteenth-Century America," directed by Stuart Levine, had a lasting impact on my scholarly interests. I was introduced to American studies and read, for the first time, works by Melville, Cooper, Norris, Frederic, Howells, and Crane.

Over the course of Levine's seminar, a familiarity with the nineteenth-century American philosophical developments made it clear to me, for example, that the pragmatic account of religion provided a rich framework through which to analyze Harold Frederic's *The Damnation of Theron Ware* and that developments in moral philosophy between 1850 and 1890 shed light on a number of ethical elements in William Dean Howells's *The Rise of Silas Lapham*. After I completed article-length treatments of a number of overlapping philosophical and literary themes in the late nineteenth-century United States, I began a book on Stephen Crane. The more of Crane I read, the more my attention was drawn to a philosophy I noticed in his works. The philosophy I found there contained most of the hallmarks of classical American philosophy: a tentative and revisable notion of truth, a progressive and melioristic morality, and an experimental and transactional metaphysics. In short, I found Crane's philosophical commitments remarkably akin to the views of William James, C. S. Peirce, Josiah Royce, John Dewey, George Herbert Mead, and George Santayana.

Though not the founder of pragmatism, William James was its popularizer, publicist, and polemicist. The movement's founder, C. S. Peirce, unhappy with what James did to his (Peirce's) carefully and precisely worked-out maxims for clarity and intellectual inquiry, responded by calling his own philosophy "pragmaticism," "a name ugly enough to be safe from kidnappers" (1934, 277). The prolific and long-lived John Dewey preferred the term "experimentalism," in part because it reinforced his hands-on and experimental theory of education that had such a profound impact on the schools in America. But James had the public's ear, and he enjoyed his near-celebrity status.

In my pre–American studies days, I believed that William James had, all by himself, worked out the main components of his philosophical vision: the strenuous and genial moods, a finite God, the stream of thought, a pragmatic theory of truth, and a pluralistic universe. But as my awareness of late nineteenth-century American culture increased, it became obvious that though James was an original and seminal thinker, his thought was a response to a cultural endowment of concepts and problems. For example, a particularly striking example of a shared interest occurred during the late 1890s when, in an attempt to capture the exhilarating and transforming impact of actions beyond the routine and ordinary, James extolled the value of the strenuous mood and Theodore Roosevelt praised the benefits of the strenuous life. Also at the same time, though Crane's preoccupation with courage and all sorts of heroism spanned his single-decade (1890–1900) meteoric writing career, his literary apogee was surely in 1895, with the publication of "A Mystery of Heroism" two months before *The Red Badge of Courage* appeared in book form and became a runaway best seller in both America and England, followed by the publication of "The Veteran" three months later. More broadly, this time period included the age of heroism, expansion, and exploration, notably the polar expeditions that inspired Frank Norris's arctic adventure tale, *A Man's Woman,* and Jack London's celebration of life in extremis in his Klondike stories, especially "To Build a Fire," *The Call of the Wild,* and *The Sea-Wolf.* These works by Norris and London all appeared in the first decade of the 1900s.

In other words, my exploration of philosophical and literary themes has taken for granted that turn-of-the-(last)-century American intellectuals responded to a common intellectual matrix. I find that the same cultural agenda that energized artists, jurists, journalists, scientists, and clergy also influenced the philosophers and novelists of that era. What follows is a sketch of classical American philosophy's expression of that agenda. (For some suggestions for further study and information on the ongoing critical editions of American philosophers, see appendix.)

C. S. Peirce: The Demise of Descartes and Science as the Model for Philosophy

Any treatment of classical American philosophy must begin with C. S. Peirce's seminal pair of articles, "The Fixation of Belief" (1877) and "How to Make Our Ideas Clear" (1878). Peirce repudiates Descartes' project of using methodic doubt to establish an indubitable foundation from which humans embark upon the project of achieving certitude. John Dewey echoes Peirce's stance that postmodern philosophy has to abandon the quest for certainty.

Peirce argues that Descartes' goal of certitude was unrealistic, even impossible, and that his strategy of manufactured doubt was at best a make-believe exercise and, at worst, could undermine confidence in our ability to understand and deal with the world. Describing Cartesian doubt as alternatively feigned and corrosive, Peirce states, "We cannot begin with complete doubt. . . . Hence this initial skepticism will be a mere self-deception, and not real doubt; and no one who follows the Cartesian method will ever be satisfied until he has formally recovered all those beliefs which in form he has given up. . . . Let us not pretend to doubt in philosophy what we do not doubt in our hearts" (1982, 211)

In its place, Peirce offers a triad of *belief* (defined as a habit of action), *doubt* (described as an irritation prompted by failure), and *inquiry* (characterized as the process of fixing a problematic situation by proposing a satisfactory plan of action in the form of a replacement belief). Instead of wondering whether my hand is before my eyes, whether I am now dreaming or whether I am being deceived by an evil genius, as the father of modern philosophy asks us to do, the founder of pragmatism suggests that the paradigm for intellectual inquiry is real-life problem solving. When my car will not start, I experience real doubt. The situation demands that I investigate the situation in order to fix the problem so that when the solution is found, I can drive down the road in a calm and satisfactory state of mind. In a masterfully compressed sketch of the intellectual development of individuals as well as the human race, Peirce argues that four strategies for fixing belief have evolved: first tenacity, then authority, followed by reasonableness, and finally the scientific method. The first three methods are infected with subjectivity and a full range of human biases. Only the fourth method allows reality itself to shape our beliefs objectively and systematically, instead of vice versa. Moreover, the scientific method is self-corrective and is the only method that can use doubt as an opportunity (instead of a threat), as it turns difficulties into additional hypotheses awaiting further testing. Close at hand are redefinitions of both meaning and truth.

If the hypothetical-deductive method is to become *the* strategy to fix beliefs, then all questions, problems, concepts, and issues will have to be translatable (without loss of content) into patterns of action. Thereby, the meaning of an idea is the behavior it prompts, and its fruitfulness (or failure) will measure its truth (or falsity) as a pattern of action. In the nearly seventy-five years between the publication of Peirce's seminal articles and John Dewey's death (in 1952), American pragmatists worked out the profit of and the problems with such a radical redefinition of truth and meaning, and more generally with a fundamental recasting of the nature of philosophy. (After Dewey's death, classical American pragmatism's influence declined precipitously, only to experience a stunning renaissance triggered by the publication of critical editions of the works of Peirce, James, and Dewey in the early 1970s and the emergence of the high-energy, high-profile neo-pragmatism of Richard Rorty in the 1980s and 1990s.) Though there are many individual differences of detail and emphasis among even the main classical American philosophers, a cluster of six commonly shared commitments can be discerned.

FAMILY RESEMBLANCE: TRAITS OF CLASSICAL AMERICAN PHILOSOPHY

The repudiation of the project of modern philosophy

As noted above, the American pragmatists rejected the search for certain, timeless, and universal answers to ultimate questions about Reality, Truth, God, and the Good. Rather than a theoretical pursuit, philosophy is seen as an instrument responding to concrete and tractable real problems. In his seminal essay, "The Influence of Darwinism on Philosophy" (1909), Dewey explains that "the bearing of Darwinian ideas upon philosophy" is that "the new logic outlaws, flanks, dismisses—what you will—one type of problems and substitutes for it another type. Philosophy forswears inquiry after absolute origins and absolute finalities in order to explore specific values and the specific conditions that generate them" (1977, 10).

Dewey further argues that all forms of intelligence are inherently critical; philosophy, because of its generality and fundamental nature, is "criticism of criticisms." Accordingly, philosophy's duty of cultural criticism is in the service of social reconstruction and the amelioration of human suffering. "Philosophy," he writes in 1917, "recovers itself when it ceases to be a device for dealing with the problems of philosophers and becomes a method, cultivated by philosophers, for dealing with the problems of men" (1987, 46).

Philosophy as a pluralistic and humanistic enterprise

A comprehensive perspective and a total picture are deemed beyond the ken of humans. Philosophy's claims are understood to be inherently partial, context-dependent, tentative, and transactional articulations of the human perspective. William James is especially keen on these characteristics; note his comments first on pluralism and then on humanism:

> But as the sciences have developed farther, the notion has gained ground that most, perhaps all, of our laws are only approximations. The laws themselves, moreover, have grown so numerous that there is no counting them; and so many rival formulations are proposed in all the branches of science that investigators have become accustomed to the notion that no theory is absolutely a transcript of reality, but that any one of them may from some point of view be useful. Their great use is to

summarize old facts and to lead to new ones. They are only a man-made language, a conceptual shorthand, as someone calls them, in which we write our reports of nature; and languages, as is well known, tolerate much choice of expression and many dialects. (1907, 33)

Laws and languages at any rate are thus seen to be man-made things. Mr. Schiller [a contemporary English pragmatist] applies the analogy to beliefs, and proposes the name of "Humanism" to the doctrine that to an unascertainable extent our truths are man-made products too. Human motives sharpen all our questions, human satisfactions lurk in all our answers, all our formulas have a human twist. . . . You see how naturally one comes to the humanistic principle: you can't weed out the human contribution. Our nouns and adjectives are all humanized heirlooms, and in the theories we build them into, the inner order and arrangement is wholly dictated by human considerations, intellectual consistency being one of them. Mathematics and logic are themselves fermenting with human rearrangements; physics, astronomy and biology follow massive cues of human preference. (1907, 116–17, 122)

Note how sweeping James's claim is: not just philosophy, literature, and the humanities in general but also mathematics, logic, and the empirical sciences are humanistic enterprises. We humans, insists James, must continually acknowledge the irreducible plurality of experiences and the inescapable lens of perspective.

An experiential, evolutionary, and process orientation

Experience, not Reality, is seen as the subject matter for reflection and analysis. John Dewey, for example, describes the project of metaphysics as the discovery of the generic traits of existence. Among the traits that Dewey examines are experience as stable, precarious, eventful, active, genuine, spurious, nurturing, hazardous, changing, continuous, practical and experimental, filled with initiations and consummations, funded with meanings, and socially orientated.

Pragmatism replaces the spectator view of knowledge that assumes that our ideas are a copy of a static universe with the view that, as knowers, we are involved participants who make and remake the universe. As part of pragmatism's war on all dualisms (subject/object, matter/spirit, appearance/reality, means/ends), James and Dewey looked for terms that would get behind (or under) the known/knower opposition. Dewey, in particular, is adamant that experience (not reality, or things or consciousness) is what is problematic and therefore in need of investigation. To further stress the active and inter-active process involved in knowing, Dewey initially described knowledge as a "transaction"; later he preferred the term "negotiation." "Experience," he writes, "is primarily a process of undergoing: a process of standing some-thing; of suffering and passion, of affection, in the literal sense of these words. The organism has to endure, to undergo, the consequences of its own actions. Experience is no slipping along in a path fixed by inner consciousness. . . . Undergoing, however, is never mere passivity. . . . Experience, in other words, is a matter of *simultaneous* doings and sufferings. Our undergoings are ex-periments in varying the course of events; our active tryings are trials and tests of ourselves" (1987, 8–9).

The impact of Darwinian evolution is pervasive in classical American phi-losophy. If all reality is in evolutionary flux, there are no immutable natures to anchor knowledge or to ground values. Given the ascent of Darwin, everything is in process.

A scientific paradigm for philosophy

As noted above, if the scientific method is the only trustworthy and defensible method of inquiry, then ideas are best understood as tools. If every belief is corrigible, our standards for knowledge must be modestly downgraded to an expectation of high probability. Dewey offers "warranted assertability" (in-stead of certainty or Truth) as a realistic and assessable goal for true beliefs. Pragmatism's anti-foundational stance treats every belief as criticizable and re-visable. Peirce, writing in 1897, observes that "no man of self-respect ever now states his result without affixing to it its *probable error*" (1934, 9)—a posture he dubs "fallibilism." He further urges that all dogmas be greeted with extreme skepticism. Peirce kept every issue open to reexamination, offering as "the first rule of reason . . . 'Do not block the road to inquiry'" (1934, 136). In his famous essay "The Will to Believe," James stresses the importance of sustaining a ten-sion between trusting and questioning our beliefs. "I live, to be sure, by the practical faith that we must go on experiencing and thinking over our experi-ence, for only thus can our opinions grow more true; but to hold any one of them—I absolutely do not care which—as if it never could be re-interpretable or corrigible, I believe to be a tremendously mistaken attitude, and I think that the whole history of philosophy will bear me out" (1897, 22).

The pragmatic notion of ideas as trustworthy tools can be highlighted by a favorite paradigm: an idea as map. Ideas do not duplicate sensations or impressions, nor do they picture reality; ideas guide. A map is an extraordinarily compact summary of past experience that literally leads us. A reliable one gets us to our destination (and a faulty one gets us lost). Note that we more naturally speak of a reliable or good or useful map, not a true one. James puts it this way. "Truth is *one species of good,* and not as is usually supposed, a category distinct from good, and co-ordinate with it. *The true is the name of whatever proves itself to be good in the way of belief, and good, too, for definite, assignable reasons.* . . . Her only test of probable truth is what works best in the way of leading us, what fits every part of life best and combines with the collectivity of experience's demands, nothing being omitted" (1907, 42, 44).

In short, for the pragmatists, reflective thought is a response to concrete, real-life problems, while truth is proximately measured by its effectiveness in accomplishing specific practical goals and ultimately gauged by its ability to promote long-term human flourishing. The classical American philosophers would be hard pressed to improve upon Frank Norris's account of pragmatic truth. Writing in the December 1901 *World's Work,* Norris explains that though unreflective persons may think truth is "an abstraction, a vague idea," it has instead "to do with practical, tangible, concrete work-a-day life. . . . [It is] as concrete as the lamp-post on the corner, as practical as a cable-car, as real and homely and work-a-day and commonplace as a boot-jack" (1901, 1158).

Meliorism, human responsibility, and a finite God

Both pessimism and optimism are rejected in favor of the view that improvement is possible. Accordingly, humans are responsible for designing workable, ongoing, revisable solutions to improve the lot of their fellows. Lest human freedom, initiative, and responsibility be compromised, God is seen as a powerful, though finite, partner in improving the world. James imagines God, at the moment of creation, putting the following case to his human co-creators: "I am going to make a world not certain to be saved, a world the perfection of which shall be conditional merely, the condition being that each several agent does its own 'level best.' I offer you the chance of taking part in such a world. Its safety, you see, is unwarranted. It is a real adventure, with real danger, yet it may win through. It is a social scheme of co-operative work genuinely to be done. Will you join the procession? Will you trust yourself and trust other agents enough to face the risk?" (1907, 139).

With regard to religion, the pragmatists are, predictably, more interested in assessing the valuable (and sometimes deleterious) effects of *belief* in God, rather than in engaging in debate about the perennial philosophical questions regarding the existence and attributes of God. In this connection, James argues that with no other reasons to believe in God, "men would postulate one simply as a pretext for living hard, and getting out of the game of existence its keenest possibilities of zest" (1897, 161). In other words, religion's chief value is as a catalyst for the strenuous mood.

An emergent, communal, and social self

Since a social and public assessment of policies is seen as essential, individual insight and personal satisfaction are relegated to the periphery. Even more fundamentally, a preexistent, inner transcendental self of the Thoreauvian sort is supplanted by a model of selfhood in which both self-awareness and self-constitution are socially and behaviorally generated.

The pragmatists' interest in psychology is striking. Following the publication of James's monumental and groundbreaking two-volume masterpiece, *The Principles of Psychology* (1890), he turned in 1895 to applied psychology, giving summer-school lectures in Boston, at the Chautauqua Institute in upstate New York, and as far away as Colorado Springs. These lectures were published as *Talks to Teachers* in 1899. Dewey's work followed the same pattern. Beginning with several volumes devoted to psychological issues, he then turned to pedagogy and related educational issues. His sustained critique of the American educational establishment's misguided views of human development and its faulty recitation/memorization curricula had a profound impact upon American society.

Also with regard to human development, the theories of second-generation pragmatist George Herbert Mead (a colleague of John Dewey at the University of Chicago), who was neither a prolific nor popular philosopher, were revolutionary and influential. His approach to selfhood is explicitly developmental and behavioristic. Note the title of one of his influential essays: "Mind Approached Through Behavior—Can Its Study Be Made Scientific?" Mead's response to his own question was, of course, yes, as his study of the behaviors of lower animals (concentrating on the growls and barks of dogs) led to his theories about human development:

How can an individual get outside himself (experientially) in such a way as to become an object to himself? This is the essential psychological problem of selfhood or of self-consciousness; and its solution is to be found by referring to the process of social conduct or activity in which the given person or individual is implicated. . . . The individual experiences himself as such, not directly, but only indirectly from the particular standpoints of other individual members of the same social group, or from the generalized standpoint of the social group as a whole to which he belongs . . . in so far as he first becomes an object to himself just as other individuals are objects to him or in his experience; and he becomes an object to himself only by taking the attitudes of other individuals toward himself within a social environment or context of experience and behavior in which both he and they are involved. . . . It is impossible to conceive a self arising outside of social experience. (1934, 138–40)

It is interesting to note that most of Mead's writings appeared from the mid-1930s onward, so there is good reason to believe that, in this instance, the vector influence went both ways—from literature to philosophy (and psychology) and vice versa. Accordingly, in the Crane/Norris/London/Dreiser focus upon behavior, environment, materialism, and the human animal, American literary realism and naturalism were important influences upon philosophers and psychologists, including Mead and Josiah Royce, who were both keenly interested in the process of self-emergence and the catalysts of community building. Ironically, while William James is often seen as the quintessential American thinker even though his education was largely European and he was a lifelong devotee of Continental travel, Royce's early life was spent on the American frontier. Royce's parents left Iowa to join the 1849 California gold rush, and Royce was born in 1855 in a mining camp. He never forgot his first experiences of moving from one mining camp to the next: "My earliest recollections include a very frequent wonder as to what my elders meant when they said that this was a new community. . . . I wondered, and gradually came to feel that part of my life's business was to find out what all this wonder meant" (1916, 122–23).

NOTES

Part of this chapter is a somewhat revised version of section of a chapter, "Pragmatism," that appeared in *American History through Literature, 1870–1920*, edited by Tom Quirk and Gary Scharnhorst, 889–93 (Detroit: Charles Scribner's Sons, 2005).

WORKS CITED

Dewey, John. 1977. *The Collected Writings of John Dewey, 1882–1952: Middle Works*. Edited by Jo Ann Boyston. Vol. 4. Carbondale: Southern Illinois University Press.

———. 1987. *The Collected Writings of John Dewey, 1882–1952: Middle Works*. Edited by Jo Ann Boyston. Vol. 10. Carbondale: Southern Illinois University Press.

James, William. 1907. *Pragmatism*. Edited by Frederick H. Burkhardt, Fredson Bowers, and Ignas K. Skrupskelis. *The Works of William James*. Cambridge, MA: Harvard University Press, 1975.

———. 1897. *The Will to Believe*. Edited by Frederick H. Burkhardt, Fredson Bowers, and Ignas K. Skrupskelis. *The Works of William James*. Cambridge, MA: Harvard University Press, 1979.

Mead, George Herbert. 1934. *Mind, Self, and Society: From the Standpoint of a Social Behaviorist*. Edited by Charles W. Morris. Chicago: University of Chicago Press.

Norris, Frank. 1901. "The Need of a Literary Conscience." In *Frank Norris: Novels and Essays*. Edited by Donald Pizer, 1155–64. New York: Library of America, 1986.

Peirce, C. S. 1934. *The Collected Papers of Charles Sanders Peirce*. Edited by Charles Hartshorne, Paul Weiss, and Arthur Burks. Vol. 5. Cambridge, MA: Harvard University Press.

———. 1982. "Some Consequences of Four Incapacities." In *Writings of Charles S. Peirce: A Chronological Edition*. Edited by Edward C. Moore. Vol. 2. Bloomington: Indiana University Press.

Royce, Josiah. 1916. *The Hope of the Great Community*. Freeport: NY: Books for Libraries, 1967.

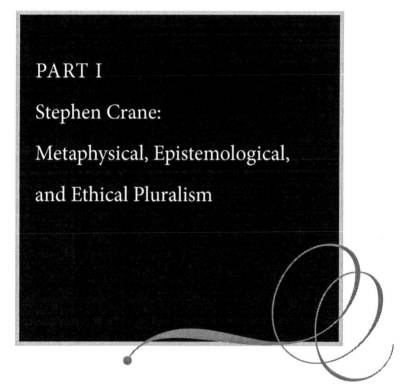

PART I

Stephen Crane:

Metaphysical, Epistemological,

and Ethical Pluralism

1

Spectators and/or Participants
Crane on Epistemological Privilege

A wound gives strange dignity to him who bears it.
—Stephen Crane

Artistically, Stephen Crane's quest was capturing experience, mostly human experience and experiencers. But his genius also disclosed the lived worlds of animals. "Experience" customarily refers to the obvious and ordinary stuff of consciousness, but as we shall see, Crane's notion of experience was more complex and sophisticated. Philosophically, the upshot of his work amounts to an epistemological and a metaphysical shakedown. Although common sense has us believe that we have a reliable grasp of what is out there (in reality) and what is inside (within consciousness), Crane was more attentive and sensitive and therefore more suspicious. He noticed that the contents and status of the inner and outer worlds are problematic and that the borderline between them is permeable. He also explored situations in which experiencers have the epistemological advantage over observers and, strikingly, the opposite—occasions wherein onlookers are in a better position to understand and assess what happens to those who undergo an experience. And so as Crane's artistic sensitivity uncovered the mystery of experience, his philosophical legacy earned him a place in a distinguished company of thinkers, beginning with Plato, who believed that wonder is the beginning of wisdom.

"Wonder" is too weak a word for Crane's artistic and philosophical accomplishment; "surprise" comes closer. His objective was not to create doubt, neither the comprehensive and corrosive upheaval wrought by Descartes' methodic doubt nor the beneficial, though unsettling, irritation of doubt that is central to the thought of Crane's American contemporary, the scientist and philosopher C. S. Peirce. Nor was it Crane's goal to address the epistemological panic that haunts postmodern theorists and deconstructionist critics. Instead, his goals were positive: to foster awareness and to cultivate openness to experience.

Scott Slovic recommends the works of Annie Dillard as an anecdote to the "anesthesia of routineness" (1992, 65). But whereas Dillard's artful and leisurely paced essays gently wake us, Crane's potent prose and poetry startle us with shocks of recognition. How powerful, how unpredictable, how disorienting it is to let Crane control one's stream of thought! His prose is so highly charged that the ozone smell of a cracking thunderstorm still lingers. A surge protector, or at least a transformer, is needed to buffer the excessive voltage of Crane's writing. Forewarned and even shielded, readers of Crane continue to discover that neither the external world nor the internal world is as it seems. For Crane, human experience is an epiphany to be explored. With Crane as tour guide and commentator, richness, complexity, wonderful surprises, and unsettling questions supplant the obvious and everyday world we ordinary mortals are used to.

A brief explanation of the term "experience" is in order. Crane's contemporaries, the American pragmatists C. S. Peirce, William James, and later John Dewey, sought to overcome the subject/object duality and the commonsense spectator view of knowledge. William James, in his *Essays in Radical Empiricism* (1912), argued that a neutral stuff, *pure experience,* is epistemologically and metaphysically basic.[1] James proposed that a bit of pure experience can be both public (out there) and private (within consciousness). Such bits of experience exist in separate but compatible histories—as an experiencer's mental biography and as an experienced fact in the world. James insisted that we cannot and do not deal with the world as detached observers. Instead, we interact and interfere with an environment. John Dewey suggested that the terms "sensation," "perception," "apprehension," and "knowledge" be replaced with more active and interactive notions. He insisted that cognition is not an affair of getting an accurate account of what is external to a disembodied knower: rather, knowledge is a process better characterized as a transaction or a negotiation that remakes the neutral stuff that is prior to both the known and the knower.[2] In this proposed renovation of our notions of both truth and reality, veracious ideas are not static, accurate mental duplicates, but road maps that prompt fruitful (or faulty) behavioral incursions. "The truth of an idea," writes James, "is not a stagnant property inherent in it. Truth *happens* to an idea. It *becomes* true, is *made* true by events. Its verity *is* in fact an event, a process: the process namely of its verifying itself, its veri-*fication*. Its validity is the process of its valid-*ation*" (1907, 97).

As I will now show, such a concept of experience (as well as similar concepts of truth and reality) function vividly in Crane's accounts of the experiences of wounds and being wounded in three short stories: "An Episode of War," "The Price of the Harness," and "The Mystery of Heroism: A Detail of an American Battle."

As it turns out, a wide range of expectations about pain and being wounded are overturned in these accounts. However, not only readers but also Crane's own fictional characters themselves discover that very little of what they expect to happen ever happens. Further, through a subtle enfolding, the reader becomes both spectator and participant. So, too, Crane's fictional characters both observe and constitute the experiences that occur. As a result, neither the spectator's nor participant's vantage point is epistemologically privileged.[3] Accordingly, at both extremes of the continuum, both being an onlooker and being a sufferer involve serious liabilities as well as significant advantages; moreover, as noted above, the "real" event that occurs is a tertium quid that is both public and private and is thus both shareable and idiosyncratic.

For Crane, perhaps the most surprising misinformation regarding wounds has to do with pain. Pain is not always agonizing. It can be an intriguing, revelatory experience. I am reminded of my own experience of twice being in shock. Both times everyone who watched grimaced and/or averted their glances, but I did neither because I was not suffering excruciating pain. Some pain can also be pleasurable. Consider this passage from Edward Abbey's journal, *Confessions of a Barbarian:* "My lips are stiff and chapped, with a small crack in my upper lip, a reliable source of a kind of interesting tiny, dry pain which I take continual delight in experiencing" (1994, 32). And I recall a provocative article in *Sports Illustrated* on athletes and pain that I read more than twenty-five years ago. In "The Face of Pain," Mark Kram relates how Los Angles Rams star (now sportscaster and actor) Merlin Olsen thought of pain as an opportunity for mental gymnastics: "Pain is an interesting thing. . . . Man is an adaptable creature, . . . and one finds out what you can or cannot do. It's like walking into a barnyard. The first thing you smell is manure. Stand there for about five minutes and you don't smell it anymore. The same thing is true of a knee. You hurt that knee. You're conscious of it. But then you start to play at a different level." Kram comments that Olsen "looks upon pain as an interesting companion, as something which arouses his contempt and inexhaustible taste for pragmatism" (1976, 62). For Crane, too, pain brings illumination and insight along with suffering.[4]

The wounding of the lieutenant in "An Episode of War" is first described as an irritating, random occurrence that disturbs a mundane routine. "The others cried out when they saw blood upon the lieutenant's sleeve" (Crane 1984, 671). They cannot see the wound, only the blood on his uniform, though they notice that their superior "winced like a man stung" (671). But Crane does not focus upon the pain—actually very little is made of the wound sufferer's suffering. Instead he stresses the ways in which the gunshot debilitates the officer. He can no longer sheath his sword; he cannot use his right arm but must carry it. That part of his body becomes an alien thing: "He held his right wrist tenderly in his left hand, as if the wounded arm was made of very brittle glass" (672).

The irony, of course, is that while pain can enfeeble, more importantly, in this case it capacitates the lieutenant. The remainder of the story dramatizes how, "as the wounded officer passed from the line of battle, he was enabled to see many things which as a participant in the fight were unknown to him" (672). The image Crane uses to capture the strangely ambiguous power of pain to innervate and empower is one of his favorites: a curtain.[5] "A wound gives strange dignity to him who bears it. Well men shy from this new and terrible majesty. It is as if the wounded man's hand is upon the curtain which hangs before the revelations of all existence. . . . The power of it sheds radiance upon a bloody form and makes the other men understand sometimes that they are little" (672).

Among the things that being wounded makes possible is the lieutenant's realization that, even as a frontline combatant, his understanding of battle is faulty. Indeed, the farther he removes himself from participating and the more distant and spectator-like he becomes, the more accurate are his (and others') observations: "He came upon some stragglers and they told him how to find the field hospital. They described its exact location. In fact these men, no longer having part in the battle, knew more of it than others. They told the performance of every corps, every division, the opinion of every general. The lieutenant, carrying his wounded arm rearward, looked upon them with wonder" (673).

More participant/spectator reorientations are in store. Even the sufferer of an injury does not automatically grasp its seriousness or significance; under the influence of shock, the patient does not feel the real damage of an injury. Further, in the lieutenant's case a rearward officer corrects the lieutenant's appreciation of his own injury. "'Why man, that's no way to do it. You want to fix that thing.' He appropriated the lieutenant and the lieutenant's wound. . . . His tone allowed one to think that he was in the habit of being wounded every day. The lieutenant hung his head, feeling, in this presence, that he did not know how to be correctly wounded" (673–74).

Interestingly, the term "appropriate" is apt for describing our dealings with things (instead of persons). As noted earlier, the arm had become an alien object to the lieutenant; in fact, both the soldier and his arm have been reified.

Soon after the lieutenant learns how to be "correctly wounded," he sees a man who is dying but who apparently does not realize it. He wonders if he should alert the dying man about his condition. "Sitting with his back against a tree a man with a face as grey as a new army blanket was serenely smoking a corn-cob pipe. The lieutenant wished to rush forward and inform him that he was dying" (674). Two additional perspectives on wounds can be found in "An Episode of War." The surgeon who tends to him treats him with "great contempt" because the doctor views the wound as having "placed [him] on a very low social plane" (674). This stands in stark contrast to the "strange dignity" with which his wound was invested by those formerly under his command. Finally, by Crane's radical questioning of the privileged or compromised positions of participants and spectators in understanding pain, the significance of an injury and the lasting impact of a wound bring the story to its pungent conclusion. "And this is the story of how the lieutenant lost his arm. When he reached home his sisters, his mother, his wife, sobbed for a long time at the sight of the flat sleeve. 'Oh, well,' he said, standing shamefaced amid these tears, 'I don't suppose it matters so much as all that'" (675).

Really? When the head of a household loses an arm, who are the observers and who are the participants? Crane's ending is as problematic as it is poignant.

In "The Price of the Harness," Crane again uses the curtain image—"the steep mountain range on the right turned blue and as without detail as a curtain" (1016)—for his exploration of the complex and confusing experience of battle. This story, one of Crane's longer short stories, examines all sorts of misapprehensions and mistakes made both by participants and observers. In Crane's American Civil War stories—for instance, in "An Episode of War"— distance from the battle is the coefficient of clarity; in his Spanish–American War stories, detachment and spectator neutrality often have the opposite effect. The drawback that comes from being too remote is symbolized by a military reconnaissance balloon that does not provide reliable intelligence but only gives away the troops' position, drawing both friendly and hostile fire. In "The Price of the Harness" the balloon is shot down, and all witness its demise: "The balloon was dying, dying a gigantic and public death before the eyes of two armies" (1022).[6] Apparently those on the ground involved in the battle are sometimes, but not always, closer to the truth. In exploring the perspective of the infantry, Crane uses a technique later exploited by Alfred Hitchcock and more recently by Steven Spielberg in *Jaws*. First false suspense is created when the men sense danger but they are safe; then false security follows when the men feel safe but are truly in mortal danger. And so, Crane explains, after a long, tense wait, when the troops are finally able to return gunfire, "a new sense of safety was rightfully upon them" (1029). Of course, then the real carnage begins.

"The Price of the Harness" tallies up the costs of war: death, destruction, wounds, and pain. Crane depicts a variety of wounded men. Some are in shock, walking rearward, looking back whence they had fought. "The wounded paused to look impassively upon this struggle. They were always like men who could not be aroused by anything further" (1028).

Others suffer terribly on the field and in the hospital. In particular, Martin (whom Crane follows for the first half of the story) is badly wounded. As in "An Episode in War," Martin shuns the surgeons' comfort and care, choosing instead to rest against a tree: "Martin saw a busy person with a book and a pencil, but he did not approach him to become officially a member of the hospital. All he desired was rest and immunity from nagging. He took seat painfully under a bush and leaned his back upon the trunk. There he remained thinking, his face wooden" (1028).

The climax of "Price of the Harness," perhaps even more emotionally wrenching than the close of "An Episode of War," concerns a soldier who is wounded and dying but does not realize it. Again the epistemological advantages and handicaps that one assumes accrue to participants and observers are undercut in Crane's account of experience. James Nolan has suffered a fatal stomach wound but believes his wound is minor. His only complaints are that he is cold and that the ground he is lying on is wet. The ground is not damp, his comrades insist. Nolan will not be persuaded:

> "Just put your hand under my back and see how wet the ground is," he said.
>
> Grierson seemed to be afraid of Nolan's agitation, and so he slipped a hand under the prostate man, and presently withdrew it covered with blood. "Yes," he said hiding his hand carefully from Nolan's eyes, "you were right, Jimmie."

"Of course I was," said Nolan, contentedly closing his eyes. "This hillside holds water like a swamp." After a moment he said: "Guess I ought to know. I'm flat here on it, and you fellers are standing up." (1031)

Crane has several soldiers well positioned to give an accurate report upon the factual matters under dispute. Above all the rest, Nolan has direct access to the situation. However, "he did not know he was dying. He thought he was holding an argument on the condition of the turf" (1031).

A brief look at the third story, "A Mystery of Heroism," reveals familiar Cranean themes dealing with battlefield trauma. The curtain image is repeated: "From beyond a curtain of green woods there came the sound of some stupendous scuffle as if two animals of the size of islands were fighting" (623–24). Again, a wounded right arm becomes an artificial appendage: "A lieutenant of the battery rode down and passed them, holding his right arm carefully in his left hand. And it was as if this arm was not a part of him, but belonged to another man" (624). Beyond these standard themes, Crane pays careful attention to some overlooked victims of war: plants, "for the little meadow which intervened was now suffering a terrible onslaught of shells. . . . And there was a massacre of young blades of grass" (624), and animals, especially horses, which suffer terribly in war. Indeed, Crane sometimes seems more attentive to the pain of the "brute-soldiers" than to that of their masters: "In this rank of brute-soldiers there had been relentless and hideous carnage. From the ruck of bleeding and prostrate horses, the men of the infantry could see one animal raising its stricken body with its fore-legs and turning its nose with mystic and profound eloquence toward the sky" (625).

Nonetheless, germane to the present analysis is Crane's account of how a spectator, along with the sufferer, is able to penetrate the mystery of being wounded. Near the end of the story, Collins, now with a bucket of water, crosses a meadow, encountering a wounded artillery officer pinned under his fallen horse. (Crane's description of the pain and suffering of the horse was just noted above.) The stricken superior officer

had been making groans in the teeth of the tempest of sound. These futile cries, wrenched from him by his agony, were heard only by shells, bullets. When wild-eyed Collins came running, this officer raised himself. His face contorted and blanched from pain, he was about to utter some great beseeching cry. But suddenly his face straightened and he

called: "Say, young man, give me a drink of water, will you?" . . .
"I can't," he screamed. . . . He ran on. (630–31).

But then Collins turns back. Reaching the wounded officer, Collins tries to give him a drink, "but his shaking hands caused the water to splash all over the face of the dying man" (631). Pain and suffering, correctly appreciated by both the patient and the onlooker and correctly responded to, have transformed a foolish caper into a genuine moral act of heroism. Accordingly, in "A Mystery of Heroism" Crane shows how battlefield pain and suffering can convert an amoral, even immoral, action into a moral one. Perhaps a compassionate response to battlefield trauma might also turn foolhardy actions into exemplary acts beyond the pale of ethics![7] Or, as Crane himself puts it in "An Episode of War," not only does "a wound [give] strange dignity to him who bears it" (672), but sometimes it can also bestow moral standing on the actions of those who are moved to respond to pain and suffering.

Philosophically speaking, Crane has used the considerable candlepower of his prose to illuminate several hidden, unnoticed, and surprising contours of the experience of battle wounds and suffering. "Experience," I hope I have shown, is the proper term for the subject matter of Crane's explorations. He has clearly transcended the traditional dualisms of subject/object and reality/appearance. I am not surprised at Crane's epistemological and metaphysical sophistication, especially his grasp of the ambiguous status and the dubious merits of spectator/participant perspectives. After all, Crane was a genius living at the turn of the (last) century when the pragmatic temper dominated the mind-set of America, an intellectual milieu that John McDermott has aptly described in the title of his fine book, *The Culture of Experience*.[8]

NOTES

This chapter is a recast version of the essay "'A wound gives strange dignity to him who bears it': Stephen Crane's Metaphysics of Experience," that appeared in *War, Literature & the Arts* 11 (1999): 116–27.

1. See my *Pragmatism as Humanism: The Philosophy of William James* for more on James's notion of pure experience.

2. For an excellent survey of Dewey's thought, see Campbell (1995).

3. For more on Crane's examination of actor/spectator perspectives, see the second chapter of my *The Pluralistic Philosophy of Stephen Crane*.

4. Along these lines, recent interest in environmental ethics has lead several theorists to revisit Darwin, especially his concepts of pain as unwelcome information (and pleasure as a reward). Callicott (1980) has been particularly influential in a renewed philosophical examination of Darwin's biological notions of pain and suffering.

5. Surely Crane's most powerful curtain image occurs in "An Eloquence of Grief," in which he describes the courtroom scream of a young woman after she is pronounced guilty as being "so graphic of grief, that it slit with a dagger's sweep the curtain of common-place" (1984, 863).

6. See "Stephen Crane's Vivid Story of the Battle of San Juan" for the same sort of trouble caused by another reconnaissance balloon.

7. The core of "A Mystery of Heroism" deals with the questionable pseudoheroism of Private Fred Collins taking supreme risks to quench his thirst—see chapter 4 for an examination of this aspect of Crane's story.

8. Equally helpful is McDermott's more recent *The Streams of Experience: Reflections on the History and Philosophy of American Culture.*

Works Cited

Abbey, Edward. 1994. *Confessions of a Barbarian.* Edited by David Petersen. Boston: Little, Brown.

Callicott, J. Baird. 1980. "Animal Liberation: A Triangular Affair." *Environmental Ethics,* 2:311–38

Campbell, James. 1995. *Understanding John Dewey: Nature and Cooperative Intelligence.* Chicago: Open Court.

Crane, Stephen. 1984. *Stephen Crane: Prose and Poetry.* Edited by J. C. Levenson. New York: Library of America.

Dooley, Patrick K. 1974. *Pragmatism as Humanism: The Philosophy of William James.* Chicago: Nelson-Hall.

———. 1993. *The Pluralistic Philosophy of Stephen Crane.* Bloomington: University of Illinois Press.

James, William. 1907. "Pragmatism's Conception of Truth." In *Pragmatism.* Edited by Frederick H. Burkhardt, Fredson Bowers, and Ignas K. Skrupskelis. *The Works of William James.* Cambridge, MA: Harvard University Press, 1975.

———. 1912. *Essays in Radical Empiricism.* Edited by Frederick H. Burkhardt, Fredson Bowers, and Ignas K. Skrupskelis. *The Works of William James.* Cambridge, MA: Harvard University Press, 1976.

Kram, Mark. 1976. "The Face of Pain." *Sports Illustrated* (March) 8:62.

McDermott, John. 1976. *The Culture of Experience: Philosophical Essays in the American Grain.* New York: New York University Press.

———. 1986. *The Streams of Experience: Reflections on the History and Philosophy of American Culture.* Amherst: University of Massachusetts Press.

Slovic, Scott. 1992. "Sudden Feelings: Annie Dillard's Psychology." In *Seeking Awareness in American Nature Writing,* 61–92. Salt Lake City: University of Utah Press.

2

"In the Depths of a Coal Mine"
Crane's Metaphysics of Experience

*The dead black walls slipped swiftly by. They were a swirling
dark chaos on which the eye tried vainly to locate some coherent
thing, some intelligible spot.*
—Stephen Crane

In early January 1894, Hamlin Garland dispatched Crane to S. S. McClure with a bundle of manuscripts and a note reading, "If you have work for Mr. Crane talk things over with him and for Mercy Sake! Dont keep him *standing* for an hour; as he did before, out in your pen for culprits" (Crane 1994, 95–96). The publication of *The Red Badge of Courage,* which would make him an overnight international celebrity, was almost two years away. Crane's first novel, *Maggie,* had appeared a year earlier. Virtually no one bought it; nonetheless, it gained him important support from critics William Dean Howells and Hamlin Garland and syndicate owners S. S. McClure and Irving Bacheller.

In April 1894, Crane offered the manuscript of *The Red Badge of Courage* to McClure. McClure and his syndicate, suffering through a brief recession, were overextended. So McClure neither accepted nor rejected Crane's war novel; instead, he kept Crane's manuscript for six months. (Incidentally, McClure held the only copy of Crane's masterpiece, and it was misplaced for several weeks. Eventually it was found in the pressroom; some of *McClure's* compositors had been reading it!) One supposes, then, that McClure felt some responsibility and remorse for delaying the career of a young writer whose work he very much admired, and so he sent reporter Crane to do a story on the anthracite coal mines of Pennsylvania's Wyoming County.

En route to the northeast corner of Pennsylvania, Crane (and his friend Corwin Linson) spent the night at Crane's sometime hometown of Port Jervis, New Jersey. The next day, the *Port Jervis Union* boasted of Crane's fame and success and reported his next assignment: "Mr. Stephen Crane, of New York city, whose novel 'Maggie' has given its author considerable literary celebrity, and whose magazine articles have many readers in this village, was in town over night, as the guest of his brother, Mr. W. H. Crane. He started for Scranton this noon, where he goes to obtain material for an article in *McClure's* magazine on the coal fields of that region. He was accompanied by Mr. C. K. Linson, the well known artist, who will furnish the illustrations for the article" (Crane 1994, 108).[1]

On May 18–19 Crane and Linson made two descents into the Dunmore mines—the first shaft was 750 feet deep, the second, 1,000 feet. Crane and Linson boarded at the Valley House in Scranton: the journalist worked on his first draft, and the illustrator, his drawings. In late July, "In the Depths of a Coal Mine" was syndicated in five newspapers. The abbreviated newspaper version contained up to three of Linson's drawings. Shortly thereafter, the full version, with fourteen illustrations by Linson, was the feature article in the August *McClure's*.

Fortunately, we have most of Crane's first draft to compare with the final *McClure's* version.[2] A comparison of these drafts reveals Crane's sure-handed self-editing as he held himself to his maxim, "Preaching is fatal to art in literature" (1988, 230). Before we look at Crane's revisions, we will examine how his extraordinary openness led him to a sophisticated metaphysical position on the nature of human experience. Hence, "In the Depths of a Coal Mine" offers both social commentary and philosophical insight.

"New Eyes": Crane's Metaphysics of Experience

Crane's philosophical contemporaries, the pragmatists William James, C. S. Peirce, and John Dewey, sought to transcend the dualisms of subject/object, knower/known, and person/thing. The subject matter for philosophical (and literary) inspection, they argued, was *experience*. Dewey proposed using neutral and interactive language. For example, he referred to experience as "a transaction" or "a negotiation" between experiencers and their experiences. (Note that both "experiencers" and "experiences" are plural.)

For his part, James took aim at two of the "Idols of the Tribe": Truth and Reality. We "naturally" suppose that experience puts us into contact with a static, given Reality, and we "naturally" assume that a detached spectator's objective report is capable of capturing the Truth about what is out there. But truths and realities are all that human experiencers can manage. Accordingly, reliable and practically useful accounts of multiple realities constituted by a variety of experiencers and realized across a spectrum of contexts form the basis of James's modest and realistic pragmatic epistemology.

For the American pragmatists (and for Crane), the first step in the philosophical reconstruction of our habitual views of Truth and Reality is a realization that all facts (as well as values, ideas, and beliefs) are theory laden and context dependent. Alert to the constitutive nature of contexts and consciousnesses, Crane maneuvers his readers into experiential contact with richness, novelty, and surprise as he has us confront a variety of incompatible versions of the same event. On precisely this point, Crane's writings are replete with observers and participants who discover that experiences grant them "new eyes."

In the second paragraph of "In the Depths of a Coal Mine," Crane notes how he and Linson react to a group of second-shift miners walking by them. "They went stolidly along, some swinging lunch-pails carelessly, but the marks upon them of their forbidding and mystic calling fascinated *our new eyes* until they passed from sight" (591, emphasis added). As capable witnesses, Crane and Linson already have "new eyes": they are neither too aloof nor too engrossed, neither too clinical nor too sympathetic. As attentive and balanced onlookers, they are not without biases and preconceived views. As epistemologically competent experiencers with prior—even firm and well-considered—opinions, they remain, crucially, open, tractable, and sensitive enough to permit, even encourage, revisions of their beliefs.

A comparison of Crane's opening and second-to-last paragraphs (both of which describe the mine, the breakers, and the area around the mine) dramatizes how Crane's subterranean tour radically reconstitutes the same scene. The sketch begins with a graphic description of the land around the mine— nature ruined and degraded: "The breakers squatted upon the hillsides and in the valley like enormous preying monsters eating of the sunshine, the grass, the green leaves. The smoke from their nostrils had ravaged the air of coolness and fragrance. All that remained of the vegetation looked dark, miserable, and half-strangled. Along the summit-line of the mountain, a few unhappy trees were etched upon the clouds. Overhead stretched a sky of imperial blue, incredibly far away from the sombre land" (590). At the end of the piece, as Crane rides the elevator up to the surface, he wonders about "the new world that I was to behold in a moment" (599–600). Reborn, he sees that the ravaged and ugly land around the mine has become Edenic—beautiful, wholesome, and natural: "Of a sudden the fleeting walls became flecked with light. It increased to a downpour of sunbeams. The high sun was afloat in a splendor of spotless blue. The distant hills were arrayed in purple and stood like monarchs. A glory of gold was upon the near-by earth. The cool fresh air was wine" (600). Of course, neither the "ravaged" land nor the "glory of gold" earth is the total, final Truth. Indeed, for Crane (and the pragmatists), experience forces us to confront a pluri-verse of multiple realities that tolerate a wide variety of opinions and adaptive strategies.

But not every opinion, however contextualized and thereby understandable, is equally valid; not every tactic, however long endorsed by habit and tradition, is equally fruitful. The arbiters of our beliefs and actions are pragmatic: success or failure, pleasure or pain, safety or danger, profit or loss, stability or precariousness. The second term in each pair looms large in Crane's account of coal mines and miners.

A coal mine is not a safe place; mining is not a healthy job. No news here! Crane's genius, however, turns these obvious and commonplace observations into emotionally charged, empathetic encounters. A number of Crane's stories and journalistic pieces skillfully exploit the irony of participants unable to understand themselves and their situations. Such is also the case with the Scranton miners.

The situation of the miners is complex; Crane is careful to preserve nuance and ambiguity. On one hand, miners "choose" to become miners. He explains how badly the slate boys want to become real miners, deep down inside the earth. On the other hand, these youngsters have had an apprenticeship in the breakers and so had to "breath[e] this atmosphere until their lungs grow heavy and hav[e] this clamor in their ears until they grow deaf as bats. Poor little ambitious lads, it is no wonder that to become miners, is the height of their desires" (602). Perhaps, suggests Crane, a boy growing up in a mining town has little choice about his future.

But when it comes to a description of the mine as a place of work, Crane is neither restrained nor cautious. It is an unfair contest. Since the miners are thieves and intruders, it is only a matter of time until Nature retaliates. Though the miners are able to probe and blast and tear away at the mine walls and ceilings, Crane and Linson cannot bring themselves to touch the walls or ceiling that bear the seams of coal: "The sense of an abiding danger in the roof was always upon our foreheads. It expressed to us all the unmeasured, deadly tons above us. It was a superlative might that regarded with supreme calmness of almighty power the little men at its mercy. Sometimes we were obliged to bend low to avoid it. Always our hands rebelled vaguely from touching it, refusing to affront this gigantic mass" (594). The miners surely understand that in the long run the odds are against them. Still, they willingly gamble their lives. Crane, however, sees the situation differently: "It is war. It is the most savage part of all in this endless battle between man and nature. These miners are grimly in the van. They have carried war into places where nature has the strength of a million giants. Sometimes their enemy becomes exasperated and snuffs out ten, twenty, thirty lives. Usually she remains calm, and takes one at a time with method and precision. She need not hurry. She possesses eternity" (596–97). Though not as unabashedly and aggressively reformist as B. O. Flower's *Arena* (which also published a number of Crane's pieces), *McClure's* nonetheless featured the writing of a number of muckrakers. Clearly then, Crane had to make decisions about the extent and explicitness of his social commentary about mines and miners. As we shall now see, Crane used art, not propaganda, to make his case. A collation of the first draft with the *McClure's* article reveals substantial shifts in tone, content, and rhetorical style.

SELF-EDITING, INDIRECTION, AND SOCIAL COMMENTARY

There are many minor alterations of the first draft. Some emendations are purely stylistic; others, seemingly trivial, are rhetorically telling and philosophically significant. Crane was careful about the uncertain situation of the miners—did they have a real choice in becoming miners, or were their lives environmentally determined? Crane's account of miners' health problems uses precisely parallel language. The magazine version has it "there *usually* comes to him an attack of '*miner's* asthma,'" while the draft version is subtly different: "there comes an *inevitable* disease, the '*mine* asthma'" (599, 606, emphasis added).

Overall the magazine version is cooler and less strident.[3] More significantly, all editorial commentary has been excised from the published version. What remains appears to be the simple reporting of the dirt, din, and danger of coal mining. There is no overt indictment of the mining industry, but by powerful indirection and effective understatement, Crane deftly leads the reader to make a social and moral assessment.

Linson recalled that Crane composed the first draft in their Scranton hotel room. In the initial version, Crane's simmering outrage and indignation leaked onto his pages; however, upon his return to New York City, his artistic sense reasserted itself. For example, the phrase comparing the mine to "a penitentiary for bandits, murderers, and cannibals" (606) was removed because it undercut the moral message that most miners did not view themselves as being trapped by the mine. Crane did not need to point out the coal industry's inhumanity to miners; the treatment of the mine mules made his moral point for him (more on the mules shortly).

Crane's most extensive and important deletions reflect a reporter's commitment to neutrality. He wondered why the miners did not organize a strong union. "When I studied mines and the miner's life underground and above ground, I wondered at many things but I could not induce myself to wonder why the miners strike and otherwise object to their lot" (605). That sentence and his sardonic comment that a coal miner's retirement bonus is "mine asthma" were deleted.

Crane eliminated four paragraphs near the end of the piece that denounced the mining industry and its place in American society. These sections discussed the fact that miners' hardship provides comfort for coal-burning homeowners, the fact that miners' grime gives livelihood to "virtuous and immaculate coal-brokers" (607), and the fact that miners' diseases bring financial health to "the impersonal and hence conscienceless thing, the company" (607). Finally, Crane refrained from saying the obvious: "One cannot go down in the mines often before he finds himself wondering why it is that the coal-barons get so much and these miners, swallowed by the grim black mouths of the earth day after day, get proportionately so little" (606).

As noted above, Crane held that preaching and literary art are incompatible. His letter to the editor of *Demorest's Family Magazine* states, "I try to give readers a slice out of life; and if there is any moral or lesson in it I do not point it out. I let the reader find it for himself. As Emerson said, 'There should be a long logic beneath the story, but it should be kept carefully out of sight'" (1988, 230).

Crane's most potent incrimination utilizes the signature characteristic of his style: irony. He skillfully contrasts the reluctant mine mules with the youngest boys, the slate pickers who are eager to be promoted deeper into the mine to become door boys, then mule boys, then laborers and helpers, and, finally, in the depths of a coal mine, "real miners" who make the blasts. The mules, which "resembled enormous rats" in their "stable [that] was like a dungeon" (597), become the vehicle of Crane's ethical point. Aghast at the condition of the miners, Crane dramatically reserves his moral condemnation, "the tragedy of it," for the lot of the animals:

One had to wait to see the tragedy of it. . . . It is a common affair for mules to be imprisoned for years in the limitless night of the mines. . . . When brought to the surface, these animals tremble at the earth, radiant in the sunshine. Later, they go almost mad with fantastic joy. The full splendor of the heavens, the grass, the trees, the breezes breaks upon them suddenly. They caper and career with extravagant mulish glee. . . . To those who have known the sun-light there may come the fragrant dream. Perhaps this is what they brood over when they stand solemnly in rows with slowly flapping ears. A recollection may appear to them, a recollection of pastures of a lost paradise. Perhaps they despair and thirst for this bloom that lies in an unknown direction and at impossible distances. (597–98)

Crane's ethical case reverses the standard *a fortiori* argument—if the stronger case holds, surely the weaker case presents no problem.[4] So then, from the opposite direction, Crane asks, if the weaker case, animal welfare, raises moral issues, how much more ought the mining industry's treatment of humans be scrutinized?

Crane continues his oblique critique in another pairing of the human and nonhuman. Darkness and silence are the natural state underground. Here "there frequently grows a moss-like fungus, white as a druid's beard, that thrives in these deep dens but shrivels and dies in contact with the sun-light" (599). The unnatural inhabitants of the mine—the men and the mules—are phototropic so they yearn for "the glorious summer-time earth" (594). But this is not in every case, suggests Crane. Apparently many miners have adjusted to "the stretches of great darkness, [and] majestic silences" (597). But not the mules. Some of them "seem . . . somehow, like little children. We met a boy once who said that sometimes the only way he could get his resolute team to move was to run ahead of them with the light. Afraid of the darkness, they would trot hurriedly after him and so take the train of heavy cars to a desired place" (598). For the mules, every return to the surface means salvation and liberation. However, inured to the mine's debilitating dangers and accustomed to silence and darkness, a coal miner's daily return to and thereafter his retirement on the surface are not always happy or healthful: "If a man may escape the gas, the floods, the 'squeezes' of falling rock, the cars shooting through little tunnels, the precarious elevators, the hundred perils, there usually comes to him an attack of 'miner's asthma' that slowly racks and shakes him into the grave. Meanwhile he gets three dollars per day, and his laborer one dollar and a quarter" (599). Many miners, like the mosslike fungus, shrivel and die when they come into prolonged contact with the fresh air and the sunlight.

In conclusion, as the elevator ascends the mine shaft, Crane reflects on the "new world" he will reenter. "In the Depths of a Coal Mine" has made us privy to new worlds of mines, mules, and miners. However, Crane's most important insight about these new worlds deals with the role of coal mining in turn-of-the-(last)-century American society.

Whereas his first draft explicitly commented upon how miners are exploited by coal-burning consumers, coal brokers, and coal companies, the *McClure's* version ends with an abstract, symbolic summary. Crane begins his article by likening miners' work to the feeding of a monster: "With terrible appetite this huge and hideous monster sat imperturbably munching coal, grinding its mammoth jaws with unearthly and monotonous uproar" (591). Crane concludes by returning to the breakers, now refashioned and recast as machines, the embodiment of American business. Note his penultimate and ultimate phrases: "Of that sinister struggle far below there came no sound, no suggestion save the loaded cars that emerged one after another in eternal procession and were sent creaking up the incline that their contents might be fed into the mouth of the breaker, imperturbably cruel and insatiate, black emblem of greed, and of the gods of this labor" (600).

NOTES

This chapter is a revised and shortened version of the chapter "Openness to Experience in Stephen Crane's 'In the Depths of a Coal Mine'" that appeared in *Caverns of the Night: Coal Mines in Art, Literature and Film,* edited by William Thesing, 186–98 (Columbia: University of South Carolina Press, 2000).

1. Corwin Knapp Linson (1864–1959), painter, illustrator, and photographer, was introduced to Crane during the winter of 1892–93. Both lived in the old Art Students League building on East Twenty-third Street in New York City, and they remained friends until 1897. In addition to his illustrations for *McClure's,* Linson's work appeared in *Century* and *Cosmopolitan. Scribner's Magazine* sent him to Athens to provide sketches of the revived Olympic Games in 1896. For reliable information on Linson's life and work, see Wertheim's entry on him in *A Stephen Crane Encyclopedia.*

2. Both the *McClure's* article and Crane's first draft are printed in volume 8 of *The Works of Stephen Crane.*

3. Whether Crane initiated the editing of his manuscript or whether it was *McClure's* censorship is a matter of scholarly dispute. The matter is further complicated

by differences between the syndicated newspaper and magazine versions of the piece. It is my view that because *McClure's* printed a number of preachy social commentary articles (including some by Crane's friend and mentor, Hamlin Garland), Crane's self-editing best explains the differences between the first draft and the complete magazine version. See my *Pluralistic Philosophy* (10–14 and 153–54, nn22 and 23) for more on this issue. For secondary comments on Crane's journalism, see chapter 9 of my *Stephen Crane: An Annotated Bibliography of Secondary Scholarship.*

4. For a clear example (its plausibility and decency aside) of the *a fortiori* ethical argument strategy, see Tooley (1984), who argues that if the stronger case, infanticide, could be made morally innocuous, then objections to the weaker case, killing fetuses, would be obviated. As noted, Crane reverses this strategy by making vivid the weaker case—animal welfare—letting his readers extend his argument to the stronger case—the use and abuse of humans.

WORKS CITED

Crane, Stephen. 1969–76. *The Works of Stephen Crane.* Edited by Fredson Bowers. 10 vols. Charlottesville: University Press of Virginia.

———. 1988. *The Correspondence of Stephen Crane.* Edited by Stanley Wertheim and Paul Sorrentino. 2 vols. New York: Columbia University Press.

———. 1994. *The Crane Log: A Documentary Life of Stephen Crane, 1871–1900.* Edited by Stanley Wertheim and Paul Sorrentino. New York: G. K. Hall.

Dooley, Patrick. 1992. *Stephen Crane: An Annotated Bibliography of Secondary Scholarship.* New York: G. K. Hall.

———. 1993. *The Pluralistic Philosophy of Stephen Crane.* Urbana: University of Illinois Press.

Tooley, Thomas. 1984. "In Defense of Abortion and Infanticide." In *The Problem of Abortion,* edited by Joel Feinberg, 120–34. Belmont, CA: Wadsworth.

Wertheim, Stanley. 1997. *A Stephen Crane Encyclopedia.* Westport, CT: Greenwood Press.

3

Ethical Tolerance and Sociological Savvy
Crane's Travels in Mexico

> *Above all things, the stranger finds the occupation of foreign*
> *peoples to be trivial and inconsequent. The average mind utterly*
> *fails to comprehend the new point of view.*
> —Stephen Crane

In January of 1895, the Bacheller syndicate sent Stephen Crane west to report on the impact of a summer of extreme drought followed by windstorms that led to one of the worst winters on record. While in Kearney, Nebraska, Crane reported (from his unheated hotel room!) winds of sixy miles per hour and a temperature of fifteen degrees below zero. After Nebraska, Crane traveled to Louisiana and Texas. From Laredo, a two-day train ride brought him to Mexico City. Over the next two months, Crane not only experienced life in the capital city but made several short trips into the surrounding provinces. All told, he wrote a half-dozen remarkably open, tolerant, and nonjudgmental dispatches recording his impressions of life in a foreign land.

While it is not my purpose to make Crane into a politically correct saint before his time, I find that his sociological maturity and his other-culture sophistication are exceptional. Beyond his journalistic dispatches dealing with Mexican life, which we will soon look at in some detail, Crane's foreign foray inspired two wonderful tales of the Mexican frontier: "One Dash—Horses" and "A Man and Some Others." The second was not published until February 1897 (with a full-page illustration by Frederic Remington) even though Crane had written the story shortly after his return to New York City from Mexico. The gap between composition and publication was partly due to *Century* editor Richard Watson Gilder's objection to profane dialogue in the story. Another reader of the manuscript version of the story, Theodore Roosevelt, offered a different objection. Crane's story tells of a confrontation between an American sheepherder, Bill, and several Mexican vaqueros who insist that he move his herd back across the U.S. border. Bill refuses and is killed in an ambush. Roosevelt disliked the story, writing to Crane, "Some day I want you to write another story of the frontiersman and the Mexican Greaser in which the frontiersman shall come out on top; it is more normal that way" (Crane 1988, 249). Regrettably, that opinion of the "more normal" way was apparently the majority view, judging by the American public's enthusiastic support of the Roosevelt administration's expansionistic, jingoistic, and imperialistic foreign policy.

In contrast, Crane's live-and-let-live posture of nationalist neutrality is drawn from his fundamental philosophical commitments. I have argued elsewhere that Crane's understanding of the nature of experience leads him to positions of metaphysical pluralism and epistemological contextualism.[1] Both, in turn, dictate a modest ethical imperative that is reluctant to make claims of cultural superiority and is loath to be critical of other lifestyles.

From his early juvenile pieces to what I believe to be his most subtle social and ethical commentary, *The Monster*, the metaphysical pluralism of Crane's writing is propelled by a curiosity of and openness to the lives of an astonishing range of experiencers, both human and nonhuman. Crane remained loyal to his deepest impulse to simply display and then move on, letting stand without judgment his depictions of a wide array of experienced realities. Note, for example, in his "Crane at Velestino," how his juxtaposition of the spectators' remove and the soldiers' agony renders the same event both gorgeous and tragic: "The roll of musketry was tremendous. From a distance it was like tearing a cloth; nearer, it sounded like rain on a tin roof and close up it was just a long crash after crash. It was a beautiful sound—beautiful, as I had never dreamed. It was more impressive than the roar of Niagara and finer than thunder or avalanche. . . . This is one point of view. Another might be taken from the men who died there. The slaughter of the Turks was enormous" (1984, 935).

Or, in a wonderful short piece, "A Lovely Jag in a Crowded Car," a drunken man enters the crosstown streetcar and, taking his seat, "put his hands on his knees and beamed about him in absolute unalloyed happiness." Because he was "on the best of terms with each single atom in space . . . his excited spirits overflowed to such an extent that he was obliged to sing" (1973, 362). His experience of "the pearl-hued joys of life as seen through a pair of strange, oblique, temporary spectacles" (364) was, for him, not only moving but also profound beyond words, and so he burst into song—a song unappreciated by the train conductor and his fellow passengers, who were experiencing a rather different world.

Logically, prior to Crane's metaphysical pluralism is his epistemological contextualism. His position on the tentativeness, revisability, and partiality of knowledge is, of course, closely linked to his contentions regarding the limitations of language. His commentary on tourist books in "Stephen Crane in Mexico" is only partly ironic: "Strangers upon entering Mexico should at once acquire a guide book, and if they fail to gain the deepest knowledge of the country and its inhabitants, they may lay it to their own inability to understand the English language in its purest terms" (1973, 442).

Then, too, Crane is cognizant of the perennial epistemological problems of induction: can we gain sufficient insight from a sample to support assertions about the whole, and can past experience provide a reliable guide to the future? On both accounts, Crane's theory of knowledge is realistic and pragmatic, content with reliable generalizations that stop far short of making any absolute claims. For instance, from his study of Mexican guidebooks, he gleans four elementary rules for dealing with peddlers:

I. Do not buy anything at all from street venders.
II. When buying from street venders, give the exact sum charged. Do not delude yourself with the idea of getting any change back.
III. When buying from street venders, divide by ten the price demanded for any article, and offer it.
IV. Do not buy anything at all from street venders. (442)

And then before he reiterates his warnings about the deception and trickery of typical scams played by street hustlers in Mexican parks and byways, Crane is careful to frame his tourist alert with a telling cautionary preface: "It is never just to condemn a class" (442).

Accordingly, then, my overall contention is that given Crane's philosophical stances of metaphysical pluralism and epistemological contextualism, it is no surprise that he is leery to claim for himself any personal competence in understanding other cultures or any special insight into the strong and weak points of other lifestyles. I see Crane employing a negative *a fortiori* argument, putting the matter in the form of a logical axiom—if it is the case that we cannot be certain in making claims about our own culture by using our own language, how much more cautious ought we be about the reliability of our grasp of an alien culture and a foreign language?[2] In "The Mexican Lower Classes" Crane is explicit about this contention: "It perhaps might be said—if any one dared—that the most worthless literature of the world has been that which has been written by the men of one nation concerning the men of another" (1984, 728). Crane goes on to urge that foreign travelers "not sit in literary judgement on this or that manner of the people." Beyond "literary judgment," his more important admonition concerns sitting in cultural and ethical judgment. But before we assess Crane's conclusion, we need to take a look at the cautionary evidence he offers against making judgments about the fashions, tastes, and occupations of others.

None of us should have the slightest difficulty agreeing with Crane's deflating comments about the fickleness of fashions and fads and the foolishness of staying in step with the latest trends. Crane's fashion report deals with "Hats, Shirts and Spurs in Mexico." Though he pokes fun at the Mexican gentlemen of fashion with their tight silver-button-edged trousers, spurs the size of "rhinoceros traps" (1973, 466), and hats "with the same artistic value as . . . a small tower of bricks" (465), Crane knows that his own outfit must look silly to the Mexicans. Wanting to take exception to the crimson shirt of a smart, with-it American tourist, he tempers his comments, conceding that "it is never wise to deride the fashions of another people, for we ourselves have no idea of what we are coming to. Within two years, New York may be absolutely on fire with crimson shirts—blood red bosoms may flash in the air like lanterns" (467).

Next he turns to preferences in tastes and smells, which are, of course, acquired and adaptable. The tourist Crane has no difficulty finding American-style cocktails, but it is the natives' preference for pulque that fascinates him. As the beverage was very cheap and available, dispensed from near-omnipresent stalls, Crane regularly witnessed its powerful impact. He notes that though "five glasses seem to be sufficient to floor the average citizen of the republic . . . the author of this article is not supposed to be transfixed with admiration because of the above facility of jag. He merely recites facts" (446). Nonetheless the smell and the taste of pulque make Crane wonder why anyone would "ever taste another drop of pulque after having once collided with it" (457). Apparently neither the smell nor the taste "relate[s] to the Mexicans." Crane continues, "This relates to the foreigner who brings with him numerous superstitious and racial, fundamental traditions concerning odors. To the foreigner, the very proximity of a glass of pulque is enough to take him up by the hair and throw him violently to the ground. . . . And it tastes like—it tastes like—some terrible concoction of bad yeast perhaps. Or maybe some calamity of eggs. . . . This, bear in mind, represents the opinion of a stranger. . . . To the Mexican, pulque is a delirium of joy" (457).

Even if tourists ought to give a wide berth to Mexican fashions and drink, one wonders whether a corresponding acquiescence ought to be extended to the poverty of their lives and the apparent pointlessness of their occupations—mostly sitting on doorsteps and sleeping. "That such and such a man should be satisfied to carry bundles or mayhap sit and ponder in the sun all his life in this faraway country seems an abnormally stupid thing. The visitor feels scorn. He swells with a knowledge of his geographical experience. 'How futile are the lives of these people,' he remarks, 'and what incredible ignorance that they should not be aware of their futility'" (1984, 728).

Visitor Crane, however, does not agree. For him, such a value judgment shows "the arrogance of the man who has not yet solved himself and discovered his own actual futility" (728).

Why do the Mexican lower classes acquiesce to their situation? "Their squalor, their ignorance seemed so absolute that death—no matter what it has in store—would appear as freedom, joy" (728–29). Though they are silent, "One listens for the first thunder of the rebellion, the moment when this silence shall be broken by a roar of war. . . . They have it in their power to become terrible" (729). To account for their submissiveness, Crane proposes "certain handsome theories" (729). For instance, it may be the case that the average Mexican peasant "has not enough information to be unhappy over his state. Nobody seeks to provide him with it. He is born, he works, he worships, he dies, all on less money than would buy a thoroughbred Newfoundland dog and who dares to enlighten him?" (729).

Crane's preferred account for the complaisance of the Mexican lower class hinges on two striking claims: despite their being apparently "poverty-stricken," he wonders what "plums in the world" (729) are lacking to them. Crane avers, "I would remember that there really was no comfort in the plums after all as far as I had seen them and I would esteem no orations concerning the glitter of plums" (729). Crane's first contention, then, is that the Mexican lower classes are not materially impoverished after all. Second, he holds that they are no worse off, from a moral point of view, than the affluent elsewhere. In fact, in important ways he finds their lives spiritually superior. "I measure their morality by what evidences of peace and contentment I can detect in the average countenance" (730). Their peace and contentment, he argues, indicates that they are not suffering any serious injustices. With justice and fairness as his standard, he offers the following negative norm: "If a man is not given a fair opportunity to be virtuous, if his environment chokes his moral aspirations, I say that he has got the one important cause of complaint and rebellion against society" (730). According to Crane's sociology of material poverty, however, nothing of real importance has been denied to the Mexican lower classes, and according to his criterion of moral opportunity, no significant ethical barriers confront them. Accordingly, neither hand-wringing nor a helping hand is in order: "It is for these reasons that I refuse to commit judgment upon these lower classes of Mexico. I even refuse to pity them. It is true at night that many of them sleep in heaps in door-ways, and spend their days squatting upon the pavements. It is true that their clothing is scant and thin. All manner of things of this kind is true but yet their faces have almost always a certain smoothness, a certain lack of pain, a serene faith. I can feel the superiority of their contentment" (731).

Crane's conclusion appears to overshout the most enthusiastic partisan of political correctness, for even the most chaste noninterference policy must have some limits!

Suppose we test Crane's live-and-let-live conclusions against semineutral transcultural standards of judgment that have been used to justify a missionary-style effort to convince and convert or, perhaps in extreme cases, would sanction forceful intervention. For example, one criterion that might justify cultural hegemony would be an egregious and/or systemic violation of basic human rights as promulgated in the United Nations Declarations of 1948 and 1966. Of course, much empirical work about conditions in Mexico when Crane visited in 1895 would be needed to support an intervention initiative on humanitarian grounds.

A more abstract and older basis for societal interference is worked out in John Stuart Mill's classic *On Liberty*. Decrying the tendency of governments and individuals to intrude paternalistically into the free space of others, Mill argues:

> That the only purpose for which power can be rightfully exercised over any member of a civilized community, against his will, is to prevent harm to others. His own good, either physical or moral, is not a sufficient warrant. He cannot rightfully be compelled to do or forebear because it will be better for him to do so, because it will make him happier, because, in the opinions of others, to do so would be wise, or even right. . . . To justify [either compulsion or punishment] . . . the conduct

from which it is desired to deter him, must be calculated to produce evil to some one else. (1859, 9–10)

Mill then adds two qualifications that seem obvious to him. His first exception regarding children, that "those who are still in a state to require being taken care of by others, must be protected against their own actions as well as against external injury" (10), is hard to argue with. His second caveat, however, is problematic: "For the same reason, we may leave out of consideration those backward states of society in which the race itself may be considered as in its nonage. . . . Despotism is a legitimate mode of government in dealing with barbarians, provided the end be their improvement, and the means justified by actually effecting that end" (10).

Given Crane's philosophical overview, especially his ethics of cultural tolerance, Mill's easy confidence about the backwardness of primitive societies seems to be little more than a bold assertion that betrays the cultural arrogance and narrow-mindedness of a society, much like America at the turn of the (last) century, which claimed political imperialism and territorial expansionism as its manifest destiny. Recall Roosevelt's comments about "the normal way" noted above; he surely must have welcomed the paternalistic prerogatives that Mill's political theory offered.

Crane's attitudes about imposing the values and religion of one's culture are diametrically opposed to Roosevelt's. An earlier travelogue dealing, in part, with his visit to the old mission at San Antonio gave Crane an opportunity to make some wonderfully satirical comments about Spanish missionary activities in Old Mexico (now Texas): "During interval of peace and interval of war, toiled the pious monks, erecting missions, digging ditches, making farms and cudgeling their Indians in and out of the church. Sometimes, when the venerable fathers ran short of Indians to convert, the soldiers went on expeditions and returned dragging in a few score" (1984, 713).

To return to Crane's intuitions about nonintervention, suppose a society whose members are in pain and lack peace, contentment, and serenity is observed. In this instance, one supposes that Crane's epistemological modesty about how well outsiders can ascertain the inner lives and psychological states of those they observe would reassert itself. Moreover, since he grants to other societies a prima facie and generous benefit of the doubt, he would be chary of indicting another society of deficiencies. The tuition that purchases such catholic tolerance is travel. In "Seen at Hot Springs" he argues that the townspeople have been enlightened by numerous visitors who have journeyed to this famous American spa: "This street thoroughly understands geography, and its experience of men is great. . . . This profound education has destroyed its curiosity and created a sort of a wide sympathy, not tender, but tolerant" (1984, 701–2). Likewise in "Stephen Crane in Mexico (1)," he notes how long and how carefully one must take in any situation before one "can begin to understand the local point of view" (1973, 439).

Crane's abiding wonder at the variety and richness of human and other lives leads him to suppose (except in obvious and intractable situations like war or coal mines or chronic sickness or serious injury) that the mix of good and evil, pain and pleasure, anxiety and contentment, is probably evenly distributed over the human race. That is, the differences between persons in one situation and the next are refractory and superficial. In other words, Crane contends that there is little variation due to time and place across the generic human situation: "It is the fortune of travelers to take note of differences and publish them to their friends. It is the differences that are supposed to be valuable. The travellers seek them bravely, and cudgel their wits to find means to unearth them. But in this search they are confronted continually by the resemblances and the intrusion of commonplace and most obvious similarity. . . . In a word, it is the passion for differences which has prevented a general knowledge of the resemblances" (1984, 706–7).

All in all, then, it seems to me that Crane's attitude toward other cultures is laissez-faire. He is suspicious of outsiders who show up to help, especially when help has not been sought. Despite his minister father and his more ambitiously proselytizing mother, Crane is leery of the missionary impulse. His wariness is symbolically underscored by the colors he uses to describe churches, colors that make it difficult for these buildings to blend in with and be seen as part of a native culture. In *George's Mother,* though the little mission chapel that George reluctantly agrees to visit with his mother "sat humbly between two towering apartment-houses" and was illuminated by "a red street-lamp [that] threw a marvelous reflection upon the wet pavements, it was like the death-stain of a spirit" (1984, 255). Or in "The Viga Canal," Crane notes "that in the midst of the swarming pulque shops, resorts, and gardens, stood a little white church, stern, unapproving, representing the other fundamental aspiration of humanity, a reproach and a warning" (1973, 434). Crane's last phrases are pregnant and significant. If the tendency to judge, correct, reprove, and interfere is a "fundamental aspiration of humanity," Crane's wise admonition is to cultivate and heed a corresponding moral imperative: learn to appreciate, and leave alone the ways of being human that are unlike our own.

Notes

This chapter is a slightly revised version of the essay "Crane's Sociological Savvy: An Examination of His Mexican Travel Dispatches," *Stephen Crane Studies* 11.2 (2002): 2–10.

1. See the second chapter of my *The Pluralistic Philosophy of Stephen Crane* for a detailed account of Crane's metaphysics and epistemology.

2. See page 30 (and note 4) in chapter 2 for Crane's use of a positive *a fortiori* argument.

Works Cited

Crane, Stephen. 1973. *The Works of Stephen Crane*. Edited by Fredson Bowers. Vol. 8. Charlottesville: University Press of Virginia.

———. 1984. *Stephen Crane: Prose and Poetry*. Edited by J. C. Levenson. New York: Library of America.

———. 1988. *The Correspondence of Stephen Crane*. Edited by Stanley Wertheim and Paul Sorrentino. 2 vols. New York: Columbia University Press.

Dooley, Patrick K. 1993. *The Pluralistic Philosophy of Stephen Crane*. Urbana: University of Illinois Press.

Mill, John Stuart. 1859. *On Liberty*. Northbrook, IL: AHM, 1947.

4

"Matters of Conscience" and "Blunders of Virtue"

Crane on the Varieties of Heroism, or Why Moral Philosophers Need Literature

Fiction is nothing less than the subtlest instrument for self-examination and self-display that Mankind has invented yet. Psychology and X-rays bring up some portentous shadows, and demographics and stroboscopic photography do some fine breakdowns, but for the full parfum *and effluvia of being human, for feathery ambiguity and rank facticity, for the air and iron, fire and spit of our daily moral adventure there is nothing like fiction: it makes sociology look priggish, history problematical, the cinema two-dimensional, and* The National Enquirer *as silly as last week's cereal box.*
—*John Updike*

Moral philosophers badly need the concrete, vivid, probing dramatizations that are the stock and trade of novelists and short story writers. The fiction of Stephen Crane is an especially rich resource in this regard. Of particular interest is the fact that his works repeatedly dramatize risk taking, courage, and heroism. The shifting and uncertain borderline between ordinary and exceptional moral actions is an area especially worthy of consideration since this topic has recently attracted renewed attention from philosophers (and theologians) who have examined heroic (and saintly) conduct as acts of supererogation.

The technical term "supererogation" comes from the Good Samaritan parable, Luke 10:30–35, which functions as *the* paradigm for actions above and beyond the call of duty. The Vulgate text of the Bible includes the phrase *quodcumque supererogaveris*—this is the only time the latter word occurs in the New Testament. Translated literally, the Samaritan tells the innkeeper that he will, upon his return, "repay if there is any further expense."[1]

In the standard philosophical account, as summarized by David Heyd, an act is supererogatory if and only if:

1. It is neither obligatory nor forbidden.
2. Its omission is not wrong, and does not deserve sanction or criticism—either formal or informal.
3. It is morally good, both by virtue of its (intended) consequences and by virtue of its intrinsic value (being beyond duty).
4. It is done voluntarily for the sake of someone else's good, and is thus meritorious. (1982, 115)

Or, somewhat differently, Gregory Mellema begins his recent monograph with the following definition: "An act of supererogation can be identified by its possession of three characteristics. First, it is an act whose performance fulfills no moral duty or obligation. Second, it is an act whose performance is morally praiseworthy or meritorious. Third, it is an act whose omission is not morally blameworthy" (1991, 3). Even more concisely put, Michael Langford's characterization is the soul of brevity: an act of supererogation is "commendable but not commandable" (1988, 444).

Although philosophers may have contributed to a theoretical understanding of conduct above and beyond the call of duty, they have failed to provide persuasive, emotionally compelling, and intellectually engaging illustrations of such conduct. Worse, such actions have been trivialized. For instance, some philosophical essays appeal to intuitions about overtricks in bridge ostensibly to aid our understanding of optional and praiseworthy actions. Or, seeking to illuminate behavior that goes beyond or stops short of doing one's duty (actions recently dubbed "suberogatory"[2]), Roderick Chisholm explores restaurant etiquette: "If the waiter is not busy, failure to tell him he has brought the wrong dessert may be supererogatory omission; but if he is told and then returns with the proper dessert, failure to say 'Thank you' may be an offense of omission; a generous tip would then be supererogatory commission and a complaint to the manager an offense of commission" (1963, 11). Similarly, Joel Feinberg examines at some length our responses to strangers: "Any reasonable man of good will would offer the stranger a match. Perhaps a truly virtuous man would do more than that. He would be friendly, reply with a cheerful smile, and might even volunteer to light the stranger's cigarette" (1970, 4). Thankfully, marginally substantive examples of doing more than is required have recently been examined. (Sadly, however, even these offer little more than lowercase illustrations.) For example, Paul McNamara explores why it is the case that when one has promised to drop off or pick up a friend at the airport, one is "not obligated to do both—though doing so is permissible, in fact supererogatory" (1996, 428).

In contrast to these superficial examples of supererogation, Crane's works supply striking and profound, and serious, instances of behaviors for philosophical analysis. In what follows, we will examine his explorations of exceptional conduct described in his signature novel, *The Red Badge of Courage*; ethical problems raised in the short stories "The Veteran" and "The Mystery of Heroism"; and several moral issues dramatized in his late novella, *The Monster*. Overlaying Crane's literary depictions on a framework that utilizes philosophical requirements for supererogation is pedagogically fruitful as engaging and vivid answers surface, and fresh and challenging questions emerge.

Readers of Crane's masterpiece, *The Red Badge of Courage*, vicariously experience three days in the life of Henry Fleming, a green, untried, naive, and sometimes romantic private. Incidentally, Crane had no combat experience; in fact, he had not even observed war when he wrote *The Red Badge* some thirty years after the Civil War armistice at Appomattox. Yet he so convincingly captured the feel of combat from the point of view of an ordinary soldier that many veterans thought he had been one. Indeed, after reading Crane's account, one high-ranking officer, Colonel John L. Burleigh, "recalled," "I was with Crane at Antietam and saw him rush forward, seize two of the enemy and bump their heads together in way that must have made them see constellations" (Crane 1994, 181–82).

In the three days wherein we see the world through Henry's eyes, unlike the mistaken Civil War veteran, we *are* alongside Crane's green private for two enemy engagements. At the start of the first battle Henry and his comrades hold their ground, but during the second wave, Henry (along with several others) throws down his rifle and runs to the rear. Wandering behind the lines, he is haunted by his cowardice: "At times he regarded the wounded soldiers in an envious way. He conceived persons with torn bodies to be peculiarly happy. He wished that he, too, had a wound, a red badge of courage" (1984, 133).[3] A short time later, his wish is granted. When he grabs the arm of a retreating soldier, he is accidentally struck by a rifle butt, which gives him his own red badge. A cheery-voiced stranger bandages Henry's bloodied head and leads him back to his regiment, where his comrades admire his bravery and his wound. Henry lets the lie stand, and as a result "his self-pride was now entirely restored. . . . He performed his mistakes in the dark, so he was still a man" (165).

Struggling to come to terms with his flight from the battlefield, he is able, for a time, to persuade himself that "he had fled with discretion and dignity" (165). Soon, however, "the ghost of his flight from the first engagement appeared to him and danced. There were small shoutings in his brain about these matters. For a moment he blushed, and the light of his soul flickered with shame" (210–11). Believing that only heroic actions could erase his cowardly ones, he prepares to face the enemy a second time. The next day Henry stands firm against the enemy's first surge; he then raises the regimental flag and leads a charge that forces the enemy to retreat.

It seems as though Crane has dramatized three different moral actions: performing one's duty (Henry's standing firm during the initial engagement of both the first and second battles), failing in one's duty (his cowardly desertion), and surpassing one's duty (Henry's spectacular and heroic dash with the regimental flag). However, a closer look at the text reveals that *none* of the three sorts of behavior described is a moral action that deserves blame or praise, let alone heroic commendation.

Beginning with the opening stages of both the first and second battles, Henry's behavior has little resemblance to actions prompted by conscious choices. Just before "he was about to be measured" (100) in the opening engagement, for example, "he instantly saw that it would be impossible for him to escape from the regiment. It enclosed him. And there were iron laws of tradition and law on four sides. He was in a moving box" (101). Later, he "fired a first wild shot. Directly he was working at his weapon like an automatic affair" (112). Indeed, he becomes a machine, devoid of human personality:

> He suddenly lost concern for himself, and forgot to look at a menacing fate. He became not a man but a member. He felt that something of which he was a part—a regiment, an army, a cause, or a country—was in crisis. He was welded into a common personality which was dominated by a single desire. For some moments he could not flee no more than a little finger can commit revolution from a hand.

There was a consciousness always of the presence of his comrades about him. He felt the subtle battle brotherhood more potent even than the cause for which they were fighting. (112–13)

Crane uses similar language to describe Henry during the initial part of the second battle. Henry is again in a "battle sleep," with both machine and animal qualities: "The youth was not conscious that he was erect upon his feet" (173). After the first interlude, his fellows "looked upon him as a war devil. . . . He had been a barbarian, a beast. He had fought like a pagan who defends his religion. . . . And he had not been aware of the process. He had slept and, awakening, found himself a knight" (175).

Henry's cowardly desertion that causes him so much shame and anguish is also little more than a biochemical reflex. The second wave of the enemy is much larger and louder, and "he caught changing views of the ground covered with men who were all running like pursued imps, and yelling" (119). The iron law and the moving box disintegrated as the lad next to Henry threw down his gun and "ran like a rabbit. . . . [Soon] others began to scamper away through the smoke. The youth turned his head, shaken from his trance by this movement as if the regiment was leaving him behind" (119). Once the battle spell is broken, Henry becomes "like a proverbial chicken. He lost the direction of safety. Destruction threatened him from all points . . . [and] he ran like a blind man. Two or three times he fell down. Once he knocked his shoulder so heavily against a tree that he went headlong" (119–20). It is clear that for Crane's young recruit, neither holding fast while the enemy is engaged at the battle line nor retreating to the rear was a conscious, freely willed, genuinely moral (or immoral) action.

Henry's heroics at the end of the second battle likewise fall short of moral actions. After Henry's regiment holds off the enemy, he takes the flag from a fallen comrade and leads the charge. But, as in Henry's other battlefield actions, the narrator admits that "the youth, light-footed, was unconsciously in advance" (182); though his grasp of the terrain and other soldiers is preternaturally acute and remained vivid even after the fact, "everything was pictured and explained to him, save why he himself was there" (183). Henry and his comrades were caught up in a mob action that "made a mad enthusiasm. . . . There was the delirium that encounters despair and death, and is heedless and blind to the odds" (183). Crane masterfully captures the frenzy that turned the soldiers, as noted earlier, into beasts and/or machines: "It is a temporary but sublime absence of selfishness" (183). Eventually the "wild battle madness" (205) subsides and the depersonalized soldiers "were men" (193) once again.

Henry's reckless, heedless, and unarmed advance (with Private Wilson at his shoulder), though deemed by his superiors exceptional and even heroic conduct—the colonel boasts, "They deserve t' be major-generals" (198)—when measured against the conditions for supererogation fails to satisfy at least two requirements: producing good consequences and being the result of voluntary choices. Henry's commanding officers notwithstanding, Crane's assessment of both Henry's ordinary soldierly duty in holding the line as well as his cowardly desertion is that these were merely amoral, unconscious, subhuman, and reflex actions.

Henry Fleming, now an old man, reappears in the short story "The Veteran." The cracker-barrel philosopher/grocer at the country store respectfully asks, "Mr. Fleming, you never was frightened much in them battles, was you?" (666). Henry comes clean. "'Well, I guess I was', he answered finally. 'Pretty well scared, sometimes. Why, in my first battle I thought the sky was falling down. I thought the world was coming to an end. You bet I was scared'" (666). The crowd at the store is nonplussed by his confession, for "they knew he had ranked as an orderly sergeant, and so their opinion of his heroism was fixed. None, to be sure, knew how an orderly sergeant ranked, but then it was understood to be somewhere just shy of a major-general's stars" (666). But Henry's grandson, little Jim, is mortified: "His eyes were wide with astonishment at this terrible scandal, his most magnificent grandfather telling such a thing" (667). Henry goes on to explain that it was his first battle and that it took him, like lots of other soldiers, a while to get used to combat.

The scene then shifts to the Fleming home. One of the hired men, a Swede, returns home drunk and overturns a lantern, setting the barn on fire. Henry enters the burning barn five times to lead out the workhorses. Next, he, his son, and the hired men are able to save all but one of the cows from the barn's basement. Crane describes their response as morally correct on the grounds that these ordinary measures involving acceptable risk had alleviated suffering. He comments that when "they returned to the front of the barn [they] stood sadly, breathing like men who had reached the final point of *human* effort" (669, emphasis added). Note Crane's careful qualification.

When the Swede remembers the colts still in the barn, ordinary moral efforts are no longer sufficient. Henry and the others have to reassess the situation: is rescuing the colts from a barn now engulfed in flames foolhardy? Is it so perilous as to make the risk immoral? Is there still a reasonable chance of rescue? Can an heroic and dangerous risk be morally acceptable? The onlookers describe the sacrifice involved as patently foolish, protesting, "Why, it's sure death!" "Why, it's suicide for a man to go in there!" (670). Henry, however, apparently believes that the risk is reasonable, for he insists, "I must try to get 'em out" (670). Crane refuses to choose either alternative; instead, he describes the sacrifice as an exceptional, extra-moral, nonrational occurrence. "Old Fleming staggered . . . [and] stared absently-mindedly . . . [and then] rushed into the barn" (670). The roof caves in, trapping Henry. The story ends with a poetic and mystical description of Henry's death: "A great funnel of smoke swarmed toward the sky, as if the old man's mighty spirit, released from its body—a little bottle—had swelled like the genie of the fable" (670).

While Old Henry's attempt to rescue the colts is indeed exceptional, does it fulfill the supererogation criteria? Several requirements are met: it is not required by duty, its omission is not blameworthy, and it was voluntarily done. However, ought it be forbidden on account of the disproportion between the risk (of human life) and the benefit (of animal welfare)?[4] That is, if the anticipated benefits cannot offset the costs, even this sort of risk to save one or more human lives might not be a justifiable moral action, even as an act of heroism. In either event, the old man's actions deserve sustained moral reflection.

Crane's most revealing study of exceptional battlefield conduct, "A Mystery of Heroism," provides an especially rich example of behavior for philosophical examination. In the midst of a fierce battle, thirsty Fred Collins spots a well in the no-man's-meadow between the two armies. He talks so much about his thirst and boasts so loudly about his fearlessness that he backs himself into seeking permission to get water. Amid his mixed motivations, his selfish desires, and the high probability of death in a trivial matter, Crane explores heroism. No one knows what to make of Collins's recklessness: "The colonel and the captain looked at each other then, for it had suddenly occurred that they could not for the life of them tell whether Collins wanted to go or whether he did not" (627). His fellow soldiers are amazed: "We ain't dyin' of thirst, are we? That's foolishness" (628). Collins cannot understand himself either. "He had blindly been lead by quaint emotions. . . . As a matter of truth he was sure of very little. He was mainly surprised" (628).

So far we have seen Crane reduce heroism to subhuman behavior in *The Red Badge of Courage* and make it mystical in "The Veteran." In "A Mystery of Heroism," he offers a religious explanation. Crane says of Collins, himself confused about why he had taken such a risk, "It seemed to him *supernaturally* strange that he had allowed his mind to maneuver his body into such a situation" (628, emphasis added). Primarily he is dazed and disappointed as he says to himself that if this is heroism, either "heroes were not much" (628) or "he was an intruder in the land of fine deeds" (629). Impelled by fear and inspired by pride, he has taken a great risk to satisfy merely personal and physical desires. Carrying a bucket on the way back from the well, (it had taken too long to fill the canteens he started with), he passes a wounded artillery officer who is pinned under his fallen horse and asks him for some water. Collins runs on, but then he reconsiders and comes back. Appropriately, despite the risk, Collins has responded to a genuine need of a fellow human being. The narrator comments, "There was the faintest shadow of a smile on [the fallen officer's] lips as he looked at Collins. . . . Collins tried to hold the bucket steadily, but his shaking hand caused the water to splash all over the face of the dying man" (631). With both good consequences and honorable intentions, Collins performed an unsullied ethical act of mercy.

Crane concludes the story by removing the confusion between false heroism and compassionate aid. Some water is still in the bucket when Collins safely returns to the regiment. "The Captain waved the bucket away, 'Give it to the men!'" (631). But two "skylarking lieutenants," fighting over the first drink, overturn the bucket and spill the water on the ground. So in the end, no one but the wounded officer gets a drink, not even Collins, because he had left the well as soon as the bucket was filled.

How do Collins's actions fare against the criteria for supererogation? His original plan to fill the canteens and return to his regiment is flawed with regard to intention and consequences—he is unsure why he is taking the risk, and his dare, at best, is in response to selfish and nonessential desires. Yet when he changes his mind and comes back to aid the stricken officer, his action is clearly voluntary and one done for the sake of someone else—someone in a great deal of pain and genuinely needing compassionate aid. It seems, then, that although the always-troublesome matter of the proportion of risk and benefit remains problematic, Collins has performed an ethically good act. Has he, however, performed a supererogatory act of heroism?

Crane's very late (appearing less than two years before his death in 1900 at age twenty-eight) novella, *The Monster,* contains extended dramatization and exploration of both ordinary and extraordinary moral actions. A fire breaks out in the laboratory of Dr. Trescott's home. Hearing the fire alarm, the Trescott's black stablehand, Henry Johnson, rushes home and breaks down the door to go upstairs to rescue young Jimmie Trescott, asleep in his bedroom. With the hallway blocked, Henry carries Jimmie, wrapped in a blanket, out the back way through Dr. Trescott's laboratory. There, overcome by the fire, Henry stumbles and falls. Jimmie, still wrapped in the blanket, rolls across the room and comes to rest under a window. Henry falls, face up, at the base of an old desk upon which are stored Trescott's chemicals.

Shortly thereafter both Jimmie and Henry are taken from the burning house. Jimmie sustained only minor injuries, but Henry was badly burned and his face horribly disfigured by the chemicals, which had exploded and spilled over the edge of the desk and dripped onto his upturned face. Dr. Trescott, Jimmie, and Henry move into the home of the next-door neighbor, Judge Hagenthorpe. It is widely expected that Henry will die, and the townspeople celebrate him as a hero. But due to Dr. Trescott's exceptional and devoted care, Henry survives—only now he is a monster.

Early on, the judge expresses doubts about Dr. Trescott's effort to save Henry. Note the careful moral language that Crane uses: "Perhaps we may not talk with propriety of this kind of action, but I am induced to say you are performing *a questionable charity* in preserving this negro's life. As near as I can understand, he will hereafter be a monster, a perfect monster, and probably with an affected brain. No man can observe you as I have observed you and not know that it was *a matter of conscience* with you, but I am afraid, my friend, that it is *one of the blunders of virtue*" (413, emphasis added).

The rest of the story traces the consequences of Dr. Trescott's nursing Henry back to health. Henry will not stay with the family Dr. Trescott has hired to care for him and wanders around town, terrorizing children and adults alike. Dr. Trescott eventually brings Henry back to his own home, with the result that Dr. Trescott is ostracized, his medical practice fails, and the family's social life vanishes.

Which (and whose) responses to the fire and to the monster Henry are supererogatory and heroic? Which of the actions is, in Crane's perceptive and apt phrases, "a matter of conscience," an act of "questionable charity," or "one of the blunders of virtue?" It might be argued that Henry's rescue of Jimmie and Dr. Trescott's medical and financial support of Henry are matters of ordinary moral duty. Dr. Trescott's decision to keep the deformed Henry at his home seems to be a dramatic example of heroism. A case can also be made, however, that Dr. Trescott's single-minded devotion goes so far beyond moral duty that it is not heroic but foolish, perhaps even immoral. First, Henry no longer needs any special medical care from Dr. Trescott. Second, since Henry lives apart from the family, above the carriage house, his living arrangements are not very different from those of a public institution. Third, Dr. Trescott effectively abandons his duty to practice medicine and shirks his duties as husband and father with regard to his family and their involvement in community life.[5]

In the some two thousand years since Jesus told the Good Samaritan parable; in the five hundred years since Aquinas, Luther, and Calvin discussed superabundant merit; and in nearly fifty years since J. O. Urmson's seminal article "Saints and Heroes" appeared, the nature of supererogation remains elusive. The most glaring omission in the recent philosophical discussion of supererogation is the dearth of substantive, concrete examples. Only two real-life examples have wide currency; both were suggested by Urmson. These are a soldier who throws himself on a live hand grenade to protect his comrades and, apparently inspired by Albert Camus' *The Plague,* the case of a doctor who volunteers to aid a plague-stricken city. What are badly needed by philosophers are explorations of realistic and believable cases like those conceived by novelists like Stephen Crane. Crane, as we have seen, paid close attention to a wide array of examples: extreme situations wherein lives are in the balance, midrange instances involving person-defining and character-testing choices, cases involving genuine heroism, and finally, cases so far beyond the pale of the duty cutoff point that they are foolish or even immoral because they involve dereliction of ordinary and more important duties.

It is clear that supererogation requires the backgrounding of duty. But what is little emphasized in technical discussions of supererogation is that, duty as a context notwithstanding, a number of other factors—training, skill, and vocation or profession, expertise, and opportunity—are invariably crucial and essential qualifiers. Especially in dealing with such qualifiers, literary examinations have much to contribute to our understanding of supererogation. Alasdair MacIntyre explains that the difficulty is one of complexity and individuality, and that the usual algorithms of moral philosophers that offer solutions by appealing to universal or even general maxims are not helpful:

> Where there is real moral perplexity it is often in a highly complex situation, and sometimes a situation so complex that the question "What ought I to do?" can only be translated trivially into "What ought someone like me to do in this kind of situation?" This is important because this translation is often not trivial all. When I am puzzled it is often useful to pick out the morally relevant features of the situation and of my position in it and, having isolated them from the particular situation, I

am in a better position to solve my problem. But, where the situation is too complex, phrases like "someone like me" or "this kind of situation" become vacuous. (1957, 335)

It is, MacIntyre concludes, precisely because novelists are concerned with this level of complexity and detail that their works are needed. For instance, "It is because Sartre and Simone de Beauvoir are concerned with morality of this kind and in this way that they present and can only present their insights in the form of novels rather than of logical analyses" (335).

So more precise and technical "knowledge about" supererogation is not what is most needed; more helpful would be a "knowledge by acquaintance" that motivates and inspires.[6] What is lacking in most philosophical analyses of supererogation is an interest in moral suasion. Indeed, recent philosophical examinations of supererogation appear to be chiefly motivated by an abstract and clinical interest in logical matters.

Ethical philosophers have not always wallowed in trifling moral acts. Turn-of-the-(last)-century American moralists[7] and novelists[8] understood themselves to be responding to an ethical calling that implied a moral responsibility to educate, motivate, and energize actions beyond ordinary duties. I conclude, then, with the suggestion that philosophers of the twenty-first century can revitalize their theorizing by regrounding it in human lives, using the vibrant narratives of gifted writers like Stephen Crane.

NOTES

1. See *New Catholic Encyclopedia*, 1st ed., s.v. "Supererogation," for a brief discussion of the theological development of the term.

2. See, for example, Driver's (1992) discussion of failing to do optional "duties."

3. The standard source for Stephen Crane is *The Works of Stephen Crane.* Most of this critical edition, published by the University Press of Virginia, has been conveniently collected in a single volume, *Stephen Crane: Prose and Poetry,* edited by J. C. Levenson.

4. Regarding the claim that it is a matter of duty to rescue humans but beyond the call of duty to rescue animals, Zimmerman states, "Some theory *might* claim that, while it is obligatory to help humans whenever possible, it is supererogatory to help non-human animals" (1993, 375, emphasis added). However, beyond a passing mention by Baron (1987), I have been unable to find any further discussion of this plausible suggestion.

5. For more analysis of Crane's ethical philosophy, see chapter 4, especially the

last section, "Good Doctor Trescott, or Ned Trescott, Martyr and Fool?" in my *The Pluralistic Philosophy of Stephen Crane.*

6. These terms are from chapter 7 of William James's *The Principles of Psychology.* For a discussion of James's distinction, see chapter 2 in my *Pragmatism as Humanism: The Philosophy of William James.*

7. The most influential late nineteenth-century works in moral philosophy were by Asa Mahan (1848), Francis Wayland (1847), and James Fairchild (1869). All three moral philosophers addressed practical questions and were keen on improving the nation's moral character. A clear case in point is Fairchild's treatment of ethical issues relating to declaring bankruptcy and whether doing so freed one from a *moral* obligation to pay back one's debts. This is precisely the same ethical terrain covered by William Dean Howells in his classic, *The Rise of Silas Lapham.* For more on late nineteenth-century American moralist/novelist cross-fertilization, see chapter 6.

8. For discussions of several important late nineteenth-century American novelists offering moral suasion in matters going beyond one's duty, see chapters 7, 10, and 12.

Works Cited

Baron, Marcia. 1987. "Kantian Ethics and Supererogation." *Journal of Philosophy* 84:237–62.

Chisholm, Roderick M. 1963. "Supererogation and Offense: A Conceptual Scheme for Ethics." *Ratio* 5:1–14.

Crane, Stephen. 1969–76. *The Works of Stephen Crane.* Edited by Fredson Bowers. 10 vols. Charlottesville: University Press of Virginia.

———. 1984. *Stephen Crane: Prose and Poetry.* Edited by J. C. Levenson. New York: Library of America.

———. 1994. *The Crane Log: A Documentary Life of Stephen Crane, 1871–1900.* Edited by Stanley Wertheim and Paul Sorrentino. New York: Columbia University Press.

Dooley, Patrick K. 1974. *Pragmatism as Humanism: The Philosophy of William James.* Chicago: Nelson-Hall.

———. 1993. *The Pluralistic Philosophy of Stephen Crane.* Urbana: University of Illinois Press.

Driver, Julia. 1992. "The Suberogatory." *Australasian Journal of Philosophy* 70:286–95.

Fairchild, James H. 1869. *Moral Philosophy: The Science of Obligation.* New York: Sheldon.

Feinberg, Joel. 1970. "Supererogation and Rules." In *Doing and Deserving: Essays in the Theory of Responsibility,* 3–24. Princeton, NJ: Princeton University Press.

Heyd, David. 1982. *Supererogation: Its Status in Ethical Theory.* Cambridge: Cambridge University Press.

James, William. 1890. *The Principles of Psychology.* Edited by Frederick Burkhardt, Fredson Bowers, and Ignas Skrupskelis. *The Works of William James.* Cambridge, MA: Harvard University Press, 1981.

Langford, Michael. 1988. "Supererogation and Friendship." In *Philosophy and Culture: Proceedings of the XVII World Congress of Philosophy,* edited by Venant Cauchy, 441–45. Montreal: Éditions Montmorency.

MacIntyre, Alasdair. 1957. "What Morality Is Not." *Ethics* 30:325–35.

Mahan, Asa. 1848. *A Science of Moral Philosophy.* Oberlin, OH: J. M. Fitch.

McNamara, Paul. 1996. "Making Room for Going Beyond the Call." *Mind* 105:415–50.

Mellema, Gregory. 1991. *Beyond the Call of Duty: Supererogation, Obligation, and Offense.* Albany: SUNY Press.

Updike, John. 1991. "The Importance of Fiction." In *Odd Jobs: Essays and Criticism,* 84–87. New York: Alfred A. Knopf.

Urmson, J. O. 1958. "Saints and Heroes." In *Essays in Moral Philosophy,* edited by A. I. Melden, 198–216. Seattle: University of Washington Press.

Wayland, Francis. 1847. *The Elements of Moral Science.* 4th ed. Edited by Joseph Blau. Cambridge, MA: Harvard University Press, 1963.

Zimmerman, Michael. 1993. "Supererogation and Doing the Best One Can." *American Philosophical Quarterly* 30:373–80.

5

Human Solidarity in an Indifferent Universe
Crane's Humanism

> *It would be difficult to describe the subtle brotherhood of men*
> *that was here established on the seas. No one said that it was so.*
> *No one mentioned it. But it dwelt in the boat, and each man felt*
> *it warm him.*
> —*Stephen Crane*

In 1895, Stephen Crane's runaway best seller *The Red Badge of Courage* made him an international literary celebrity at the age of twenty-three. Five years later, Crane was dead. From his Asbury Park (New Jersey) shore dispatches for the news bureau (run by his brother Townley) to his deathbed dictation of two-thirds of *The O'Ruddy,* Crane's writing career spanned a mere twelve years. Even so, as a journalist, war correspondent, poet, novelist, and short story writer extraordinaire, he produced a substantial body of literature that espouses a bold and robust humanism.

Crane's maternal great-uncle, Jesse T. Peck, was a noted Methodist bishop and president of Syracuse University, where Crane attended one of his two semesters of college (the other being at Lafayette College). At both schools, Crane spent most of his time playing baseball and cutting classes to conduct his own direct study of humanity.

Commenting on his Syracuse semester, Crane confessed to fellow New York City reporter John Northern Hilliard, "I did little work at school, but confined my abilities, such as they were, to the diamond. Not that I disliked books, but the cut-and-dried curriculum of the college did not appeal to me. Humanity was a much more interesting study. When I ought to have been at recitations I was studying faces on the streets, and when I ought to have been studying my next day's lessons I was watching the trains roll in and out of the Central station" (1988, 99).

Both Crane's parents were ministers. He was the fourteenth and last child of Jonathan Townley Crane and Mary Helen (Peck) Crane. His reaction to being a PK (preacher's kid) involved cultivating the vices of card playing, dancing, drinking, and smoking that his father condemned in a series of popular pamphlets. Crane shunned organized religion but did not reject so much as redefine humanistically religious experience.

Crane shares with his contemporaries, the American philosophers William James and C. S. Peirce and later John Dewey, the belief that experience (not Truth, Reality, or the Good) is the starting point and the culmination of philosophical reflection. For these pragmatic humanists[1] and for Crane, humans confront realities instead of Reality, and because experiencers, in part, constitute realities, the worlds of spectators and participants are not just different but often incompatible. Given Crane's suspicions about the existence of Truth and Reality and his insistence upon the legitimate standing of multiple perspectives, his metaphysics forces readers to question the existence of a comprehensive scheme or even a widest possible context, and his epistemology casts doubt on ultimate answers and final assessments. Since experiencers are fundamental to Crane, moral agents have ethical obligations toward humans as well as other experiencers. As a result, Crane's moral reflections range from the preethical (duties toward animals) to the properly ethical (conduct toward humans in ordinary situations) to the optional and supererogatory (heroic actions above and beyond ethical obligation). Crane was unwilling to undermine the integrity of lived experience or to diminish the significance of human effort vis-à-vis philosophical absolutes or theological dogmas. Still, especially in his poetry, Crane scrutinized religious experience, eventually settling on a belief in a finite God who as a co-worker and an ally can further our projects but cannot guarantee their success. Crane's commitment to the importance of human projects and his acknowledgement of both the efficacy and limitations of our efforts form the core of his philosophical outlook.

Crane's Bowery works, principally *Maggie* (1893) and *George's Mother* (1896), along with numerous newspaper pieces and other early sketches, lean toward an environmental determinism that threatens to invalidate human actions. However, a journalistic trip to the West and Mexico in 1895 and the defining experience of his life—his open boat ordeal in 1897—confirmed for

Crane the value of human effort and the importance of human solidarity in an indifferent universe.

While Crane believed in human freedom before his western trip, the West significantly altered his view of human action and his opinion about individual initiative. Previously, his Sullivan County tales and New York City newspaper sketches portrayed confused and ineffectual actions. After his western trip, competence and optimism surfaced in his writings. Both East versus West and city versus nature are involved in the evolution of Crane's view of human action. Why the East and the city enervate while the West and nature energize is a complex matter for Crane. For example, out West, Crane discovered a demanding world, an environment in some ways harsher than the Bowery. Why should a winter storm make the population of an eastern city passive and reclusive while a blizzard summons the ingenuity and combative instincts of Nebraska farmers? Crane suggests that the constructed world is fraught with whim and caprice, whereas events in the natural world have sufficient regularity and enough loose play that human actions can make a difference.

The open, unpopulated, natural areas he visited in Nebraska, Texas, and Old Mexico triggered Crane's evolving view of human actions. There he discovered that human beings are not given extra consideration or extended special dispensation. Individuals of the human or any other species are neither helped nor handicapped. Nature is neutral and unbiased toward results. Secondly and significantly, Crane's western stories and his Mexican sketches explain that even though individual tragedies might be inconsequential against the backdrop of an indifferent nature, human courage and human efforts remain indispensable. Out West Crane was impressed with the value of courage and the worth of trying, whether or not effort produced success. Indeed, "Nebraska's Bitter Fight for Life," "The Five White Mice," and "A Man and Some Others" focus on struggles in which steadfastness, courage, and initiative are crucial to outcomes.

Crane's western experiences prepared the way for the mature philosophy of human action that is expressed in his greatest short story, "The Open Boat." There he celebrates the value of the resourceful human efforts characteristic of his western tales and, in addition, offers the possibility of real success and genuine brotherhood born of joint effort.

Crane's January 6, 1897, newspaper dispatch, "Stephen Crane's Own Story," set out the facts that he retold six months later in a *Scribner's Magazine* story, "The Open Boat," subtitled "A tale intended to be after the fact. Being the experience of four men from the sunk steamer *Commodore*." The four men are the cook, the oiler, the correspondent, and the injured captain. Crane was commissioned by the Bacheller newspaper syndicate to slip into Cuba to report on the Cuban revolution in late December 1896. On New Year's Eve, the *Commodore*—loaded with munitions and Cuban insurgents, and with Crane, an able seaman, onboard—struck a sandbar when leaving the port of Jacksonville. Damaged while being towed off the sandbar, the ship took on water and two days later sank at sea. All the lifeboats were launched, leaving Crane and three others with a small "dingey." His story retells some thirty hours of exposure, rowing, and suffering before the small "dingey" capsized on the breakers, forcing the four to swim a half-mile to shore at Daytona Beach. As in his western stories, the setting, in this case the ocean, is natural. However, in place of solitary or unorchestrated efforts, the four men struggle in unison. They find that their shared trial discloses human solidarity as each of them encounters an efficacious, social self:

> They were a captain, an oiler, a cook and a correspondent, and they were friends, friends in a more curiously iron-bound degree than may be common. The hurt captain, lying against the water-jar in the bow, spoke always in a low voice and calmly, but he could never command a more ready and swiftly obedient crew than the motley three of the dingey. It was more than a mere recognition of what was best for the common safety. There was surely in it a quality that was personal and heartfelt. And after this devotion to the commander of the boat there was this comradeship that the correspondent, for instance, who had been taught to be cynical of men knew even at the time was the best experience of his life. (1984, 890)

In their ordeal, solidarity, instead of rancor and mistrust, flourished because the survival test put to them is neither impossible nor routine. It is a stern but fair trial of wits and determination.

The existential disinterest of nature is only apparent after painful struggle. Initially, the correspondent finds the "dingey" to be overmatched by waves, which are "most wrongfully and barbarously abrupt and tall" (885). He soon discovers that any particular wave mastered is not "the final outburst of the ocean, the last effort of the grim water" (886). It is only a wave and soon there will be another. "A singular disadvantage of the sea lies in the fact that after successfully surmounting one wave you discover that there is another behind it just as important and just as nervously anxious to do something effective in the way of swamping boats" (886). The four are silent in the struggle; neither optimism nor hopelessness is expressed. They see a lighthouse, then the land, then the beach, and they conclude that they will be safe in an hour. It had turned out to be an easy contest, so they celebrate. Three dry matches and four good cigars are produced, and "the four waifs rode impudently in their little boat, and with an assurance of an impending rescue shining in their eyes, puffed at the big cigars and judged well and ill of all men. Everybody took a drink of water" (892–93).

But no one on shore sees them; they are not rescued. The slowly setting sun brings anger but not despair. They are bitter because no one recognizes their plight or appreciates their efforts:

> As for the reflections of the men, there was a great deal of rage in them. Perchance they might be formulated thus: "If I am going to be drowned—if I am going to be drowned—if I am going to be drowned, why, in the name of the seven mad gods who rule the sea, was I allowed to come thus far and contemplate sand and trees? Was I brought here merely to have my nose dragged away as I was about to nibble the sacred cheese of life? It is preposterous. If this old ninny-woman, Fate, cannot do better than this, she should be deprived of the management of men's fortunes. She is an old hen who knows not her intention. If she has decided to drown me, why did she not do it in the beginning and save me all this trouble." The whole affair is absurd. (894)

Finally a man on the beach waves to them. He is then joined by a crowd from the resort hotel, and all the people on the land wave merrily to the four "fishermen" in their tiny boat.

The resorters do not recognize the men's plight, and with nightfall, both the lighthouse and the shore disappear. Through the long, painful night they spell each other at rowing. Crane uses the seriousness of the task to point up the precariousness of human existence. Their small boat has two fragile oars, each "a thin little oar and it seemed often ready to snap" (885). They cannot let the boat drift, so they must row continually. Crane likewise skillfully exploits the hazards of taking turns at the oars:

> The very ticklish part of the business was when the time came for the reclining one in the stern was to take his turn at the oars. By the very

last star of truth, it is easier to steal eggs from under a hen than it was to change seats in the dingey. First the man in the stern slid his hand along the thwart and moved with care, as if he were of Sèvres. Then the man in the rowing seat slid his hand along the other thwart. It was all done with the most extraordinary care. As the two sidled past each other, the whole party kept watchful eyes on the coming wave, and the captain cried: "Look out now! Steady there!" (889)

They row and row. During the night a great shark circles their boat. Finally, at dawn, still alive and still forced to struggle, the correspondent realizes humanity's situation in nature. Since shipwrecks are merely natural events, "*apropos* of nothing" (891), and since they are less than "the breaking of a pencil's point" (903), the correspondent learns that nature places no special significance or insignificance upon individual lives. "When it occurs to a man that nature does not regard him as important, and that she feels she would not maim the universe by disposing of him, he at first wishes to throw bricks at the temple, and he hates deeply the fact that there are no bricks and no temples" (902).

In the early morning light, the wind tower reappears: "This tower was a giant, standing with its back to the plight of the ants. It represented in a degree, to the correspondent, the serenity of nature amid the struggles of the individual—nature in the wind, and nature in the vision of men. She did not seem cruel to him then, nor beneficent, nor treacherous, nor wise. She was indifferent, flatly indifferent" (905). The four decide to risk a run through the breakers onto the beach. A half-mile from shore, the "dingey" capsizes and they must swim. Later, after a wave tosses the correspondent over the upturned boat, he finds himself in waist-deep water. A man on shore drags the cook, the captain, and the correspondent to safety. Billie the oiler drowns.

The stern ordeal over, the three survivors understand the serene indifference of nature. That night, on the beach, amid the perpetual sea wind and the ceaseless waves as they meditate upon nature's abiding message, "they felt that they could then be interpreters" (909). Through their confrontation with the indifferent universe, the survivors appreciate both the limits and possibilities of human effort and human community.

A consummate ironist, Crane was neither a pessimist nor an optimist. He was rather a meliorist who believed that improvement is possible. But though Crane held that progress was possible, some of his best writing captures the perversity, and more often the apathy, through which humans cause death

("The Upturned Face"), alienation ("The Blue Hotel"), loneliness ("A Duel Between an Alarm Clock and a Suicidal Purpose"), greed ("In the Depths of a Coal Mine"), racism (*The Monster*), and imperialism ("Death and the Child"). Crane's poignant, powerful depiction of the risks and the demands, but more so his account of the rewards and satisfactions that can be won in a world that is neither menacingly hostile nor benevolently supportive but merely indifferent, captures the project of serious and sober, realistic and effective, humans of goodwill.

Crane's writings frequently praise the competence of such everyday heroes. For instance, just six months before his death, midway through "War Memories" he attempted to capture Admiral Sampson, who was, for Crane, the most interesting personality in the war in Cuba. "The quiet old man . . . a sailor and admiral" seemed at first bored with the war and indifferent to details. But once the action started, "hidden in his indifferent, even apathetic, manner, there was the alert, sure, fine mind of the best sea-captain that America has produced since—since Farragut? I don't know. I think—since Hull" (1970, 239). Unimpressed with the common seaman's eager devotion and reverence of him, Admiral Sampson thought not of glory but "considered the management of ships" (240). Crane's summary strikes, as it so often does, precisely the right note—Sampson's record was "just plain, pure, unsauced accomplishment" (240).

Other everyday heroes also received Crane's attention. In an early piece, "In the Depths of a Coal Mine," he salutes the elevator operator: "Far above us in the engine-room, the engineer sat with his hand on a lever and his eye on the little model of the shaft wherein a miniature elevator was making the ascent even as our elevator was making it. . . . My mind was occupied with a mental picture of this faraway engineer, who sat in his high chair by his levers, a statue of responsibility and fidelity, cool-brained, clear-eyed, steady of hand" (1984, 614). In "Nebraska's Bitter Fight for Life," Crane cites Mr. L. P. Ludden, secretary and general manager of the relief commission, who "works early and late and always. But he is the most unpopular man in the State of Nebraska. He is honest, conscientious and loyal; he is hard-working and has great executive ability" (693). Crane's most effusive praise of ordinary competence is reserved for the railroad engineer in "The Scotch Express." The engineer's skills, indispensable though they are, are generally overlooked: "One finds very often this apparent disregard for the man who . . . occupies a position which for the exercise of temperance, of courage, of honesty, has no equal at the altitude of prime-ministers" (1973, 743). The engineer's matter-of-fact attitude and the deceptive ordinariness of his tasks intrigue Crane: "He was simply a quiet, middle-aged man, bearded and with little wrinkles of habitual geniality and kindliness. . . . This driver's face displayed nothing but . . . cool sanity. . . . The engine-driver is the finest type of man that is grown. He is the pick of the earth. He is not paid too much. . . . But for outright performance carried on constantly, coolly, and without elation by a temperate, honest, clear-minded man he is the further point" (746).

In a word, Crane strongly endorses the central plank in the humanistic and melioristic platform of the classical American pragmatists: the reality of human freedom.[2] Those philosophers and Crane are of one mind that to a large degree the fate of the world generally, and human welfare in particular, rests in human hands. Compare, for example, the thrust and trajectory of Crane's worldview with William James's "Pragmatism and Humanism," where James argues:

> In our cognitive as well as in our active life we are creative. We *add,* both to the subject and to the predicate part of reality. The world stands really malleable, waiting to receive its final touches at our hands. Like the kingdom of heaven, it suffers human violence willingly. Man *engenders* truth upon it. . . . *The alternative between pragmatism and rationalism, in the shape in which we now have it before us, is no longer a question in the theory of knowledge, it concerns the structure of the universe itself.* On the pragmatists' side we have only one edition of the universe, unfinished, growing in all sorts of places, especially in the places where thinking beings are at work. (1907, 123–24)

However, going even beyond James, Crane's humanism underscores the fact that our successes are won by the regular and reliable work of everyday heroes and through the energy-releasing catalyst of human solidarity. While our successes may be neither easy nor total, they are nonetheless significant, for even if all four in "The Open Boat" were not saved, three were.

Notes

This chapter is an expanded and revised version of "The Humanism of Stephen Crane" that appeared in *The Humanist* 56 (1996): 14–17.

1. For more on William James's humanism, see chapter 5 of my *Pragmatism as Humanism: The Philosophy of William James* and my "William James on the Human Way of Being."

2. The credo of the American Humanist Association is "The Humanist Manifesto," which was largely the work of a second-generation pragmatist, Roy Wood Sellars. Among the early and influential signers and promoters of American humanism was John Dewey. See Delaney (1969) for a good introduction to the pragmatism of Sellars.

Works Cited

Crane, Stephen. 1970. *The Works of Stephen Crane.* Edited by Fredson Bowers. Vol. 6. Charlottesville: University of Virginia Press.

———. 1973. *The Works of Stephen Crane.* Edited by Fredson Bowers. Vol. 8. Charlottesville: University of Virginia Press.

———. 1984. *Stephen Crane: Prose and Poetry.* Edited by J. C. Levenson. New York: Library of America.

———. 1988. *The Correspondence of Stephen Crane.* Edited by Stanley Wertheim and Paul Sorrentino. Vol. 1. New York: Columbia University Press.

Delaney, C. F. 1969. *Mind and Nature: A Study of the Naturalistic Philosophy of Cohen, Woodbridge, and Sellars.* Notre Dame, IN: Notre Dame University Press.

Dooley, Patrick K. 1974. *Pragmatism as Humanism: The Philosophy of William James.* Chicago: Nelson-Hall.

———. 1990. "James on the Human Way of Being." *The Personalist Forum* 6:75–85.

James, William. 1907. "Pragmatism as Humanism." In *Pragmatism.* Edited by Frederick Burkhardt, Fredson Bowers, and Ignas K. Skrupskelis. *The Writings of William James.* Cambridge, MA: Harvard University Press, 1975.

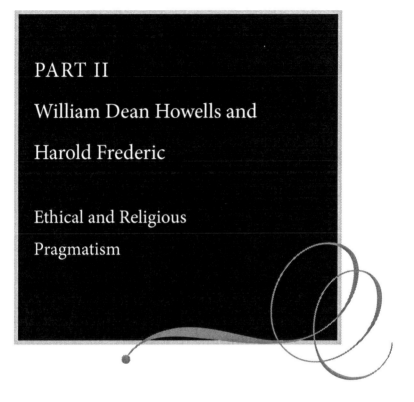

PART II

William Dean Howells and

Harold Frederic

Ethical and Religious

Pragmatism

6

Nineteenth-Century Business Ethics and *The Rise of Silas Lapham*

Caveat emptor.

It has been obvious to mid- and late twentieth-century readers of *The Rise of Silas Lapham* that William Dean Howells intends to provide moral education. To this end, he utilizes two plots—a love story and a bankruptcy—to explore the tensions involved in both a private and a social moral dilemma. What is surprising is that Howells's ethical point was frequently missed by the first readers of this novel. They focused on the love plot, all but ignored the bankruptcy plot, and had difficulty discerning any moral lesson in the novel.

The reading given to *Silas Lapham* by Howells's good friend Francis Parkman is an especially vivid case in point. In one of his memoirs Howells relates, "I remember his talking to me of *The Rise of Silas Lapham,* in a somewhat troubled and uncertain strain, and interpreting his rise as the achievement of social recognition, without much or at all liking it or me for it. I did not think it my part to point out that I had supposed the rise to be a moral one . . . but he had those limitations which I nearly always found in the Boston men" (1900, 141). There is good reason to believe that many more of the first readers of *The Rise of Silas Lapham* frequently, if not almost always, missed its moral point. By his insistence that morality applies to business dealings, Howells challenged his society's views of both commerce and ethics. An examination of the early reviews of *The Rise of Silas Lapham* will support the contention that Howells's novel was frequently misread; an analysis of the leading moralists will reveal that until the later years of the nineteenth century, business ethics was considered a new, strange, and even contradictory notion.

INITIAL REVIEWS OF *THE RISE OF SILAS LAPHAM*

In 1884, while William Dean Howells was having a new house built on Beacon Street in Boston, he began writing *Silas Lapham.* The novel was serialized in *Century Magazine* from November 1884 until August 1885. In September of 1885 it was published in book form by Ticknor and Company of Boston. Even before it appeared in book form, *Silas Lapham* attracted an enthusiastic readership and elicited wide-ranging critical commentary. Clayton Eichelberger's standard resource on Howells's commentary, *Published Comment on William Dean Howells through 1920: A Research Bibliography,* annotates some thirty-nine items relating to *Silas Lapham* from January 1885 to the early winter of 1886. (In early spring 1886 the reviewers' attention shifted to Howells's new publications, *Indian Summer* and *Tuscan Cities.*) Eichelberger's list covers announcements, notes, brief reviews (some as short as a brief paragraph), and what he terms either "major reviews" or "full reviews." In this last category he identifies sixteen commentaries; I have found two additional commentaries that I will also discuss. These reviews range in length from a half-dozen paragraphs to a twelve-page study; in discernment they range from total misperception to penetrating insight. We will look at them in three groups, beginning with the most superficial and ending with the most perceptive.

Silas Lapham as decadent realism

There were seven such reviews. The worst of the lot, "Contemporary Literature, Belles Lettres" in the *Westminster Review,* was one of the last to appear. This reviewer finds Howells's title "a misnomer for the narrative of a rapid descent from the height of prosperity to hopeless insolvency." The reviewer begins by recommending the book as "a gallery of illustration of various phases of transatlantic life and manners . . . [that succeeds in] throwing light on many obscure corners of human consciousness." Still he finds the book disappointing: "We are promised an ascent—"The Rise of Silas Lapham"— and as a matter of fact the story's course is all down hill ending in gloom and bankruptcy. This cannot be an inadvertence on the part of such an artist as Mr. Howells. No doubt it is intended, and contains a subtle lesson, but our eyes are sealed and we cannot see it"(*Westminster Review* 1886, 303).

In November of 1885, *Catholic World* carried a long review article on Howells and *Silas Lapham* titled "Novel-Writing as a Science." Once again alternative titles are suggested. Since "novels like *Silas Lapham* mark a descent,

[a] degradation" (*Catholic World* 1885, 278), other titles such as "Treatise on Commonplace People" or "Treatise on Drabs" or "Treatise on Drunkards" (280) would be more appropriate. Although Howells apparently intended moral edification, he utterly failed: "It has seldom been our duty to read a book whose moral tone was so unpleasantly, so hopelessly bad; it is a book without heart or soul, neither illumined by religion nor warmed by human sympathy. This is all the more astonishing that Mr. Howells seems convinced that he is fulfilling a high moral purpose in writing it" (279). The reviewer explains that Howells's effort could be attributed to the doctrine of total depravity, but more likely its impetus simply follows "the logic of the downward progress of godless science" (279). Therefore Howells ought to give up fiction and turn directly to science; his fiction is more akin to a series of scientific diagrams than it is to an inspiring painting or even an accurate photograph. Despite all this degradation and "descent to dirt" (279), there is no need for excessive alarm: "Mr. Howells will be read only by a species of scientific and hard-minded people, which we are led to understand flourish best in Boston; and this species is past harming" (280). That is, the people who like these kind of books will not be offended by the scene in the bar with Silas, the young woman Z'rilla, her tipsy-sailor husband, and Z'rilla's drunken mother, or even that "the worthy Mrs. Lapham suspect[s] her husband of infidelity" (279).

The third review in this first group also refers to the sort of people who might enjoy *Silas Lapham*. In this review, part of a larger article, "Recent Fiction," published by the *Dial* in 1885, William Payne comments on *Silas Lapham* and twelve other books. Payne says nothing about the plot, the bankruptcy, the love story, or, for that matter, any incidents in the book. He explains that "it is almost a new species of work . . . the business man's novel." And then he offers a throwaway comment: "People who do not care for novels ordinarily can hardly fail to like this one. . . . Here at last are such people as one meets in every-day life, and who talk in a natural and familiar way." Payne predicts that the novel's impact will be temporary; it will only be valid "as long as people continue to talk and act in just the way which it describes" (1885, 122).

A similar stress on *Silas Lapham* as chiefly an examination of business practices, especially with regard to buying and selling, was made in an 1885 review, "Silas Lapham and the Jews," in the *American Hebrew*. This reviewer comments that Howells's treatment of the legal and moral technicalities involved in selling the mines to the English agents was "spun out to such distinctions as would make a Talmudic casuist regard Howells with envy" (*American Hebrew* 1885, 122).[1]

In the August 16 "New Publications: Mr. Howells's Last Story, *The Rise of Silas Lapham,*" the reviewer for the *New York Daily Tribune* is not surprised that Howells is unsympathetic with his own characters, as the reviewer also finds them worthy of little sympathy. The *Nation's* review similarly takes offence with Silas. Curiously, although this reviewer comments that Howells has endowed Silas with "moral courage," his overall assessment is negative: "There is no inspiration for anyone in the character of Silas Lapham. It rouses no tender or elevating emotion, stirs no thrill of sympathy, suggests no ideal of conduct, no notion that the world at large is or can be any less ugly than Lapham and his paint" (Nation *1885,* 401)

The final negative and superficial review is the longest. Titled "A Typical Novel" and written by Hamilton Mabie, it occupied thirteen pages of the *Andover Review* in 1885. The article offers a general analysis of "the dominant school of contemporary fiction . . . recent realism" (1885, 417). After a lengthy commendation of Howells's skill at observation and description, Mabie states his case: "*The Rise of Silas Lapham* is an unsatisfactory story; defective in power, in reality, and in the vitalizing atmosphere of imagination. . . . It throws no spell over us; creates no illusions for us, leaves us indifferent spectators. . . . It leaves the reader cold when he has finished it" (420). For those who would like to be convinced that Howells is too cool, too detached, too factual, Mabie offers this litmus-paper test: "Perhaps nothing more decisive on this point could be said of Mr. Howells's stories than that one can read them aloud without faltering at the most pathetic passages" (421). As a matter of fact, Mabie finds it even worse. Howells and other realists are "crowding the world of fiction with commonplace people; people whom one would positively avoid coming in contact with in real life; people without native sweetness or strength . . . or accomplishment, without that touch of the ideal" (423). Mabie totally misses Silas's moral rise; he finds that modern realism examines "feeble, insolute[,] unimportant men [and it analyzes] motives that were never worth an hour's serious study" (423). He diagnoses "a mental or a moral disease [that makes] Mr. Howells . . . concern himself with men and women of very slender endowments and very superficial conceptions of life" (423–24). He concludes that realism in general and *Silas Lapham* in particular are malignant. The novel's "vigor is mainly on the side of *moral pathology*" (424).

Hence, none of these first seven reviews sees any evidence of a moral struggle, let alone a moral rise for Silas Lapham. All agree that Howells turned the high and lofty art of fiction into a depressing, even degrading, depiction of the commonest of common men. Finally, these reviewers share the hope that

Howells's crass, morbid realism will have only a temporary impact on such a small audience that other writers will resist the temptation to emulate him.

Silas Lapham as faithful realism

Here eight reviews praise Howells's realism, especially his ability to reveal the American character. Tellingly, however, whenever they speak of plot, these reviews focus on the Lapham family's fortunes in love, high society, and finance. For them the driving force of the novel is a failed attempt to climb the social ladder—Silas's moral struggles are little (if at all) noticed.

A very favorable review in the *Saturday Review* appeared in October of 1885. This review praises Howells's realism and his Americanness: "Now Mr. Howells knows his America. . . . He remains an American to the backbone. . . . *The Rise of Silas Lapham* is a novel which no one can neglect who cares to understand American character" (*Saturday Review* 1885, 517). The most skillfully done parts of the book, for this reviewer, are the interview with Bartley Hubbard, Silas's steady movement to inevitable financial ruin, and "the effect of these apparent [financial] fluctuations on the family, on the wife and on the two daughters who are the heroines of the story" (518). This last assessment is reinforced in the reviewer's summary appraisal, which is that the work is "a love story with a happy ending" (518). And so, while the *Saturday Review* likes *Silas Lapham* for its presentation of the American character and for its love interest, neither Silas's moral struggles nor his moral rise is given the briefest of mentions.

A shorter but still very positive review was published in October of 1885 by the *Independent.* Again it is Howells's realism, "his power to deal with American life, particularly middle-class life . . . every day life," that is seen as his forte: "We must again applaud the accuracy of the study" (*Independent* 1885, 1294). The reviewer is undecided as to "which is better handled in the novel: the groping but persevering ascent of the paint-manufacturer's household toward a level of society to which their equipment unfits them . . . or, the cool and dignified patronage of the Coreys" (1295). No mention is made of the love plot, the bankruptcy, or Silas's moral struggle. The reviewer explains that Silas's rise is social, for Howells is able to turn "an unromantic battle for social recognition of *un noveau riche* . . . into a dignified prose epic" (1295).

The London *Athenaeum*'s essay, "Novels of the Week," likewise commends the book as accurate sociology: "The book is charactistically American. . . . Mr. Howells's careful attention to details and to the machinery of his story is observable throughout. Every character is perfect in its way, and only on a few occasions does the writer slip into the American habit of overdoing the study of a person's state of mind" (*Athenaeum* 1885, 396). Apparently, however, deeming that Howells overstresses the conscious reflections of the central figure, this reviewer fails to grasp the significance of the close attention that Howells paid to Silas's *inner* moral struggles. In a similar vein, the *New York Sun*'s "Some New Books: Mr. Howells's Last Novel" is content to praise Howells's descriptive skills; *Lippincott*'s "Literature of the Day" commends Howells's sure handle of realistic detail as he ventures "into the broad arena of real life, with its diversity of actors and its multiplicity of interests" (Lippincott's *1995, 57*).

Three newspaper reviews extolling the faithful realism of Howells's most enduring novel complete this category. The *Boston Evening Transcript*'s "Mr. Howells's *Rise of Silas Lapham*" on August 14, 1885, offers faint and backhanded praise: historians of turn-of-the-century America will find Howells's fiction more illuminating than the actual histories of the period. The *Philadelphia American* keeps its focus on Howells's portrait of Silas, calling it "entirely successful, and the whole story, designed to develop this character, and to present it as one type of American men, has artistic unity and completeness" (65–66). The *Critic*'s review is likewise content to concentrate on the main character, observing that "Silas was a good subject" (122).

The *New York Times* review, "New Publications: Mr. Howells's Novel," published September 27, 1885, also praises Howells's skill in depicting "a typical American businessman. . . . Silas Lapham in his crudeness and shrewdness . . . his ostentation . . . gathers up in himself the traits of many self-made men of our cities and towns." We are told of the paint-business success, the house building, the love story, the dinner party (the reviewer mistakenly has both daughters at the party), and finally the business crisis. In his summary statement, the reviewer describes the book's two halves: part 1, "the outsetting, the placing of the characters on the scene, and the painting of the background," and part 2, "the love crisis of Penelope and the business crisis of her father." According to the reviewer, the first half of the book is undoubtedly better, for the second has "an overstrained note." The reviewer also gives a curious analysis of the struggles of Silas: "The paint works fail and Col. Lapham goes back to his native hills a sadder, but the novelist wishes it understood a better . . . man." The reviewer knows that Howells intended to describe some sort of rise. But he is not sure if Howells meant that rise to be social, financial, or moral. So he offers an ingenious mix; Silas returns to his native hills a better man, that is, "a more *commercially moral* man" (emphasis added). This observation is confused and halting. But after more than a dozen reviews, the moral point of *Silas Lapham* is finally noticed!

In sum, the reviews of the second group are favorable. They appreciate Howells's realism and they admire his craft. They treat both the financial and love crises. One reviewer suspects some sort of moral rise. Let us now turn to the readers in our final group, who are both perceptive and confident about the moral lesson of the novel.

Silas Lapham as moral drama

The *Literary World*'s review is explicit about Howells's moral purpose. Three ironies must be noted. First, this was one of the earliest reviews to appear; secondly, despite Howells's reservations about the literary and social faith of Boston men, the *Literary World* was published in Boston; and finally, this review *totally* ignores the love plot. This review is decidedly positive and enthusiastic. We are told that *Silas Lapham* is even better than *A Modern Instance*. Both novels are marked by a "fresh, unsparing, almost pitiless realism," and in addition, *Silas Lapham* "touches throughout a higher plane." There is no doubt that this reviewer fully understands Silas's rise to be a moral one. He finds in Silas "an underlying stratum of honesty. . . . He is the protagonist in a great moral drama." The book "discerns and emphasizes the moral element which exists in every phase of poor humanity . . . , [and it] proclaims the inherent strength of humanity in the rough"! Finally, though Silas is uncouth, crude, awkward, ill at ease socially, and gets drunk at a dinner party, "He has in him the elements of genuine manhood. . . . When the supreme moment of trial comes he rises to a dignity of achievement when his supercultivated acquaintances would perhaps have succumbed." Thus *Silas Lapham* is not decadent fiction; it is even more than faithful realism; it is an uplifting moral drama, "as impressive . . . as a Greek tragedy" (*Literary World* 1885, 299).

Although the *Literary World* reviewer bypasses the love plot of the story, Horace Scudder, writing for the *Atlantic,* finally does justice to Howells's skill in all three areas: the attempted social climb, the love plot, and Silas's wrestle with his moral dilemmas. Scudder's review, "Recent American Fiction," is above all an accurate reading of *Silas Lapham*. Scudder stresses that Howells's central concern is not the love story, not the "mere vulgar rise in society through the marriage of a daughter to a son of a social prince, [nor] the possession of a house on the water side of Beacon street." Instead, the reader sees "in the case of Mr. Howells' hero . . . the achievement of a moral solvency unglorified by any material prosperity" (1885, 555).

Scudder also makes the striking suggestion that the foil for Lapham is not his business partner, Rogers, but the journalist Bartley Hubbard (reintroduced from Howells's successful *A Modern Instance*). Scudder suggests "a possible comparison between Hubbard and Lapham. They are both self-made men, but Hubbard is essentially vulgar, while Lapham is only accidentally so; the former thrusts his vulgarity through the thin covering of education and aptitude for the world, the latter thrusts his essential manliness through the equally thin covering of an uneducated manner and a hopeless condition of social outlawry" (556). Scudder provides a clear, perceptive statement of Howells's moral intent: he "has convinced himself of the higher value to be found in a creation which discloses morals as well as manners" (554). Howells, he writes, "never intended to waste his art" on a mere love story. He "was using all this realism of Boston society as a relief to the heavier mass contained in the war which was waged within the conscience of the hero" (555). Unfortunately, as we have seen, only two of Howells's initial three-dozen reviewers understood his moral point.

Inattentiveness to the full meaning of *Silas Lapham* was not confined to early reviews; similar misreadings continued through the 1920s. Alexander Harvey, in *William Dean Howells: A Study of the Achievement of a Literary Artist*, argues that "from the standpoint of literature regarded as fine art, I consider *The Rise of Silas Lapham* the greatest novel ever written" (1917, 147). Harvey avers that the book provides the most moving love story since *Romeo and Juliet*, and that the scene in Penelope's bedroom when Irene is told that Tom Corey never loved her is "the most thrilling scene in fiction" (146). In Howells's main character, however, Harvey sees neither moral struggle nor moral rise. Instead Silas represents "the unredeemed ugliness of the material prosperity of his type [and] . . . race. He is typically American in his ignorance of human nature, of beauty, of ideas. . . . [He is one of] the last survivors of the barbarian world . . . the American savage" (154, 155, 158).

A decade later, in his full-length work *William Dean Howells: A Study,* Oscar W. Firkins describes *The Rise of Silas Lapham* as a love story complicated by the tale of the business difficulties of the father of the family. Firkins explains that Howells had two plots, "a love-affair and a bankruptcy. . . . As it happens, the bankruptcy story is late; it is so much of a laggard that it has almost the look of a trespasser" (1924, 71–72). Unfortunately, concludes Firkins, the Johnny-come-lately bankruptcy plot seriously weakens the novel.

Although mid- and late twentieth-century commentators quibble over whether the love plot and the bankruptcy plot are co-plots or a main plot with a subplot, there is no longer any controversy about the strong moral message of the novel.[2] Nowadays Silas's moral struggle and rise are emphasized; the love plot is downplayed, even ignored. Why did earlier reviewers, Howells's Bostonian friends like Parkman, and critics like Harvey and Firkins misperceive the novel's moral messages?

I am sure several explanations are possible. For example, one might explain that Howells was attempting to recast the nature and purpose of novels. His contemporaries did not recognize, let alone appreciate, the sort of innovation Howells contemplated. Certainly many of the reviewers cited here seem to fit this explanation. Without disputing such accounts, I wish to provide a nonliterary, complementary explanation: *Silas Lapham* was misread, for although Howells saw business and ethics as connected, many of his contemporaries did not. An analysis of moral philosophy texts from 1835 to 1895 reveals the very slow emergence and eventual acceptance of business ethics. At first, no special ethical demands were associated with business; next, a confused mixture of legal principles and accepted practices was applied to moral conflicts in business; and finally, a genuine business ethic was worked out. Early readers of *Silas Lapham* had not caught up to this third stage, so they misread the book; later readers, accustomed to applying morality to commercial transactions, saw Howells's moral point as obvious.

NINETEENTH-CENTURY MORAL PHILOSOPHY

In the six decades from 1835 to 1895, American moral philosophy was dominated by three college president–moral philosophers: Francis Wayland of Brown University, and Asa Mahan and James H. Fairchild of Oberlin College. All three men wrote popular and well-regarded textbooks. The most popular of all was Wayland's *The Elements of Moral Science*. It went through four editions in its first two years and sold 200,000 copies between 1835 to 1895. All three men used their college presidencies to exert influence on the ethical questions of the day. All were highly visible and antislavery, and Mahan and Fairchild were active abolitionists.

There were, however, important differences in the moral positions advanced by these ethicists. In regard to business ethics, Mahan's *A Science of Moral Philosophy* all but ignored the topic, Wayland's *The Elements of Moral*

Science presented a simplistic and confused position, and Fairchild's *Moral Philosophy: The Science of Obligation* laid out a clear, sophisticated, and practical set of moral principles as they apply to business.

Textbook treatments of general moral obligations

Before we look at business ethics, a brief comment on nineteenth-century moral philosophy is in order. A typical moral philosophy of this period devoted most of its attention to personal and interpersonal ethical obligations but practically none to civil and social duties. The divorce of the private from the public and the separation of personal from social duties were not accidental or unconscious. Especially in view of the slavery issue, nineteenth-century moral philosophers worried a great deal about the ethical obligations of individual citizens. What should a moral man do in the concrete?

The most influential of these three moral philosophers, Wayland, advanced the standard, conservative position in *The Limitations of Human Responsibility* in 1838. After a lengthy caution about the dangers of moral fanaticism and excessive zeal (he cites temperance societies), Wayland states his central principle: "Our responsibility for the *temper of mind* is *unlimited* and *universal,* our responsibility for the *outward act* is *limited* and *special*" (1838, 19, emphasis added). That is, we are responsible for our motives but not all the consequences of our actions. For example, in the case of the clear evil of slavery, even as we are obliged to preach the Gospel, we are not required to convert our fellow citizens. For Wayland the crux is "what *manner* it be proper [to use] to remove or to arrest the evil . . . ?" (162). Wayland's remedy is to preach the immorality to the slaveholder and leave the rest to God:

> [The slave holders] have as good a right to their ears, as we have to our tongues. Hence, if they will not hear us, our responsibility is at an end. We have no right to force our instructions upon them, either by conversation, or by lectures, or by the mail. If they still determine to go on, in what we believe to be wrong. we must leave them to God, who is perfectly capable of vindicating his own laws, and executing justice among the children of men. If they will not hear us, the indication is plain, that God does not mean to use *our* instrumentality in this affair. We must retire and leave the case in his hands, and turn our attention to the doing of good, in some other way. (185)

Wayland then opts for a narrow zone of personal responsibility.[3] How circumspect he believes our responsibilities to be can be seen in another concrete moral assessment he makes.

Exactly what is involved in our duty to tell the truth? Wayland gives an interesting answer. Not only is this answer repeated in his ethical textbook, *The Elements of Moral Science,* but it is exactly the same *moral* advice that Rogers will give to Silas regarding the mills and the English buyers. Wayland's advice is that "the moral precept respecting veracity, is not a positive but merely a negative precept. It does not command us *to bear witness,* it merely forbids us to bear *false witness*" (1847, 68, emphasis added).

Two aspects of an individual's moral obligations need to be stressed. First, according to Wayland, those obligations are very limited. Second, and more important, the demeanor of the moral agent is passive, not active; one should not be immoral, but then again, one need not be a crusader.

If the nineteenth-century reader was accustomed to thinking of morality as limited to personal, even private, matters, does it not seem natural for that reader to focus on the love story and the ethical questions involved in the Tom-Irene-Penelope triangle? Would not that reader, like the reviewers cited above, either see Lapham's bankruptcy as a superfluous plot or fail to perceive the ethical dilemmas that confront Lapham in his business dealing with Rogers? Let us now turn to the matter of business ethics. I will confine my treatment to Wayland and Fairchild since Mahan did not develop a formal position on these matters.[4]

Business ethics

Francis Wayland's treatment of business ethics occurs in the section of *The Elements of Moral Science* titled "Justice in Respect to Property," especially in a subsection called "Modes in which the right of property may be violated by the individual" (1847, 216). Although this subsection is detailed and gives a wide assortment of concrete examples, the norms espoused by Wayland are shifting and vague. In the last analysis, it is clear that the principles of Wayland's business ethics are nonmoral. Wayland is candid: both the buyer and the seller know the business of business, and each knows he must look after his own interest. "Hence . . . a seller . . . is under no obligation to assist the judgment of the buyer *unless* the article for sale is defective, and then he is under obligation to reveal it" (219, emphasis added). But even this proviso about declaring defects is suspended in cases where known risk is involved, say, at an auction or in a speculative enterprise. Apparently buying mills in a foreign country would be just such a speculative enterprise. Later Wayland asserts that "the seller is under no obligation to set forth the quality of his merchandise, yet he is at liberty to do so, confining himself to the truth" (220). However, in the examples that Wayland analyzes to illustrate his truth-in-merchandising principle, his advice is quite simple: one must not lie, but one need not volunteer information. As above, no need to bear witness!

The tenor of Wayland's business ethics is most clear in his position on three issues: liability for the delivery of defective goods, exorbitant interest rates, and bankruptcy. In the case of the delivery of defective goods, he concludes that liability "must be settled by precedent; and can rarely be known in any country until a decision is had in the courts of law" (223). As for exorbitant interest rates, "If it be said, men may charge exorbitant interest, I reply, so they may charge exorbitant rent for houses, and exorbitant hire for horses. And, I ask, how is the evil of exorbitant charges remedied? The answer is plain. We allow a perfectly free competition" (224)

Finally, regarding bankruptcy, "The question is often asked whether a debtor is *morally* liberated by an act of insolvency" (226, emphasis added). Wayland's reply is tentative and qualified: "I *think* not, if he ever afterward have the means of repayment" (226, emphasis added). Notice that in all three of these issues it is not a moral principle; rather, it is a practical consideration, a prudential judgment, or a legal precedent that provides the "moral" solution. What is even more surprising is that Wayland seems not to have noticed his own slippage from morality to legality. He does not realize that he is no longer functioning as a moral philosopher because he is codifying existing business practice instead of furnishing a business ethic.

Wayland pawns off another descriptive and legal treatment of business as a normative and ethical treatment in a second well-known textbook, *The Elements of Political Economy*. This book was first published in 1837 and by 1860 had sold 30,000 copies. Here again Wayland convolutes values and facts: "The principles of Political Economy are so closely analogous to those of Moral Philosophy, that almost every question in one, may be argued on ground belonging to the other" (1837, vi). But for Wayland, business practices, not moral principles, are primary. On the question of whether contracts are binding, he explains, "With this question, Political Economy has nothing to do. Its only business is, to decide whether a given contract were or were not *wise*" (vi, emphasis added). In other words, in business the prudential is the moral. Further, the prudential is what is customarily allowed and legally permitted. For Wayland, then, writing a business ethic is not a normative project; it is a descriptive exercise.

James H. Fairchild's *Moral Philosophy: The Science of Obligation* is very different in tone and result. He is precise in his separation of the realms of morality and legality. He carefully and consistently maintains that, in business, what is legal may have little or nothing to do with what is ethical. His premise is the opposite of Wayland's: "The ordinary business maxim, to assume that every man in trade will attend to his own interests, is, by no means, a safe [that is, an acceptable ethical] principle of conduct" (1869, 249). When Fairchild treats the duties of sellers, he does not waver; he speaks of "commercial honesty," "an honest bargain," and "true commercial integrity" (247–48). He judges monopolies, artificial shortages, and market glutting to be "utterly unjustifiable" (249). Whereas Wayland only tentatively and reluctantly linked morality and bankruptcy, Fairchild does so without doubts or reservations: "Morally, debts are never outlawed. . . . There is, doubtless, propriety in the law which set a limit to the collectability of a debt, but such a law cannot discharge the moral obligation. The proper force of bankrupt laws, is not in any power to release the debtor from his moral obligation. They have no such power; but it is in the protection they afford to the debtor, in his effort to recover himself, and acquire the ability to meet his obligations. The release from indebtedness is technical and legal, not real" (253). Thus with regard to bankruptcy, conduct morally permissible to Wayland would be immoral for Fairchild. The difference between Wayland and Fairchild is vast. In the end it comes to this: Wayland sees business in legal, not moral, terms, while Fairchild holds that there are moral obligations in business that are more extensive and binding than *merely* legal obligations. In a word, Wayland is concerned with avoiding fraud; Fairchild seeks to promote honor and honesty.

In any number of situations wherein Fairchild would see a moral duty, Wayland would judge the situation in practical and legal, that is, in *amoral,* terms. Chapter 21 of *Silas Lapham* describes such a situation. Rogers announces to Lapham that he has found some English parties interested in buying the mills. Lapham explodes: Why had Rogers not told him that the railroad intended to buy the mills? "You lie. . . . You're a thief. . . . You stole" (Howells, 1885, 241). Through all of this, Rogers maintains "self-possession" (241). After he is called a liar, Rogers calmly sits, "listening, as if respectfully considering the statements. . . . [He] sat wholly unmoved . . . with dry tranquility ignoring Lapham's words, as if they had been an outburst against some third person, who probably merited them, but in whom he was so little interested that he had been obliged to use patience in listening to his condemnation" (242–43).

The fact that details about the railroads had not been volunteered is, for Rogers (as for Wayland), a practical matter, a matter of business savvy and shrewdness. If Lapham had bothered to ask, Rogers might have shared this information with him; but as it stood it was Lapham's, not Rogers's, responsibility. However, for Lapham (and for Fairchild), Rogers's craftiness is immoral and despicable. Thus the same action, viewed by two different people from the perspective of two different ethical systems, is either highly unethical or blandly amoral. Perhaps Rogers is not putting up a front at all; perhaps he is not morally callous. He can confront Lapham with "dry tranquility," for although Lapham finds Rogers's conduct morally outrageous, Rogers himself sees it as standard business practice.

Or witness Rogers's notion of the limits of personal responsibility. In chapter 25, Lapham will not sell the mills. Rogers offers a way out: "Then why don't you sell to me? Can't you see that you will not be responsible for what happens after you have sold?" (290). Clearly, Rogers is appealing to a Wayland-like concept of limited personal responsibility.

If Rogers dramatizes the ethical stance of Wayland, then Lapham amounts to a moral exemplar for Fairchild. Lapham is clear about legal and moral responsibilities; because he responds to the latter and not the former, he loses his fortune. Much has been written about the moral quandaries and ethical calculations of Lapham. My point is more basic. Lapham's ethical intuitions are sometimes clear and decisive, at other times clouded and halting. But his eventual actions are clearly ethical, as opposed to prudential or legal; Lapham responds to *a business ethic*. I will cite only three examples.

First, although Lapham claims that his "conscience is easy" (41) about buying Rogers out of the business, his conscience is not clear. Listening to his conscience and to his wife leads him to loan Rogers the money that will initiate Lapham's financial plunge. But even if Lapham is slow to recognize his moral duty, when he does, he acts resolutely.

Again, in the climactic chapter 25, after the meeting with the English parties, Rogers comes to the Lapham home with a final offer. He argues that if Lapham sells the mills to him, the matter (and the responsibility) will be out of Lapham's hands: "It was perfectly true. Any lawyer would have told him the same. He could not help admiring Rogers for his ingenuity, and every selfish interest of his nature joined with many obvious duties to urge him to consent. He did not see why he should refuse. There was no longer a reason. He was standing alone for nothing" (290). But after wrestling through the night, Lapham ends by "standing firm for right and justice [even] to his own destruction" (292).

Third, in the concluding chapter, Lapham and his family live in near poverty until "every dollar, every cent, had gone to pay his debts; he had come out with clean hands" (318). Lapham has not sought, in Fairchild's words, the technical and legal release of bankruptcy. Lapham has discharged, as Wayland puts it, the *real* moral responsibility of his debts.

When readers of *Silas Lapham* are ignorant of changes in nineteenth-century moral philosophy, including the emerging business ethics, shallow readings result. Misreadings were common with early readers, and superficial readings are just as common among contemporary readers.

Just how commonly was *Silas Lapham* superficially read by Howells's contemporaries? This is certainly an arguable point. But Howells's own comments, all but three of eighteen initial reviews, and some early commentators indicate that (at least early on) the moral point of *Silas Lapham* was not understood. Important confirmation of this claim can be found in a most unlikely place, the *Andover Review*. This was the same journal that published Hamilton Mabie's review, "A Typical Novel." As we have seen, that review missed Howells's moral point and misread *Silas Lapham,* concluding that "its vigor is mainly on the side of moral pathology" (1885, 424). Seven volumes and four years later, the *Andover Review* published its own rebuttal, "The Moral Purpose in Howells's Novels." In this article Anna Laurens Dawes laments that Howells's moral purpose in writing has "been too little considered" (1889, 23). Indeed, she is saddened that Howells's moral purpose has been "*altogether* ignored or . . . deplored as an acknowledged lack" (24, emphasis added). Dawes argues that "a distinct ethical intention" (25) has always marked Howell's works and wonders how he could have been more obvious about it. Nonetheless, "The general reader, as well as the critic, has somewhat captiously misunderstood Mr. Howells" (26). The body of the article delineates the moral purpose in all fourteen of Howells's novels, from *Their Wedding Journal* (1872) to *Annie Kilburn* (1889). For those still unconvinced, Dawes offers three additional items of evidence. First, an ethical concern permeates Howells's poetry, even his sketches, and his "Editor's Study" (especially his book reviews) consistently stresses ethical elements. Finally, she cites Howells's brave "petition for clemency to the Anarchists" (35).

Accordingly, I have argued that the moral point of *Silas Lapham* was frequently missed by his early readers. If they liked the book, they saw it as a love story with a happy ending; if they didn't, they saw it as decadent realism. The moral dilemmas involved in the bankruptcy plot escaped them. I believe that a lack of awareness of changing moral standards, especially in business ethics, best explains this blind spot. Early readers, not yet accustomed to connecting business and ethics, saw Silas's bankruptcy struggles as a financial, not an ethical, matter. Only the more perceptive, ethically sensitized readers and critics appreciated the moral drama in Howells's groundbreaking novel. Following the lead of the moralist James Fairchild, business ethics gradually gained popular awareness and support. And, too, the moral drama of *Silas Lapham* came to be widely appreciated, eventually coming to be regarded as the main message of the novel.

And what of shallow readings given by current readers? The figure of Rogers is the key here. Rogers is quickly and universally dismissed as a scoundrel. Rogers, if he is noticed, is seen as the ignoble foil of the exemplary Lapham. But such a reading fails to capture the complexity of Howells's task. Howells was quite aware that in the eyes of his own contemporaries, Rogers would be seen as crafty and moral at the same time. In Francis Wayland's views of moral responsibility and ethical practices in business, Roger's schemes are moral. Howells strongly disagrees and writes a novel to convince his contemporaries, in effect, to reject Wayland's hair-splitting, casuistic morality. Howells and moralists like Fairchild were successful. They were so successful that it is now difficult to fathom Rogers as a moral figure. But that must have been as obvious to the nineteenth-century readers as Lapham's moral excellence is to us. In *The Rise of Silas Lapham,* William Dean Howells was attempting to change theory in novel writing and ethical practice in business. His success in *both* tasks deserves acknowledgment.

NOTES

This chapter is an expanded and thoroughly recast version of two articles: "Nineteenth-Century Business Ethics and *The Rise of Silas Lapham*" and "Moral Purpose in Howells's Realism" that appeared in *American Studies* 21 (1980): 17-32 and *American Studies* 25 (1984): 75-77.

1. See the Norton Critical Edition (Howells, 1885, 343–46) for the exchange of letters between Cyrus L. Sulzberger and Howells on a section of the second chapter of

the original serial version of *The Rise of Silas Lapham* that was prejudicial to Jews. The amended book version of this chapter can also be also found in that edition.

2. For example, Pizer (1960) offers a helpful discussion that links the love plot and the moral dilemma plot, and Vanderbilt offers interesting comments on "the story of Silas' business rise and his conflict between moral integrity and the gospel of wealth . . . [and] the Cory-Lapham 'sub-plot'" (1962, 310). On the role of the love plot and the class conflict plot, see Li and Prioleau.

3. See Madden (1962) for a detailed analysis of this work by Wayland. For more on the issue of slavery and northern moral philosophers (some forty-eight are treated), see Smith, who contends that "Protestant churches and churchmen in America have been concerned primarily with the problems of the individual in society rather than with the problems of society as a whole" (1956, 197).

4. Mahan (1848, 367–69) makes scattered observations on ethics and business, but his commentaries are unsystematic and usually amount to disclaimers. For instance, he explains that a contract, business or otherwise, is only a mutual promise and hence needs no special treatment beyond what he has already given concerning promises.

WORKS CITED

American Hebrew. 1885. "Silas Lapham and the Jews." September 4, 1885:50. Reprinted in George Arms and William B. Gibson, "'Silas Lapham,' 'Daisy Miller,' and the Jews."

Arms, George, and William B. Gibson. 1943. "'Silas Lapham,' 'Daisy Miller,' and the Jews." *New England Quarterly* 16:118–22.

Athenaeum. 1885. "Novels of the Week." Reprinted in William Dean Howells, *The Rise of Silas Lapham.* Edited by Don L. Cook, 395–96. Norton Critical Edition. New York: W. W. Norton, 1982.

Catholic World. 1885. "Novel-Writing as a Science." 42:274–80.

Critic. 1885. "Review of *The Rise of Silas Lapham.*" September, 12:122

Dawes, Anna Laurens. 1889. "Moral Purpose in Howells's Novels." *Andover Review* 11:23.

Eichelberger, Clayton L. 1976. *Published Comment on William Dean Howells through 1920: A Research Bibliography.* Boston: G. K. Hall.

Fairchild, James H. 1869. *Moral Philosophy: The Science of Obligation.* New York.

Firkins, Oscar W. 1924. *William Dean Howells: A Study.* Cambridge, MA: Harvard University Press.

Harvey, Alexander. 1917. *William Dean Howells: A Study of the Achievement of a Literary Artist.* New York.

Howells, William Dean. 1885. *The Rise of Silas Lapham.* Edited by Don L. Cook. Norton Critical Edition. New York: W. W. Norton, 1982.

———. 1900. *Literary Friends and Acquaintances.* New York.

Independent. 1885. Review of *The Rise of Silas Lapham* 37:1294–95.

Li, Hsin-Yin. 1996. "For Love or Money: Courtship and Class Conflict in Howells's *The Rise of Silas Lapham.*" *Studies in American Fiction* 24:101–21.

Lippincott's. 1885. "The Literature of the Day." 36:421–22. Excerpted in Eichelberger, *Published Comment on William Dean Howells,* 372.

Literary World. 1885. Review of *The Rise of Silas Lapham.* 16:299.

Mabie, Hamilton Wright. 1885. "A Typical Novel." *Andover Review* 4:416–28.

Madden, Edward H. 1962. "Francis Wayland and the Limits of Moral Responsibility." *Proceedings of the American Philosophical Society* 106:348–59.

Mahan, Asa. 1848. *A Science of Moral Philosophy.* Oberlin, OH.

Nation. 1885. Review of *The Rise of Silas Lapham.* Reprinted in Howells, *The Rise of Silas Lapham,* 400–402.

New York Daily Tribune. 1885. "New Publications: Mr. Howells's Last Story: *The Rise of Silas Lapham.*" August 16:8.

New York Times. 1885. "New Publications: Mr. Howells's Novel." September 27:5.

New York Sun. 1885. "Some New Books: Mr. Howells's Last Novel." August 23:4.

Payne, William Morton. 1885. "Recent Fiction." *Dial* 6:122.

Philadelphia American. 1885. Reviews. August 29:265–66. Excerpted in Eichelberger, *Published Comment on William Dean Howells,* 54–55.

Pizer, Donald. 1960. "The Ethical Unity of *The Rise of Silas Lapham.*" *American Literature* 23:322–27.

Prioleau, Elizabeth Stevens. 1983. "*The Rise of Silas Lapham*: The Sexual Subplot." In *The Circle of Eros: Sexuality in the Works of William Dean Howells.* Durham, NC: Duke University Press.

Saturday Review. 1885. Review of *The Rise of Silas Lapham.* 60:517–18.

Scudder, Horace. 1885. "Recent American Fiction." *Atlantic,* October, 554–56.

Smith, Wilson. 1956. *Professors and Public Ethics: Studies of Northern Moral Philosophers before the Civil War.* Ithaca, NY: Cornell University Press.

Vanderbilt, Kermit. 1962. "Howells among the Brahmins: Why 'The Bottom Dropped Out' during *The Rise of Silas Lapham.*" *New England Quarterly* 36:291–317.

Wayland, Francis. 1837. *The Elements of Political Economy.* New York.

———. 1838. *The Limitations of Human Responsibility.* Boston.

———. 1847. *The Elements of Moral Science.* 4th ed. Edited by Joseph Blau. Cambridge, MA: Harvard University Press, 1963.

Westminster Review. 1886. "Contemporary Literature, Belles Lettres." 125:303.

7

Howells's Ethical Exegesis in
The Rise of Silas Lapham

> *Silas Lapham is a fine type of the successful American . . . Simple,*
> *clear, bold, and straightforward in mind and action . . . [he] is, in*
> *the best sense of that much-abused term, one of nature's noblemen.*
> —William Dean Howells

A keen sense of the ethical in both its personal and social aspects gave William Dean Howells's editorial commentary and fiction a clear purpose and a forceful goal: moral suasion. His adept moral analyses and his ability to dramatize the ethical dimension of human lives reached their high point in *The Rise of Silas Lapham.* The traditional reading of this novel regards it as a classical locus for moral dilemmas—both personal and business—and for moral exemplars—both virtuous and vicious. Some recent commentaries on *The Rise of Silas Lapham* advance a line of argument that stresses the complexities, contexts, and contingencies that infect human lives to the point that, at best, moral accountability is severely compromised and, at worst, is silly, even ridiculous.[1] My examination of moral questions in this turn-of-the-(last)-century American masterpiece reaffirms the traditional reading. That is, I argue that Howells was acutely aware of the maddening confusion and the painful ambiguity that surround ethical matters, and he amply appreciated how a myriad of factors threaten to overwhelm moral decision makers and their actions. Still, on the reality of the force, genuineness, and validity of *morality itself,* Howells remained clearly affirmative.

Through the events of the story, Howells carefully considered the whole range of normative matters—morality, etiquette, aesthetics, and the supererogatory.[2]

He paid close attention to both motivation and consequences in moral questions as he explored ethical growth and stagnation as well as emotional and intellectual development in key characters. Of course, the central player is the paint king and millionaire Silas Lapham. His fortitude as well as his foibles, his ethical clarity as well as his moral confusion, his waffling as well as his resolve, are deftly examined. Lapham's decisions, character, and actions become a backdrop for the rest of the moral, amoral, and immoral developments in the story.

All sorts of rises and falls—social, financial, aesthetic, and moral—enliven Howells's story, as he has nearly every character on a roller-coaster ride. But above all the others, Silas profits from experience as paradoxically he recaptures a basic decency and a clear conscience.

SILAS LAPHAM'S BASELINE INTEGRITY

Repeatedly, Howells comments that Silas is a good man. He is described as shrewd, sensible, and sharp, but also a man of integrity who is without guile. Tom Corey's assessment of him as a "very simple-hearted and rather wholesome" person is widely shared (Howells, 1885, 59). Silas's business is paint; he is devoted to it, and his successes have been won without shortcuts or ill gain.

Goodness and lack of duplicity are hallmarks of Silas's character. His rapport with people is free of staging or guise. The urbane and jaded Bartley Hubbard is struck by Silas's "free and unembarrassed interview" (19) with him. Similarly the narrator describes the Laphams' marriage: "She knew that he would tell her if ever things went wrong, and he knew that she would ask him whenever she was anxious. . . . They liked to talk to each other in that blunt way; it is the New England way of expressing perfect confidence and tenderness" (29).

Silas is candid and unpretentious. For instance, in the introductions before the dinner party, Mrs. Corey addresses him as "General Lapham." "'No, ma'am, only Colonel,' said the honest man" (167). Or when the Lapham parents call upon Rev. Sewell for advice about handling the emotional pain that will follow from straightening out the courtship misunderstandings, we are told that Silas lays out all the facts with "a simple dignity" (211). Silas's straightforward approach prompts a similar directness from Rev. Sewell: "I thank you for coming—for trusting your troubles to me" (212).

Silas is a clearly a solid, honest man. More so, at several points in the story, without much effort or deliberation, Silas goes beyond what is morally required. Still, he is no saint. Like Aristotle's "continent man," Silas struggles to do what is right and usually succeeds. Howells's detailed exploration of Silas's moral integrity revolves around two business deals that test it: buying out his partner, Rogers, and his refusal to sell out to Rogers and the British agents.

Silas's First Character Test: The Rogers Buyout

Persis is bothered by Silas's treatment of his former partner, but Silas is not. Silas's conscience is clear, as it ought to be. Milton K. Rogers appears very early in the book, three chapters from the beginning, and exits late, three chapters from the end. And as Persis notes, his appearance is always a dark omen. "'I don't see how he always manages to appear just at the moment when he seems to have gone fairly out of our lives, and blight everything,' she whimpered" (41).

Unannounced, Rogers calls upon the Laphams as they are inspecting their half-built mansion; their conversation is limited to pleasantries. After Rogers departs, Persis "turned her face toward [Silas, and] her cheeks were burning, and tears that looked hot stood in her eyes. 'You left it all to me!' she cried. 'Why couldn't you speak a word?'" (41). Silas replies that he had nothing to say to Rogers. On the way home, she continues to cry, for she cannot blink away the guilty memories. Silas, to the contrary, repeats, "I tell you, . . . it was a perfectly square thing. And I wish, once for all, you would quit bothering about it. My conscience is easy as far as he's concerned, and it always was" (41). But Persis insists that the buyout ruined Rogers. Silas reiterates that he never wanted a partner, and so as soon as he could, he dissolved the agreement: "He got his money out again and more, too" (41). As the minority partner, Rogers lacked leverage to buy out Silas. To Persis that means that Rogers had no real choice in the matter. On the contrary, "'It was a business chance,' replied Silas" (41). Persis remains adamant and tenacious: "No; you had better face the truth, Silas. It was no chance at all. You crowded him out. A man that had saved you! No, you had got greedy, Silas. You had made paint your God and you couldn't bear to let anybody share in its blessings" (42). Silas repeats that since Rogers got his money (and more), "It's an even thing, as far forth as that goes" (42). Putting the money issue aside for a moment, Persis strives to change Silas's mind by absolving him of malice. Even if he meant no wrong, she argues, he still "took an advantage" (42).

Silas's final rebuttal is elaborate, appealing to fairness, a clear conscience, and common business practices: "What do you want I should own up about a thing for when I don't feel wrong? I tell you Rogers haint got anything to complain of, and that's what I told you from the start. It's a thing that's done every day. I was loaded up with a partner that didn't know anything, and couldn't do anything, and I unloaded; that's all" (42). Silas explains that his business boom was due to timing and favorable conditions. Further, he insists that it was *his* business acumen that made the difference: "I had a right to it. I made the success" (42). Persis finally ends the discussion with a broadside against Silas's pride and joy, the new house, as she announces that she never wants to return to it. "You can sell it, for all of me. I sha'n't live in it. There's blood on it" (42).

While Silas feels no guilt, Persis's conscience is besieged. However, a strong and sincere feeling that an action is wrong (or right) is no guarantee that the action is actually forbidden (or required or even permissible). Whose ethical judgment is correct? On what grounds and for what reasons? Howells masterfully captures the signature characteristic of any serious ethical dilemma: persuasive arguments can be made for several courses of action. Since the Silas-Persis disagreement is important and complex, Howells proceeds very carefully.

Each time he presents Persis's judgment, Howells leaves the reader at arm's length with a disclaimer: "this wrong, *if any* . . . this wrong, *if it were a wrong*" (44, emphasis added). He also comments that their difference of opinion "was one of those things in life, which seem destined to wait justice," but then immediately adds a correction and a caveat. Perhaps, he comments, one ought to say that their disagreement was one of those things in this life that await "judgment, in the next" (43).

Howells's acute awareness of the moral/supererogatory borderline is clear in his contention that while what Silas did was permissible and allowable, and hence his treatment of Rogers just, Silas might have responded with greater generosity and gratitude. "Happy is the man forever after who can choose the ideal, the unselfish part in such an exigency! Lapham could not rise to it. He did what he could maintain to be perfectly fair" (44). Silas's options included going *beyond* morality, but he had not and need not have practiced moral heroism.

The disagreement between Silas and Persis will not disappear, in part, because in their marriage her moral support, "her zeal and courage[,] formed the spring of his enterprise" (43). She had been the conscience of family, "she had sense and principles, and in their simple lot she did what was wise and right" (43). Yet as the story spins itself out, in both the courtship triangle and in the bankruptcy struggle, Persis is out of her ethical depth. Fortunately, Silas's ethical resources, his New England heritage, and his basic decency serve him well.

In a conversation about how much will be spent on the new house, Silas informs Persis that he has been playing the stock market and that he has lent money to Rogers—the two actions that will cause his financial ruin. Persis quickly passes over the first news because she is so pleased with the second. Silas reiterates his sense of the matter: "I never felt the way you did about Rogers, but I know how you always did feel" (115). Silas confesses that he is unsure why he acceded to Rogers's request. Persis, however, claims that she knows why: she is certain that Silas was moved to correct a wrong and that he felt a need to assuage guilt. Lapham rejects both explanations, stating that in going over the matter, he and Rogers agreed that there had been no wrong. Persis still hungers for reparation and absolution. Notice, from her point of view, that in lending money to Rogers, Silas did what was morally required; from his perspective, the loan was an optional and supererogatory gesture. She believes that he removed "the one spot—the one *speck* off you that was ever there" (116). He disagrees: "There wa'n't ever a speck there" (116). For him, in the theological language of supererogation, his act of kindness produced a saintly surplus of merit. Ever wanting the last word, Persis demurs, explaining that she "was content to have told him that he had done his duty" (116). He does not answer, but neither does he "explicitly deny her forgiving impeachment" (116).

Silas's Second Character Test: The British Agents and Rogers's Schemes

The final third of the novel revolves around truth-telling quandaries that Rogers and Lapham must confront. Though he told Persis that he never planned to sell the mill stocks Rogers offered as collateral for the loan, his own market speculations and a lack of orders for his paint make his financial situation precarious. Rethinking his stand on Rogers's mills, Silas travels to Iowa to gauge their worth. One of the mills' attractive features is accessibility to rail service. But because a new railroad recently leased the line, it controls freight rates and train schedules, giving it the upper hand (just as Silas had in buying out Rogers).

Upon his return to Boston, Silas confronts Rogers with what he has discovered: "You knew the road wouldn't give a fair price for the mills. You knew it would give what it chose, and that I couldn't help myself, when you let me take them. You're a thief, Milton K. Rogers, and you stole money I lent you"

(241). When Silas expresses his determination to unload the mill if necessary, even at a portion of its worth, Rogers announces, "There are some English parties who have been making inquiries in regard to those mills" (242).

That evening Persis's confused moral principles begin to show themselves. When Silas admits that he is in deep financial trouble, she jumps to the conclusion that he has lent more money to Rogers. Although she had long pressed Silas about his "duty" to make reparations to Rogers, Persis now backpedals. "I know who's to blame, and I blame myself. It was my forcing Rogers on you" (244). Losing her ethical grip, she suggests how he might recover the loan: "If you could get your price from those English parties before they knew that the G. L. & P. wanted to buy the mills, would it let you out with Rogers?" (245). Silas quickly rejects this strategy; his resolve is clear. "Most likely Rogers was lyin', and there ain't any such parties; but if there were, they couldn't have the mills from me without the whole story. Don't you be troubled, Persis, I'm going to pull through all right" (246).

Although the financial pressures grow, Silas and Persis are able to keep each other from backsliding on the question of coming clean about the railroad's ability to depreciate the mills. However, as Silas's financial slide worsens and insolvency looms larger, the Laphams feel increasingly severe economic and ethical stress. Young Corey's uncle, James Bellingham, whom Silas had asked for financial advice, gives this assessment: "There's been a terrible shrinkage in his values" (264).[3] Howells's pun is neat. Silas's material decline—a West Virginia paint company had struck a natural gas vein on their works, enabling them to bake the iron paint at one-tenth of Silas's costs; he and the other paint manufacturers have glutted the market; his own paint works have been shut down for the first time; and his new house has burned to the ground—is mirrored in his moral rise. Ironically, the beginning of the end, both ethical and financial, is marked by a stroke of moral luck. Silas accidentally sets fire to his new house. (Inadvertently, he had let the insurance on it lapse.) "'I had a builder's risk on it, but it expired last week. It's a dead loss.' 'Oh, thank the merciful Lord!' cried his wife. 'Merciful!' said Lapham. 'Well, it's a queer way of showing it'" (276). Silas bravely bears the loss of his house alone, as he would also have to face alone Rogers's tempting stratagems.

Rogers calls at Silas's office with the news that he has arranged a conference with the English parties. Though both former partners understand that the railroad will soon devalue the mills to ten cents on the dollar, Rogers insists: "I've come here to tell you that these parties stand ready to take the mills off your hands at a fair valuation—at the value I put upon them when I turned them in" as collateral for his loan from Silas (282). Silas asks if he has informed the English parties about the railroad and the mill. "I did not think that necessary" (282). Silas denounces the scheme with a sneer; the narrator comments that Silas's "sneer was on behalf of virtue, but it was still a sneer" (283). Rogers is aware that Silas is scrambling to raise capital and that a deal with the English parties might rescue his affairs. Though Rogers offers the possibility of an eleventh-hour reprieve, Silas scoffs at the idea: "I shall want money a great deal worse than I've ever wanted it yet, before I go into such rascally business with you" (283).

Silas senses that he ought to put an end to the matter then and there but procrastinates—a dangerous flaw in an otherwise sound character—as he tell Rogers he will at least meet with the English parties. Even as he postpones the matter, Silas notices that his moral bearing has "somehow drifted from his moorings by Rogers's shipping intelligence" (283). Howells continues the nautical metaphor when he explains that Silas is "trying to drop another anchor for a fresh clutch on his underlying principles" (283). Rogers presses on, for he knows he can prey on what Howells correctly describes as Silas's "scrupulosity" (281): since Lapham has agreed to speak to the English parties, he "perceive[d] his moral responsibility in it" (284). Agreeing to be at the hotel at eight o'clock, he adds, "'I won't keep you five minutes when I get there,' . . . but he did not come away till ten o'clock" (284). Howells's account of their two-hour meeting (and Rogers's subsequent visit to the Lapham house) is one of the finest examinations of moral argumentation and analysis in American literature. Given his gift for ethical discernment, how Howells must have relished these scenes!

The extent of collusion between Rogers and the English parties and the degree to which they have set out to defraud the unknowing English backers, "rich people [who] could bear" an investment failure as a trifle (288), are only two of the delightful complexities that Howells deftly introduces. In addition, he explores important differences in the moral responsibilities of individuals and corporate entities. Further, the overlap of legal/moral, moral/supererogative matters is given attention.

Silas begins with a flat refusal to sell, explaining how the railroad had decimated the mills' value. The English agents regard his refusal to sell as a bluff and negotiating ploy. Caveat emptor now stands in abeyance: the English parties have made clear that they themselves already investigated the mills. Howells next has the English agents clarify their own situation and role: "They developed further the fact that they were not acting solely, or even principally, in their own behalf, but were the agents of people in England who had projected the colonization of a sort of community on the spot, somewhat after the plan of other English dreamers, and that they were satisfied, from a careful inspection, that the resources and facilities were those best calculated to develop the energy and enterprise of the proposed community" (285). What a surprising and clever development![4] The mills' usefulness for the English investors might have little to do with an ability to produce goods at profit. Instead their chief value might be as the setting for an Owenite or Fourierite communal venture.[5] In any case, the agents acknowledge that they are "quite willing to assume the risks he had pointed out" (285).

What more need be said? Why should Silas have any obligation to prevent what he only suspects *might be* "treachery" (285) on their part? Were not his moral obligations dispatched by a sincere and vigorous effort to spell out the facts? Contrary to an earlier narrator's comment, it is now clear that Rogers has not duped the English parties (and Silas has been assured about this). Why would Lapham have any responsibility to block the arrangements?

As Howells puts it, the contest is between Silas's desire for a "show of integrity" and the other side's ability to look on these business matters with "a certain comfortable jocosity" (285). First, the loss, if any, will be spread out over the membership of a corporation. Second, even if there is a loss, the consequences will be a trifling matter for wealthy investors. Only a moral zealot would worry.

Though price gouging would be objectionable, what would be wrong with Silas's naming a fair market-value price? Although the narrator initially characterized the English parties' explanation as "sophistry," the indictment is quickly softened. Perhaps, considering a moral assessment based on greater-good/lesser-evil calculations, what is involved is not even "potential immorality" (286).

Silas's (and Howells's) qualms about "potential immorality" extend to two other considerations. First, Silas is leery of basing moral judgments on the "spreading out" of loss and pain over a larger number of individuals; second, he is suspicious of preying upon corporate entities. However, all these areas of "potential immorality" remain unaddressed because Silas leaves the hotel meeting. Again Lapham does not end the negotiation; he leaves the door open, stating, "You must let me have time to think it over" (286).

Howells has additional quandaries for his readers. Is Silas's brother's-keeper response ethically required or is it an optional, nonobligatory act beyond the pale of morality?

Silas's stand is considerably beyond customary business practices.[6] Moreover, the Rogers–English parties offer is sanctioned by legal prescription. Recall that in the Silas-Persis debate about the Rogers buyout, whenever there was any mention of a possible wrong or injustice, Howells quickly added a qualifier: "if there were any." Now when exploring what Silas ought to do, Howells makes similar unsettling disclaimers. The narrator explains that the choice is totally in Silas's hands: "It was for him alone to commit the rascality—*if it was* rascality—or not" (287, emphasis added).

Leaving the hotel after the two-hour negotiation, Silas walks home only to find Rogers there pleading with Mrs. Lapham. Rogers, in the meanwhile, has added several elements to his case. First, he seeks consideration of the impact on his family: "Here am I without a cent in the world; and my wife is an invalid. She needs comforts, she needs little luxuries, and she hasn't even the necessaries; and you want to sacrifice her to a mere idea!" (288). "Mere idea," precisely stated. Because neither the railroad nor any other potential buyer has tendered an offer, the mills technically and practically retain their presumed fair valuation. Second, Rogers revives his appeal to minimal loss and trivial pain principles. Even if there should be a loss, "the investors are rich people, and could bear it if it came to the worst," and in addition, "if there was any loss, it would be divided up among them so that they wouldn't any of them feel it" (288). Rogers then adds a bold new element:

> "I want you should sell to *me*. I don't say what I'm going to do with the property, and you will not have an iota of responsibility, whatever happens." . . .
> . . . "The question is, Will you sell, and, if so, what is your figure? You have got nothing whatever to do with it after you've sold." (290)

Silas is stunned. The narrator comments on how compelling the ethical and legal arguments are. "It was perfectly true. Any lawyer would have told him the same. He could not help admiring Rogers for his ingenuousness, and every selfish interest of his nature joined with *many obvious duties* to urge him to consent. He did not see why he should refuse. There was no longer a reason. He was standing out alone for nothing, any one else would say" (290, emphasis added). Actually, three sorts of norms—customary business practices, defensible legal opinions, and acceptable moral principles—seem to concur with Rogers's analysis. For a third time, Silas does not end the matter;

again he asks for more time. Upon taking his leave, Rogers probes a long-standing sore spot. When Silas forced Rogers out, he worried only about his own interests and advantage. Why, asks Rogers, is Silas now so "particular" about watching out for others? "Lapham winced. It was certainly ridiculous for a man who had once so selfishly consulted his own interests to be stickling now about the rights of others" (291).

Silas paces the floor all night. He faces the crisis alone. Interestingly, at daybreak he still has not decided what to do. His first words to Persis are "I don't know what I'm going to say to Rogers" (291). What has become clear is that Silas's standard procedure is to postpone making ethical decisions. And in this case, Silas deliberates (and delays) so long that he no longer has to decide. After his sleepless night, he goes to the office, where waiting for him is the offer from the Great Lacustrine and Polar Railroad. The conflict was over; neither decision nor action was needed! When Rogers calls at the office at the prearranged time, Silas hands him the bid. Rogers sizes up the situation quickly—taking "all in at a glance, and [he had] seen the impossibility of negotiating any further now, even with victims so pliant and willing as those Englishmen" (292).

Curiously, the narrator credits Silas with resolute moral action: "This was his reward for standing firm for right and justice to his own destruction: to feel like a thief and murderer" (292). But, in fact, all he did was delay; he held out so long that the practical consequences made any moral decision moot.

In the next chapter, Howells describes Persis's regret that she did not help Silas make the correct decisions. She blames herself for not seeing through Rogers's "piece of roguery" (293). Furthermore, although she had long embraced the traditional Victorian role of wife and mother as moral guardian, "she admired and revered [Silas] for going beyond her" (294). Actually, because she has regressed morally, Silas has gone considerably beyond her. Persis's distance from Silas becomes clear when she accuses him of infidelity. After a couple of frantic trips to the office to locate Silas (who is off to New York and places beyond to raise capital in a last attempt to stave off bankruptcy), she finally realizes that the very pretty typewriter is Zerrilla Dewey, daughter of Jim Millon. Whereas Persis is sure that Silas had long ago wronged Rogers, she could never accept Silas's sense of debt to his fallen Civil War comrade Jim Millon. "It was a perfect superstition of his; she could not beat it out of him" (298). Notice that Silas's decision not to abandon Zerrilla can be explained as an ethical matter, as an act of justice. But then, too, Silas's monetary aid to Zerrilla and her mother can be seen as an act of charity, an optional matter beyond morality. Howells, however, deliberately and effectively leaves the moral status of Silas's acts of fairness/generosity unresolved. Indeed, he subtly poses an additional useful ambiguity: does Persis continue to regard his actions as ethically heroic, or does she come to appreciate the simple decency of his concern?

A few days later, at the end of the end, reflecting upon Silas's moral fiber, Persis admires his "simple, rude soul . . . [which] had been equal to its ordeals, and had come out unscathed and unstained" (308). For his part, in his early and late dealings with Rogers (and the English parties), Silas "believed that he had acted right . . . and he was satisfied; but he did not care to have . . . anybody . . . think he had been a fool" (309). Perhaps he had been a fool.

The Full Spectrum of Moral Evaluation in *The Rise of Silas Lapham*

Howells's dramatization of the complexities that Silas confronts in his refusal to sell to Rogers and the British agents admits of four distinct ethical assessments. Silas's refusal can be seen as heroically beyond morality, ethically required, immoral (and foolish), and amoral. Howells's analyses offer persuasive arguments for each evaluation, leaving his readers with numerous moral and philosophical questions to ponder.

Bromfield Corey, among others, thinks Silas's resolve is *heroic*. The elder Corey, sensing "a delicate, aesthetic pleasure in the heroism with which Lapham had withstood Rogers and his temptations—something finely dramatic and unconsciously effective" (315–16), writes to Silas to commend him. Corey realizes that standing up to Rogers was the final stroke that brought about the collapse of Silas's financial house. Declaring bankruptcy, the Laphams move back to the ancestral farm home, which was also the site of the original paint mine. Silas continues to manufacture his premium Persis brand of paint and uses the proceeds to pay back all his creditors, even though bankruptcy cleared him legally (and perhaps morally) of this "duty." "One thing he could say: he had been no man's enemy but his own; every dollar, every cent had gone to pay his debts; he had come out with clean hands" (318).[7] Going beyond legality, and perhaps morality, paying off his debts and helping out both Zerrilla and Mrs. Dewey are additional instances of supererogatory impulses in Silas's character.

When Rev. Sewell calls on the Laphams at the Vermont farm, Silas recounts the whole series of events, starting with the Rogers buyout and ending with his refusal to sell to the English parties. Silas reiterates that he thought he had done

Rogers no wrong; Sewell concurs. Sewell goes further, however, suggesting that perhaps any lingering doubts about ending the partnership empowered him, as "your fear of having possibly behaved selfishly toward this man kept you on your guard, and strengthened you when you were brought face to face with a greater . . . emergency" (320).[8] Regarding Sewell's theory and Rogers's temptations, Silas confesses that his reasons both then and now remain opaque to him: "Well, I don't know what it was," he says. "All I know is that when it came to the point, although I could see that I'd got to go under unless I did it, that I couldn't sell out to those Englishmen and I couldn't let that man put his money into my business without I told him just how things stood" (320).

Were Silas's actions *moral*? This evaluation has already been treated at length. It boils down to what Bartley Hubbard described in his opening interview as "sterling morality . . . the simple virtues of the Old Testament and *Poor Richard's Almanac*" (5). That is, Silas's moral duties were obvious: tell the truth and refuse to become an accomplice in the moral complicity of others. Howells's summary description is precise and careful. Because of what Silas did *not* do, the matter was settled: "'Well, it don't always seem as if I done it,' replied Lapham. 'Seems sometime as if it was a hole opened for me, and I crept out of it. I don't know'" (321).

Might Silas's actions have been *immoral* (and foolish)? Though Howells does not explicitly examine the possibility, this assessment can be inferred from his treatment of the courtship plot in the novel. Was Silas's stubborn refusal to sell a pseudoheroic act of self-sacrifice? At the dinner party, the popular novel *Tears, Idle Tears,* with its "dear old-fashioned hero and heroine in it, who keep dying for each other all the way through and making the most wildly satisfactory and unnecessary sacrifices for each other" (174), is denounced for its intellectual and moral mischief. Rev. Sewell calls such behavior "psychical suicide" (175). When the Irene-Tom-Penelope courtship confusion is revealed, precisely the same sort of unnecessary, and pseudoheroic, sacrifices are contemplated. Silas's clergyman, Rev. Sewell, suggests that the Laphams consider an "economy of pain" (212) strategy that examines the dilemma in terms of the greatest happiness of the greatest number and/or the least harm to the fewest.

If an economy-of-pain principle is applied to Silas's refusal to sell, his action appears to be a pseudoheroic act of self-sacrifice. In other words, perhaps his brother's-keeper mentality is foolish and quixotic.[9]

Whose interests ought to be foremost in an economy-of-pain calculation? Rogers appeals to Silas on behalf of his wife and children. Also to be considered are Silas's wife and daughters, as well as the employees and their families, who will be displaced if his paint business fails. If Silas sells the mills back to Rogers and if these funds facilitate a financial recovery, his refusal to sell violates the greatest-good/least-evil principles. The large number of English investors and their ability to sustain a small loss need to be part of the calculation, too. In other words, according to the economy-of-pain principle, it can be argued that Silas's "standing firm for the right and justice" (292) was foolish and immoral.

Silas could rebut the contention that he acted immorally. He and his wife and children are surviving quite well back in Vermont. In addition, Rogers and his family have enjoyed the benefit of Silas's largess. Further, Rogers had already dissipated several fortunes; his latest reversal has had no connection with Silas. As for the families who depend on the paint business, Silas has already expressed his opinion. When he tells Persis that he has to shut down the paint works because the market is glutted and his warehouse full, Persis worries. "'I don't know what's going to become of the hands in the middle of the winter, this way. . . . I don't care what becomes of the hands,' cried Lapham. 'They've shared in my luck, now let 'em share the other thing'" (253). In the final analysis, then, it remains unclear whether the economy-of-pain principle supports or undercuts Silas's refusal to act.

The fourth and final possibility is that Lapham's actions are not heroic, not moral, not immoral, but *amoral*. Getting clear about Silas's intentions is central here. If neither ethical imperatives nor good/bad consequence calculations can account for Silas's actions, what else remains? Perhaps it is simply a matter of the dollars involved. Consider the helpful long-standing moral maxim "Ought implies can." That is, one is ethically obligated only when one's actions can make a difference. Conversely, when one's actions cannot make a difference, then one is absolved of ethical responsibility. Accordingly, in this case, if there was not enough money in Rogers's schemes to save his business, monetary considerations alone might account for Silas's refusal to cooperate.

It is difficult to determine precisely the amount of his debt and how much relief can be gained by selling to the English parties. With regard to his own indebtedness (due to his stock speculations and other losses), no figures are given; with regard to the Rogers dealings, however, Silas comments, "I've used up a hundred and fifty thousand dollars" (289). Initially, Silas loaned Rogers $20,000, secured by $5,000 worth of stocks as collateral. Silas explains to Persis that Rogers wanted $20,000 because "he had got hold of a patent right that he wanted to go into on a large scale, and there he was wanting me to supply him the funds" (115). Thereafter Rogers borrowed more money. The last loans were secured from Rogers's property in Iowa, "saw mills and grist mills and lands" (279).

How much might the mills be worth? Persis wonders what would happen if Rogers were able to produce the English agents. Silas observes, "I'd let them have the mills at the price Rogers turned 'em in on me at. I don't want to make anything on 'em" (245). Persis continues, "'If you could get your price from those English parties before they knew that the G. L. & P. wanted to buy the mills, would it let you out with Rogers?' 'Just about,' said Lapham" (245).

Later, in a last-ditch effort, Rogers appears at the Lapham home to propose that Silas sell the mills back to him. The price Rogers apparently has in mind is $150,000: "I've come here to tell you that these parties stand ready to take the mills off your hands at a fair valuation—at the value I put upon them when I turned them in" (382). Rogers reiterates, "If we should succeed in selling, I should be able to repay you your loans" (282).

In fact, estimates Silas, the mills' value is only about $15,000, "worth ten cents on the dollar" (282). And indeed, as Howells puts it, the offer from the railroad proves to be "the verification of his prophetic fear" (292) about his last shrinkage in values.

If we could audit Silas's books, we would want to look at two amounts: how much money he has lost and how much he needs in order to go into partnership with the rival West Virginia paint company. Their business is sound, and a partnership with them is very attractive to Silas: "He found the West Virginians full of zeal and hope, but in ten minutes he knew that they had not yet tested their strength in the money market, and had not ascertained how much or how little capital they could command. Lapham himself, if he had so much, would not have hesitated to put a million dollars into their business" (278). But he did not have the million. About the price for a partnership, Howells first tells us that it was "a certain sum" (279), but later we are informed "that the price asked [for the partnership] was enormous" (292). Let us suppose, then, it was half a million, a sum Silas could have easily raised, save for his recent reversals and gambles.

How much is Silas worth? Bellingham (Tom Corey's uncle and Silas's sometime investment advisor) is skeptical of Silas's own estimate that he is worth one million dollars. When "Bellingham . . . subjected his figures to an analysis that wounded Lapham more than he chose to show at the time . . . it proved that he was not so rich and not so wise as he had seemed" (281). Even if he is not a millionaire, Silas's liquidity should be in the $500,000 range—

about what the West Virginia brothers want him to invest in their business and approximately the amount Silas has lost ($150,000 to Rogers, $100,000 in the new house, and $150,000 to $250,00 in stock losses, commissions, and his overstocked and devalued paint stores): "He thought ruefully of that immense stock of paint on hand, which was now a drug in the market, of his losses by Rogers and by the failures of other men, of the fire that had licked up so many thousands in a few hours; he thought with bitterness of the tens of thousands that he had gambled away in stocks, and of the commissions that the brokers had pocketed whether he won or lost" (280).

The point of all this fiscal detail is that even $150,000 from the English parties will not rescue Silas. He still needs another $300,000 to $400,000. Given the depth of Silas's money troubles, the English parties' offer, substantial though it is, would be as ineffective as Tom Corey's earlier offer to invest $30,000 in Silas's paint business or the $30,000 Silas can still raise by mortgaging his Nankeen Square home and his Beacon Street lot.

This analysis of Silas's indebtedness, if correct, means that Lapham spent the night pacing back and forth getting to the financial (and, if "cannot" implies "ought not," the moral) bottom line. For though he tells Persis, "*I don't know what I'm going to say to Rogers*" (291), he apparently settled on "standing firm" (292), as he decided, on the basis of either ethical or financial reasons (or on both grounds), not to sell. On this reading, then, Silas's refusal to sell was so much a matter of arithmetic that nonmoral consideration ruled the day.

The game is not quite up, though, and Silas's moral fiber must withstand one last temptation. Along with the G. L. & P. offer comes the news that the West Virginia paint brothers have agreed to accept Silas as a partner, provided he can raise the necessary capital. By day's end he has secured half of what he needs, and he sets off to New York to meet an interested investor. He then takes his potential investor to visit his paint works. The narrator stresses the significance of a fresh source of capital. Here, perhaps, is at last a way out, because this man "wanted to put money in the business . . . [and] his money would have enabled Lapham to close with the West Virginians" (307). With the deal all but signed, Silas feels compelled to volunteer information about his financial straits. Returning home, he tells Persis what happened. "All I had to do was keep quiet about that other company. It was Rogers and his property right over again. He liked the look of things, and he wanted to go into the business, and he had the money—plenty; it would have saved me . . . But I *had to tell* him how I stood. I *had to tell* him all about it, and what I wanted to do. He began to back water in a minute, and the next morning I saw that it was up with him. He's gone back to New York. I've lost my last chance" (307–8, emphasis added). Once again Howells's exceptional insight into fine-grained moral distinctions is evident. On one hand, customary nineteenth-century business ethics required only that the seller not deceive the buyer; thereby any clean-breast declaration surpassed morality. But, on the other hand, some turn-of-the-(last)-century American moralists sought to extend the zone of personal responsibility—beyond the injunction forbidding fraud and deceit—to a practice of aggressive honesty. Accordingly, Silas's enthusiastic integrity with regard to the New York buyer can be seen as heroically super-erogatory or as morally required. In either case, and significantly, unlike the lingering doubt about whether moral or financial considerations controlled Silas's decision not to sell to the English agents, in this last temptation ethical imperatives alone empower Silas.

After *The Rise of Silas Lapham,* Howells's investigation of moral matters turned from depictions of the individual moral arena to forceful studies of chronic and systemic injustices in American society—to wit, *The Minister's Charge* (1887), *Anne Kilburn* (1888), and, most notably, *A Hazard of New Fortunes* (1890). Still, *The Rise of Silas Lapham* is Howells's best and most enduring novel. Beside the usual reasons given for revisiting this minor classic, it is now, I hope, abundantly clear that *Silas Lapham* is a remarkable resource for ethical exegesis.

In conclusion, we have seen Howells alert to ethical complexity and sensitive to the vagaries of both motive and consequence. My analysis has highlighted his exceptional ability to dramatize how a variety of qualifiers, especially ethical theories, render the same action moral (and required) or supererogatory (and optional). Further, Howells has shown us how an optional action can be beyond morality in a number of ways: it can be foolish or heroic or immoral or amoral. In a word, gaining insight into Howells's gift for laying open the systemic ambiguity that moral agents confront is the real reward of a close study of his masterpiece, *The Rise of Silas Lapham.*

NOTES

This chapter is a slightly revised version of "Ethical Exegesis in William Dean Howells's *The Rise of Silas Lapham*" that appeared in *Papers on Language and Literature* 35 (1999): 363–90.

1. The trajectory of many of the challenging articles in *New Essays on "The Rise of Silas Lapham,"* edited by Donald Pease, especially the pieces by Dimock, Seeley, and O'Hara, is to deconstruct the ethical claims of the novel. Surveying these and other recent commentaries in his introduction to the 1996 Oxford University Press edition of *The Rise of Silas Lapham,* Crowley wonders if the fact that the novel admits of such radically opposite readings does not "suggest its self-contradictory nature . . . [and perhaps ultimately its] fundamental incoherence" (1996, xxvi).

2. See chapter 4 for a brief discussion of the term "supererogation."

3. This intriguing phrase appears in at least three other places in the novel. Early on, the elder Corey has misgivings about his son working for a living. "Here is a son of mine whom I see reduced to making his living by *shrinkage of values*" (83, emphasis added); in an earlier conversation, the narrator explains that the considerable Corey wealth had gradually melted away: "In process of time the money seemed less abundant. There were *shrinkages* of one kind and another, and living had grown much more expensive and luxurious" (62, emphasis added). And, at the height of Silas's money troubles, his bookkeeper Walker remarks that though the other paint companies have suspended production, the Lapham works have not. "I look at the stock we've got on hand. There's going to be *an awful shrinkage* on that now! And when everybody is shutting down, or running at half time, the works up at Lapham are going full chip, just the same as ever" (240, emphasis added). For an interesting discussion of this phrase and its connection with the suppressed anti-Semitic passages of the novel, see Crowley's note on the text.

4. An early review of the novel in the *American Hebrew* comments that Howells's account of the legal and moral technicalities involved in selling the mills to the English agents was "spun out to such fine distinctions as would make a Talmudic casuist regard Howells with envy" (*American Hebrew* 1886, 122). In another early essay, Dawes (1889) stresses Howells's grasp of moral distinctions.

5. See my "More's *Utopia* and the New World Utopias: Is the Good Life an Easy Life?" for an examination of the lively interest in real utopian communities in America in the 1800s.

6. For more on morality and nineteenth-century business practices, see chapter 6.

7. Foster (1978) makes a compelling case for the unmistakable similarities between *The Rise of Silas Lapham* and Balzac's *The Rise and Fall of Cesar Birotteau* (1839), noting that in both stories there is an aesthetic education by an architect and that in the end both protagonists make a heroic effort to repay all the creditors. Hedges examines a piece by Howells in *Harper's* (June 1886) that discusses "acts of generosity [that is, acts of supererogation] toward the righteous bankrupt" (1962, 170).

Arms (1942) suggests that the theme of eschewing unethical means to avoid bankruptcy in *The Rise of Silas Lapham* was inspired by Howells's reading of *The Bankrupt*

(1874) by Bjorstjern Bjornson. For a more contemporary account of the relationships between, on one hand, the supererogatory and the mandatory and, on the other, morality and legal enforcement, see Heyd (1988) and Feinberg (1970).

8. Earlier Persis made the opposite case: Silas's selfishness toward Rogers had enervated him morally. "Before she slept she found words to add that she had always feared the selfish part he had acted toward Rogers had weakened him, and left him less able to overcome any temptation that might beset him; and that was one reason why she could never be easy about it" (116).

9. Vanderbilt argues that the economy-of-pain principle "will solve Silas's own ethical dilemma with Rogers and the English financial agents" (1968, 131). Manierre remarks that "clearly the world of big business would consider Silas' scruples ridiculous" (1962, 361). However, big business versus personal responsibility is not at issue here; it is, instead, a recognition that a correct application of utilitarian morality requires that the act that promotes the greater happiness (pleasure) or prevents lesser unhappiness (pain) *is* the moral act.

WORKS CITED

American Hebrew. 1885. "Silas Lapham and the Jews." September 4:50. Reprinted in George Arms and William B. Gibson. 1943. "'Silas Lapham,' 'Daisy Miller,' and the Jews." *New England Quarterly* 16:118–22.

Arms, George. 1942. "The Literary Background of Howells's Social Criticism." *American Literature* 14:260–76.

Carter, Everett. 1950. *Howells and the Age of Realism*. New York: J. B. Lippincott.

Crowley, John W. 1996. "Introduction and Note on the Text." In William Dean Howells, *The Rise of Silas Lapham*, vii–xxxv. New York: Oxford University Press.

Dawes, Anna Laurens. 1889. "The Moral Purpose in Howells' Novels." *Andover Review* 11:23–36.

Dimock, Wai-Chee. 1991. "The Economy of Pain: Capitalism, Humanism and the Realistic Novel." In Pease, *New Essays on "The Rise of Silas Lapham,"* 67–90.

Dooley, Patrick K. 1985. "More's *Utopia* and the New World Utopias: Is the Good Life an Easy Life?" *Thought* 60:31–48.

Feinberg, Joel. 1970. "Supererogation and Rules." In *Doing and Deserving: Essays in the Theory of Responsibility*, 3–24. Princeton, NJ: Princeton University Press.

Foster, S. 1978. "W. D. Howells: *The Rise of Silas Lapham*." In *The Monster in the Mirror: Studies in Nineteenth-Century Realism*, edited by D. A. Williams, 149–78. London: Oxford University Press.

Hedges, Elaine R. 1962. "*Cesar Birotteau* and *The Rise of Silas Lapham*." *Nineteenth-Century Fiction* 17:163–74.

Heyd, David. 1988. "Moral Subjects, Freedom, and Idiosyncrasy." In *Human Agency*, edited by Jonathan Dancy, J. M. E. Moravsck, and C. C. W. Taylor, 152–69. Stanford, CA: Stanford University Press.

Howells, William Dean. 1885. *The Rise of Silas Lapham.* Edited by Don L. Cook. Norton Critical Edition. New York: W. W. Norton, 1982.

Manierre, William R. II. 1962. "*The Rise of Silas Lapham:* Retrospective Discussion as Dramatic Technique." *College English* 23:357–61.

O'Hara, Daniel T. 1991. "Growing through Pain: The Practice of Self in *The Rise of Silas Lapham.*" In Pease, *New Essays on "The Rise of Silas Lapham,"* 91–105.

Pease, Donald, ed. 1991. *New Essays on "The Rise of Silas Lapham,"* Cambridge: Cambridge University Press.

Seelye, John. 1991. "The Hole in Howells / The Lapse in *The Rise of Silas Lapham.*" In Pease, *New Essays on "The Rise of Silas Lapham,"* 47–65.

Vanderbilt, Kermit. 1968. *The Achievement of William Dean Howells.* Princeton, NJ: Princeton University Press.

8

Fakes and Good Frauds

Pragmatic Religion in *The Damnation of Theron Ware*

> *Since belief is measured by action, he who forbids us to believe*
> *religion to be true, necessarily also forbids us to act as we should*
> *if we did believe it to be true. The whole defense of religious belief*
> *hinges upon action.*
> —*William James*

Pragmatism's hold on the cultural life of America has been remarkable. From 1880 to 1910, its dominance was nearly total. Its influence remained strong through the 1930s, and since the mid-1970s, there has been sustained and lively interest in this classical American philosophy.

When pragmatism was at its zenith, Harold Frederic's *The Damnation of Theron Ware* was published. It was among the top-ten best sellers of 1896 (Ziff, 1966, 212).[1] *Theron Ware* is clearly and thoroughly pragmatic in its outlook. Although numerous critics mention pragmatism with *reference* to the novel,[2] only Scott Donaldson has offered a sustained treatment of this theme. Unfortunately, Donaldson's understanding of pragmatism is somewhat shallow, and his examination is confined to a single character, Sister Soulsby.[3]

For many, pragmatism is synonymous with crassness, compromise, and cunning. Indeed, even William James himself grew weary of the simple-mindedness of his fellow citizens' understanding of pragmatism. In a 1906 letter to H. J. Wells, James expresses chagrin that such superficiality is "understandable in onlooking citizens only as symptom of the moral flabbiness born of the exclusive worship of the bitch-goddess SUCCESS. That—with the squalid cash interpretation put on the word success—is our national disease" (James 1920, 260).

In reality, however, pragmatism is a technical and sophisticated epistemological position designed to settle the perennial questions of the nature and meaning of truth. Pragmatism's answer is that truth can only be ascertained in practice, *via* concrete experiences. Therefore truth, for humans at least, amounts to workable approximations, giving us truths rather than Truth. Pragmatists arrived at this conclusion by exploring the connection between beliefs and actions, and the relationship of ideas to useful practices.

Although C. S. Peirce, the founder of pragmatism, envisaged it as a tough-minded and scientific philosophy, the version of William James was more popular and influential. His pragmatism was tender minded, aimed at illuminating rather than undercutting the higher experiences of the "whole person." The core of James's pragmatism was a sympathetic analysis of artistic, moral, and religious experiences. As we shall see, Frederic too found that pragmatism might be a strong ally of religion.

It must be recalled why religion needed an ally in the 1890s. The answer is, of course, Charles Darwin. By 1890, Darwin's theories had been bolstered by thirty years of archeological and paleontological findings. Organized religion was severely threatened. Specifically, the biblical accounts of the origin and age of the earth and the special creation of man had been discredited. To the extent that religious truth depended upon the Bible, the impact of Darwin and science was all but fatal. The only intellectually honest option appeared to be to abandon religion and accept science.

The pragmatists, especially William James, sought to provide another option. James was convinced that religion provided unique benefits to individuals and to society. In several works, especially *The Will to Believe* (1897) and *The Varieties of Religious Experience* (1902), he displayed and defended the consequences of belief in God. For example, he showed that men and women must be highly motivated if they are to forsake the comforts of the "genial mood" of prudence and shoulder the challenges of the "strenuous mood" of moral courage. James argued that the quickest and most effective stimulus to the strenuous mood was the personal companionship of a loving God. In general, James sought to show that the consequences of religious belief were valuable.

Eventually, James drew this bold conclusion: the truth of religion and religious belief is its beneficial consequences and valuable effects. That is, religious truths are not statements of historical fact or claims about supernatural entities.

Instead the value of religious truths resides in the advantageous consequences that come with belief in God. Therefore, by reinterpreting the nature of truth, James provided a way for religion to accommodate, rather than capitulate to, Darwin and science.

Many welcomed James's pragmatism despite the fact that his bold redefinition of truth sparked a long and lively philosophical controversy. The most persistent allegation in the philosophical debate was a technical one. It was argued that James had confused the *logical* consequences of a proposition with the *practical* consequences of believing a proposition. More simply put, the charge was that James had collapsed the difference between the truth of a belief and the useful consequences of holding a belief. Except for a few academic philosophers like Bertrand Russell, for example, most people were not aware of or concerned with the technical difficulties of pragmatism. What interested them was pragmatism's ability to save religion.

Harold Frederic perceptively grasped the situation: apparently much of the American population had adopted a philosophy unaware of its inherent problems. Further, Frederic appreciated the technical, subtle, and abstract nature of pragmatism's difficulties. He decided that these flaws needed to be dramatically illustrated, not just lucidly explained. Thus my contention is that *Theron Ware* is a remarkable cultural document and an illuminating philosophical critique. In Frederic's depiction of the clergy, the reader experiences pragmatism as a philosophy of life and confronts a powerful criticism of that philosophy. Hence, in addition to its exceptional literary and dramatic qualities, *Theron Ware* deserves note for its accurate display of American life of the late 1890s and for its penetrating examination of the dominant philosophy of that era.

Let us return for a moment to the technical difficulties of a pragmatic interpretation of religion. Both James and Frederic saw difficulties in reducing truth to utility. With regard to religious truth, some of the following questions emerge. Is there actually a God, or is faith in God merely a belief with beneficial effects? Is the truth of a belief in God reducible to these beneficial effects? Supposing there is no God, or that the believer does not believe in God but only "makes believe" and acts as if there is a God, can false beliefs or beliefs held insincerely have beneficial effects? These possibilities needed to be sorted out. William James did just that in 1890. In a note titled "Is this a moral universe?" he wrote:

> Suppose human beings so constituted that belief in God be necessary
> to keep the moral world going, and yet that God did not exist. Could

the success of the moral world make the existence of God, in any sense, a truth? No!

There is a triple alternative:

1. It may be better for the moral world to admit the truth of atheism and then expire. This would show adhesion to truth to be the chief moral duty.

2. Or to go on believing a lie, which would make truth a subordinate moral value.

3. Or maybe the hypothesis is contradictory and not to be entertained at all.[4]

Neither James nor Frederic seriously entertained the first alternative. As we have seen, in response to Darwin, James designed his pragmatism to prevent the necessity of choosing between science and religion. The first option amounts to just the sort of choice James and Frederic were unwilling to make.

In his formal epistemology—*Pragmatism* (1907) and *The Meaning of Truth* (1909)—James embraced the third of his alternatives. He maintained that what is beneficial is true and, conversely, what is true is beneficial; what is false cannot be beneficial.[5]

Frederic deftly and subtly explores the second of James's alternatives. In *Theron Ware,* he examines the effects, beneficial and otherwise, of believing and living a lie. More carefully and accurately put, Frederic examines characters who, though they insincerely believe in God, act as if they are "true believers." None of the central religious figures in the novel—Ware, Forbes, or the Soulsbys—believe in God in the ordinary literal sense. Yet each is skilled in the *manufacture* of the beneficial effects of religion and belief in God. Notice, for example, that during the course of the novel, the less Ware believes, the more effectively he preaches. Ware, both embarrassed and proud of this, worries about being a fake; the Soulsbys and Forbes do not. They are at ease, for they see themselves as "good frauds" (Frederic 1896, 179). Let us now look at each of these characters in detail.

THE REVEREND MR. THERON WARE

Ware's religious pragmatism is progressive. It is first unconscious, then uneasy, and finally unworried. Compare the pristine Ware with the jaded Ware on the matter of preaching. The pristine Ware is a good preacher; he knows his craft.

Awaiting the assignments of new posts at the Nedahma Conference, Theron and Alice, the young couple in the front of the church, have "simple pride in the triumph of the husband's fine sermon" (6). At the old parish of Tyre, Ware had worked hard at becoming "a great pulpit orator. He set to work now, with resolute purpose, to puzzle out and master all the principles which underlie this art, and all the tricks that adorn its superstructure. He studied it, fastened his thoughts upon it, talked daily with Alice about it. . . . He practiced effects now by piecemeal, with an alert ear, and calculation in every tone" (21).

Ware is so proficient by the time he arrives at Octavius that he can squeeze a good sermon out of anything scriptural. In fact, he is confident that he can manage a good book almost as easily: "Familiarity with the process of extracting a fixed amount of spiritual and intellectual meat *from any casual* text, week after week, had given him an idea that anyone of many [book] subjects would do" (38, emphasis added).

Ware is an accomplished, persuasive preacher. He understands what has to be said and the effective ways of saying it. His skill is wholesome, for he preaches the noble art of preaching: it is for a good end *and* he also believes what he preaches. In his congregation, Ware is admired for "his innocent candor and guileless mind, for his good heart, his pious zeal, his modesty about gifts notably above the average" (17).

A little later, when there is still a happy congruence between what Ware believes and what Ware preaches, Frederic mentions preaching "tricks" (21). For a couple of Sundays, Ware had tried a cautious morning sermon and a flashier evening one. But since the same people heard both sermons, his double effort was wasted. In any case, his congregation seemed to prefer the staid morning version. Worse yet, at one of the liberal, literary evening sermons, the richest banker in Octavius appeared. Ware nimbly excised the section that might have offended this man of the world. Alas, the banker never returned; afterward, Ware felt "self-disgust [at] the eager, almost tremulous pains he himself took to please this banker. . . . He was ashamed . . . of his *trick* with the sermon" (111–12, emphasis added). This trickery is offensive to him because he compromised his message to please the man who probably most needed to hear it. Three months later, Ware's scruples have vanished.

At the September camp meeting of Octavius and Thessaly, Ware is "the veritable hero of the week" (231). He preaches an impromptu sermon that heals the division splitting the Methodists on the point of opening the gates on Sunday. His sermon is facile enough to appease both factions. His arguments are "clothed with so serene a beauty of imagery, and moved in such a lofty and rarified atmosphere of spiritual exaltation" (230), that everyone succumbs "to the influence of [his] graceful diction and delicately balanced rhetoric" (230–31). He is a spellbinder, "a mature, well-fed, and confident man" (231), a consummate performer. No qualms, no doubts, no worries. Now he dismisses his earlier scruples as "foolish trifles and childish perplexities" (232). The triumphant Ware leaves the Methodist camp meeting and while on a walk happens upon the Catholic picnic.

Ware's counterconversion is now complete.[6] He has a whole new set of attitudes about religion, preaching tricks, and what is wholesome. He is tired of his Methodist parishioners, and he finds that he prefers Father Forbes's flock, the Irish sinners: "I've had five days of the saints . . . and they've bored the head off me" (237). He is tired of his wife, too. Celia is a better match. In his walk in the woods with Celia, Ware announces his new confident mastery of himself, his work, and his parishioners: "I've learned to be a showman. I can preach now far better than I used to, and I can get through my work in half the time, and keep on the right side of my people, and get along with perfect smoothness" (251). No longer does he worry about trickery, whether for God's purposes or his own; he does not fret that he does not believe what he preaches. His only concern is success—worldly success at that. Ware *is* successful; he has become consciously, comfortably, even crassly pragmatic about religion.

FATHER VINCENT FORBES

The urbane Father Forbes is the most unabashed and sophisticated of Frederic's pragmatic clergy. Ware is in awe of Forbes's poise and command of social situations. Just when Ware is diligently expanding his preaching repertoire, he discovers that Forbes does not preach; he just talks. Forbes understands his vocation in secular terms: he has been called to perform social tasks. He explains to Ware why the church is needed: "It is needed, first and foremost, as a police force. It is needed secondly, so to speak, as a fire insurance. It provides the most even temperature and pure atmosphere for the growth of young children. It furnishes the best obtainable social machinery for marrying off one's daughters, getting to know the right people, patching up quarrels, and so on. . . . Their theology is thrown in as a sort of intellectual diversion, like the ritual of a benevolent organization" (243). Precisely. Theological discussions are, for Forbes, mental gymnastics. His usual partner in these exercises is an atheist, Dr. Ledsmar.

A contrast of Forbes with Ware is helpful. As noted above, when Ware compromised his theological principles by changing his sermon to accommodate the rich banker, his conscience bothered him. Gradually Ware's qualms disappeared. Forbes long ago progressed far beyond Ware. Forbes has none of the same compunction; he could not, given his "theology." Forbes believes in no creed; he adheres to no dogma; his allegiance is to a gospel of expediency.[7]

During Ware's first visit to the Catholic pastorate, Ledsmar and Forbes discuss theology with him. First they explain, gently, that Abraham was not a real person. Later, and not so gently, Forbes shocks Ware with his casual offhand reference to "this Christ-myth of ours" (71). Ware is stunned. How can a priest dismiss the revelation of both the Old and the New Testaments?

After Forbes leaves, Ledsmar explicates. It is not orthodoxy of belief that is the measure of a good priest: "What *is* wanted of him is that he should be the paternal, ceremonial, authoritative head and centre of his flock, adviser, monitor, overseer, elder brother, friend, patron, seigneur—whatever you like—everything except a bore" (74). Much later on, Forbes confirms Ledsmar's interpretation. Ware had assumed that the Catholic Church was rigid; Forbes explains that, on the contrary, "the Church is always compromising" (242). It must be flexible so it can fulfill its social role of being a "restful house" (243). Forbes maintains that his pragmatic view accurately reflects the official church position. The church, he contends, understands herself as a temporal institution, necessary for a stable society. Within that communal framework, Forbes and his fellow priests perform social roles: "The priesthood earn their salaries as the agents for these valuable social arrangements" (243).

This is all quite revolutionary for Ware. He had thought the church was a spiritual, religious entity concerned with dogmas, souls, and the afterlife. But according to Forbes (and Ledsmar), the church serves a secular, civic function. Therefore, dogmas are not particularly relevant; perhaps belief in God is not even required. It is success in the social scheme that counts.

The suave pragmatic priest does not shun the most radical claim of pragmatism: "The truth is always relative" (326). This is not to say that whatever one believes is true, but that different contexts and different perspectives can yield radically different versions of one and the same thing. For example, church ceremonies look one way from the pulpit and quite another from the pew. Frederic devotes a great deal of space to the duality of the pastor's versus the parishioners' viewpoints. Even more basically, Frederic shows how the clergy perform so that the congregation might respond. His depiction of the production of church ceremonies is a central element in Frederic's pragmatic analysis of religion.

Frederic stresses two facts: religious experiences are manufactured, and one does not have to be pious to produce religious experiences.[8] Frederic illustrates these facts with Forbes. (Later and more emphatically, he also demonstrates this with the Soulsbys.)

Forbes knows that he and his church manufacture a reassuring, comforting, secure, and mysterious ecclesiastical atmosphere. This is the point of the Latin, the cassock, the vestments, the chant, the candles, and the special music. Even a suspicious outsider like Ware is captivated by the power of the organ music, the emotional impact of the Latin chant, the smell of the candles and the incense, and the charm of the stained-glass windows.

Secondly, Frederic shows that Forbes's personal piety is not a factor in the religious experiences he creates. In fact, Forbes is quite worldly. His rectory is modern and well appointed. There is no apology for the wine, cigars, books, paintings, and "the mass of littered magazines, reviews, and papers at either end of the costly and elaborate writing-desk" (68). Forbes may claim that he is only a humble servant doing God's work, but he is clearly the boss. The parishioners know their place, and he knows his. Theirs is to wait, and his, when it suits him, is to "run down[stairs] and get rid of the people in the hall" (72). Forbes can be both nonbeliever and a "good" priest. Ware marvels: "Father Forbes could talk coolly about the 'Christ-myth' without even ceasing to be a priest, and apparently a very active and effective priest. Evidently there was an intellectual world, a world of culture and grace, of lofty thoughts and the inspiring communion of real knowledge, where creeds were not of importance, and where men asked one another, not 'Is your soul saved?' but 'Is your mind well furnished?' Theron had the sensation of having been invited to become a citizen of this world" (131–32). Gradually Ware understands the proper context for evaluating a "good" priest. He learns that what counts is a priest's social impact, not the correctness of his beliefs; he discovers that a priest is not devout with reference to his prayer life, but with reference to the sacred atmosphere he creates for his flock. Finally, when Ware actually experiences what Forbes meant, when Ware triumphs with his camp meeting sermons, he brags. The blasé Forbes does not boast or even mention his successes. Forbes knows that measured against the appropriate pragmatic standard, the successful performance of his several social roles, there is no doubt that he is a "good" priest.

SISTER CANDACE SOULSBY

In his exuberance, William James explained that pragmatists were interested in the "cash-value" of ideas. Frederic is scarcely less subtle, calling his debt raisers the Soulsbys.[9] Actually they do not so much buy souls as auction grace. Though both of these hucksters enliven Frederic's novel, it is Candace Soulsby who does the talking. Since it is her tutoring that leads Ware from embarrassment to boasting about the tricks of the trade, I will examine her.

The Soulsbys come to Octavius at a critical time for Ware. Forbes, Ledsmar, and Celia have dazzled him. He has glimpsed religion from the perspective of the clergy and from the perspective of the congregation. Gradually he has come to grips with the fact that the same event takes on graphically different characteristics from these two perspectives. This is unsettling for Ware, but since it is unavoidable, he learns to accept it.

The Soulsbys are quite another matter. Ware has understood religion and religious emotions to be natural; for the Soulsbys, both are artificially contrived phenomena. Their ministry is a carefully crafted, rehearsed, and orchestrated production. Beyond that, the Soulsbys are quite blunt about it. They talk of flexibility, tricks, and maneuvers. Their vocabulary is commercial; they even talk of selling religion. Sister Soulsby explains: "One place can be worked, managed, in one way, and another needs quite a different way, and both ways would be dead frosts—complete failures—in a third" (140) and "A little butter goes a long way, if it's only intelligently warmed" (141). Later she says, "Leave this whole thing to me. I'll pull it into shipshape for you" (142). Because Ware lacks "*sabe*—common sense" (142), Sister Soulsby takes charge. She suggests that he "leave the whole show absolutely to me" (143). And what a show!

From the very beginning, the mood is magical. At the second service, the love feast, Ware joins forces with the Soulsbys. For the occasion, he dusts off an old sermon from Tyre, one of style more than substance, one "planned as the framework for picturesque and emotional rhetoric rather than doctrinal edification" (150). At the third service, the evening prayer meeting, Sister Soulsby returns to center stage: "What Sister Soulsby said did not matter. The way she said it" did (153). Over half of the congregation responds. Even Alice comes forward, and after her the skeptical lawyer, Levi Gorringe.

Afterward Sister Soulsby chides Ware for his naïveté. He is disgusted with the trickery, the staging, and the machinery. She scolds him; she talks of the kitchen behind a lovely hotel dinner and the backstage of a play or theater. She is the spokesperson for Frederic's two-perspectives theme: "The performance looks one way from where the audience sits, and quite a different way when you are behind the scenes. *There* you see that the trees and houses are cloth, and the moon is tissue paper, and the flying fairy is a middle-aged woman strung up on a rope" (171).

It is not only fund-raising revivalists who understand staging. Priests, too, says Sister Soulsby, appreciate it: "They've got horse-sense, those priests. They're artists, too. They know how to allow for the machinery behind the scenes" (173). Still, Ware is bothered by the dishonesty and hypocrisy. In Sister Soulsby's response to this charge, Frederic presents his most elaborate pragmatic examination of religion.

Sister Soulsby's *apologia pro vita sua* involves an explanation of the difference between fakes and good frauds and an account of the nature of religion. Sister Soulsby begins by describing her own and Soulsby's past. They were actors, gamblers, and confidence men. Despite their show-business training and background, she explains, "We found that we had both soured on living by fakes, and that we were tired of the road, and wanted to settle down and be respectable in our old age" (177). The difference between a fake and a good fraud, she explains, is not the means, but the end. Means are neutral. A fake uses means for low purposes (like Brother Soulsby's being an advance man for a British Blondes Show), while a good fraud uses them for good purposes (like a religious revival). More importantly, there can be no doubt about the goodness of the Soulsbys' revivals, for they produce religion.

This is her second point. What she and Soulsby produce is genuine religious experience. What they elicit are not sham, surface, or counterfeit emotions; what they produce is the real thing. They and their audiences are "sincerely converted . . . genuinely convicted of sin" (178). For example, at the love feast, Alice and Levi Gorringe were converted. The Soulsbys have been, she says, converted "dozens of times—I may say every time. We couldn't do good work if we weren't" (178). Their skillful singing and preaching evoke powerful emotions. These emotions are religion, for religion is "a matter of temperament—of emotions" (178). Hence Frederic's analysis holds that the Soulsbys utilize neutral means to a good end. Further, because religious emotions—genuine religious emotions—are generated at their revivals, the Soulsbys are "good frauds" (179).

Later in the novel, the Soulsbys are described as genuine people. This remarkable expression of pragmatism occurs in a conversation between Dr. Ledsmar and Theron. Ledsmar begins by calling the Soulsbys "very interesting"; warming to the task, he observes they are "quite out of the common" and declares, "I don't know when I've seen two such really genuine people" (217).

Ware says he might agree with Ledsmar's first two descriptions. He even concedes that "there was a time, I dare say, when I should have believed in their sincerity" (217). But after he found out about their past and after he saw from the inside how they work, he could not acknowledge that they were "genuine." There is a further complication. Ware wonders if he any longer knows what is genuine and what is not. He explains that Forbes, Ledsmar, Celia, and the Soulsbys have so changed him that he has been totally transformed: "I can use no word for my new state short of illumination" (218). Unfortunately, Ware's illumination is not as complete as Ledsmar's, Forbes's, or the Soulsbys'.

Ledsmar's pragmatic point, too advanced and too subtle for Ware, is that the Soulsbys are genuine people. They are good at what they do. They are genuine ministers in the same way in which good actors and good showmen are genuine. A genuine actor is an effective actor; a genuine minister is an effective minister. One does not ask whether there is a correspondence between the actor's internal emotional and mental states and his actions. The relevant question is, do the actor's actions depict and evoke the intended emotional reactions? The very same is the proper context of a pragmatic evaluation of the clergy. In this light the Soulsbys are genuine and the religion they produce is real. As Sister Soulsby already explained to Ware, each time they stage a revival, they and their audiences are "sincerely converted . . . genuinely convicted of sin" (178). Of course they employ acting and showmanship, but since their aim is religion and since religion is emotion, the Soulsbys are genuine people. The Soulsbys are good frauds.

In *Theron Ware*, Frederic explored William James's suggestion (the second alternative above) that, for the sake of beneficial effects, one should go on believing a lie. This is what Ware, Forbes, and the Soulsbys do. None believes in God, yet all are involved in the manufacture of religious emotions.

Is religion emotion? Surely belief in God does produce, in the believer, useful effects and valuable emotions. But is belief in God equivalent to (or reducible to) these effects? Is there a God independent of the emotions of the believer?

There seem to be two distinct questions here. Does belief in God evoke valuable religious emotions? And does God exist? A pragmatic account of religion asserts that the first question is the pragmatic equivalent of the second. That is, "Does God exist?" pragmatically means "Is belief in God valuable?" The question "Is there a God?" means "Does belief in God induce beneficial emotions?" James was convinced that what has beneficial effects is true. Belief in God produces beneficial effects; therefore, it is true that God exists.

Frederic was not so satisfied with a pragmatic rendering of religious belief, and he was not as confident that utility equals truth. Why else would he have provided such strong counterexamples in the novel?

Alice's literal and ordinary belief in God—she actually believes that God exists—is clearly distinguishable from the pragmatic beliefs of Ware, Forbes, and the Soulsbys. Celia's brother Michael is a second counterinstance. He gives Ware the testimony of a dying man. Michael's warning is not a pragmatic assessment; his estimation of Ware is just the brutal truth: "You are much changed, Mr. Ware, since you came to Octavius, and it is not a change for the good" (295). And later: "Only half a year has gone by, and you have another face on you entirely. I had noticed the small changes before, one by one. I saw the great change, all of a sudden, the day of the picnic. I see it a hundred times more now, as you sit there. If it seemed to me like the face of a saint before, it is more like the face of a barkeeper now!" (297–98). Surely Frederic would not have had Alice and Michael stand in such sharp contrast unless he had reservations about reducing religion to its pragmatic utility, and, at that, the word "reservations" badly understates it. Frederic had very severe doubts—doubts so severe that both the reader and Frederic are confronted with several basic and difficult ambiguities.

Was Ware's transformation "damnation" or "illumination"?[10] It is as difficult for the reader to decide this as it was for Frederic. Is a pragmatic account of religion satisfactory? Frederic was not sure. He did not decide but instead forces the reader to face the question. Frederic's skill is apparent, for it remains unclear whether Rev. Mr. Theron Ware, Father Vincent Forbes, and Sister Candace Soulsby are "good frauds" or merely "fakes."

NOTES

This chapter is a slightly revised and expanded version of "Fakes and Good Frauds, Pragmatic Religion in *The Damnation of Theron Ware*" that appeared in *American Literary Realism* 15 (1992): 16–27.

1. Garner gives month-to-month sales figures leading up to his summary: "Overall, the book was the fifth best-selling novel of 1896. The four ahead of it were less than memorable, for the most part religious and historical fiction. It was ahead of *The Red Badge of Courage,* which was in eighth place for the year" (1985, 394).

2. For example, Carter explains that "the novel . . . maintains the general sense of pragmatic attitude and morality" (1960, xiii); Briggs comments, "Those who wish to make Frederic a spokesman for pragmatism have not dealt adequately with the

thoroughly pragmatic Dr. Ledsmar" (1969, 131); Garner labels the Soulsbys "two pragmatic confidence men turned evangelists" (1969, 33–34); Raleigh cites Sister Soulsby's
"pragmatic wisdom" (1958, 221); Luedke refers to "the social pragmatism usually attributed to Frederic" (1975–76, 85); Heddendorf notes "that pragmatism enters [the
novel] . . . for better or worse, as a potent, transformative option" (1990, 271); and
Johnson quips that Sister Soulsby is "a pragmatic troubleshooter for impoverished
churches and troubled psyches" (1962, 365).

3. Donaldson proposes as his thesis that Sister Soulsby, "the true villain of the
piece" (1974–75, 441), causes Theron's downfall. A superficial understanding of pragmatism weakens his case. Pragmatism is for Donaldson an "unholy gospel of expediency" (446), a "grubby philosophy" (451). He explains that "her pernicious gospel of
pragmatism" (452) makes Sister Soulsby a "pragmatic temptress" (449). Donaldson
speculates that many critics have "probably gone wrong . . . because of an insufficient
awareness of the novel's epistemological basis" (448). Unfortunately, Donaldson does
not fully understand pragmatic epistemology and he makes the mistake of assuming
that pragmatism is hostile to religion. As a result, Donaldson fails to appreciate the
sophistication of Frederic's pragmatic analysis of Sister Soulsby. Further, though this
is somewhat beyond his topic, he overlooks Frederic's treatment of the pragmatic
religion of Ware and Forbes.

4. Included in folder E5 of James's unpublished papers. Released with the kind
permission of Houghton Library of Harvard and Mr. Alexander James.

5. For more on James's stand on truth, utility, and belief in God, see my "William
James' Concept of Rationality and A Finite God."

6. For an excellent analysis of the theme of counterconversion, see Suderman
(1969). More recently, Bramen (1998) comments on the several stages of "Theron's
deconversion from Methodist insularity" (1998, 75, emphasis added) and calls attention to the frequency with which the word "illumination" appears in the novel.

7. Donaldson argues that after Sister Soulsby arrives in Octavius, "The rest of the
novel traces his [Ware's] downfall, as he attempts to organize his life around the *unholy*
gospel of expedience which Sister Soulsby preaches" (1974–75, 446, emphasis added).
It is, to be sure, a gospel of expedience, but it need not be an "unholy gospel." This is
exactly what Donaldson does not understand about a pragmatic account of religion.

8. See chapter 15 for Cather's exploration of precisely the same point: the rogue
priest Padre Martínez's skill at arousing religious fervor (in his congregation) is belied
by his own unbelief.

9. For interesting comments on Frederic's game with several of the characters'
names, see O'Donnell (1975) and Deratzian (1980).

10. See Garner (1985) on the two titles of Frederic's masterpiece. Incidentally,
Garner points out the Frederic mulled over a third title for his novel, *Snarl*. Bennett
devotes the fifth chapter of her full-length study of Frederic to *The Damnation of
Theron Ware,* including the ambiguity surrounding the book's ending. Earlier in her
book, Bennett remarks, "Theron aspires to be a 'good fraud'" (1997, 140).

WORKS CITED

Bennett, Bridget. 1997. *The Damnation of Harold Frederic.* Syracuse, NY: Syracuse University Press.

Bramen, Carrie Tirado. 1998. "The Americanization of Theron Ware." *Novel* 31:63–86.

Briggs, Austin, Jr. 1969. *The Novels of Harold Frederic.* Ithaca, NY: Cornell University Press.

Carter, Everett. 1960. Introduction to *The Damnation of Theron Ware*, by Harold Frederic, iii–xxiv. Cambridge, MA: Harvard University Press.

Deratzian, David L. 1980. "The Meaning and Significance of Names in *The Damnation of Theron Ware.*" *Literary Onomastic Studies* 11:51–76.

Donaldson, Scott. 1974–75. "The Seduction of Theron Ware." *Nineteenth-Century Fiction* 29:441–52.

Dooley, Patrick K. 1976. "William James' Concept of Rationality and a Finite God." In *Bicentennial Symposium of Philosophy: Collected Papers,* 356–61. New York: CUNY Press.

Frederic, Harold. 1896. *The Damnation of Theron Ware, or Illumination.* Edited by Charlyne Dodge. Lincoln: University of Nebraska Press, 1985.

Garner, Stanton. 1969. *Harold Frederic.* Minneapolis: University of Minnesota Press.

———. 1985. "History of the Text." In Frederic, *The Damnation of Theron Ware,* 353–415.

Heddendorf, David. 1990. "Pragmatists and Plots: *Pierre* and *The Damnation of Theron Ware.*" *Studies in the Novel* 22:271–81.

James, William. 1920. *The Letters of William James.* Edited by his son Henry James. Vol. 2. Boston: Atlantic Monthly Press.

———. 1897. *The Will to Believe.* Edited by Frederick H. Burkhardt, Fredson Bowers, and Ignas K. Skrupskelis. *The Works of William James.* Cambridge, MA: Harvard University Press, 1979.

Johnson, George. 1962. "Harold Frederic's Young Goodman Ware: The Ambiguities of a Realistic Romance." *Modern Fiction Studies* 8:361–74.

Luedke, Luther. 1975–76. "Harold Frederic's Satanic Soulsby: Interpretations and Sources." *Nineteenth-Century Fiction* 30:82–104.

O'Donnell, Thomas F. 1975. "Theron Ware, the Irish Picnic and *Comus.*" *American Literature* 46:528–37.

Raleigh, John. 1958. "The Damnation of Theron Ware." *American Literature* 30:210–27.

Suderman, Elmer F. 1969. "*The Damnation of Theron Ware* as Criticism of American Religious Thought." *Huntington Library Quarterly* 33:61–75.

Ziff, Larzer. 1966. *The American 1890s: Life and Times of a Lost Generation.* New York: Viking.

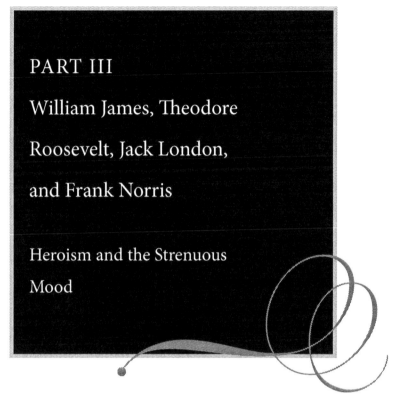

PART III

William James, Theodore Roosevelt, Jack London, and Frank Norris

Heroism and the Strenuous Mood

9

Public Policy and Philosophical Critique

The James-and-Roosevelt Dialogue on Strenuousness

> *He rather conceives of life as a duty and struggle and conquest, life which should be high and full, lived for oneself, but above all for others . . . [and he] wants man to be active and to engage in action with all his energies. It conceives of life as a struggle in which it behooves a man to win for himself a really worthy place, first of all by fitting himself (physically, morally, intellectually) to become the implement required for winning it. Therefore, life is serious, austere, and religious; all its manifestations are poised in a world sustained by moral forces and subject to spiritual responsibilities.*
> —Benito Mussolini

Commentators on classical American philosophers seem to have been unaware of, or perhaps simply reticent to acknowledge, the extent to which a shared cultural matrix drew them into conversation with the leading public figures of the day. The dialogue between Theodore Roosevelt and William James on strenuousness presents an instructive case study wherein the pronouncements of a popular and high-profile president confronted the philosophical criticism of America's most influential and respected academician.

The James-Roosevelt relationship spanned more than thirty years, beginning in 1877 when an energetic Harvard undergraduate was wont to stand up and interrupt his young, not yet well-known, comparative anatomy instructor. As reported by classmates, assistant professor of physiology William James, MD, realizing that little would be gained in a debate, responded by "settling back in his chair, in a broad grin . . . and waiting for T.R. to finish" (Perry, 1935, 313).[1] Later, upon Roosevelt's assumption of the presidency, James thought him unusually energetic, but sometimes about the wrong things.

In what follows, I will look at how these two proponents of seriousness explored whether a life of increased energy could make individual lives, and the life of the nation as a whole, worth living, and at the intriguing dialectic of theory and practice and of real-life experiences and philosophical critique that emerged in the process.

WILLIAM JAMES

Although his only advanced degree was in medicine, the closest James came to practicing medicine was teaching anatomy and physiology. After a few years he moved to Harvard's psychology department; shortly after the publication of his hugely influential *The Principles of Psychology* in 1890, he moved on to a full-time position in philosophy. James's initial interest in increased energy states prompted his physiological and psychological investigations into the phenomenon of "second wind."

James's exploration of the strenuous mood in "The Energies of Men" (1906) and its sequel, "The Powers of Men" (1907), begins with a common-sense observation that, for most of our lives, we make "use of only a small part of our possible mental and physical resources" (1982, 131). Continuing in this prosaic vein, James appeals to experience to argue that if we can raise our usual fatigue threshold, we will be able to sustain higher levels of vitality:

> The existence of reservoirs of energy that habitually are not tapped is most familiar to us in the phenomenon of "second wind." Ordinarily we stop when we meet the first effective layer, so to call it, of fatigue. We have then walked, played, or worked "enough," and desist. That amount of fatigue is an efficacious obstruction, on this side of which our usual life is cast. But if an unusual necessity forces us to press onward, a surprising thing occurs. The fatigue gets worse up to a certain critical point, when gradually or suddenly it passes away, and we are fresher than ever before. We have evidently tapped a level of new energy, masked until then by the fatigue-obstacle usually obeyed. There may be layer after layer of this experience. A third and a fourth "wind" may supervene. (132)

After examining a variety of types of physical overreaching, James turns to energy-releasing potential moral and religious ideas. Further, in "The Powers of Men" James searches for "*a methodical programme of scientific inquiry*" (1982, 150) to discover mechanisms that might foster a group "second wind": "How can men be trained up to their most useful pitch of energy? And how can nations make such training most accessible to all their sons and daughters?" (149). Notice the areas of interest to James. First, he wants to find out how to release extra levels of energy. Second, he is curious to understand how (and why) humans are persuaded to abandon routine lives of ease and comfort and to embrace risky, taxing, challenging, and even very dangerous tasks. Third, he explores how to channel increased energy states into improving the human condition. In that vein, not only was James a vocal critic of imperialism, jingoism, and other foreign policy excesses, but he sought a positive alternative as he searched for "The Moral Equivalent of War." Finally, in both a series of essays on the moral life and *The Varieties of Religious Experience,* James looked for ways to blunt the excesses of moral and religious zealots. That zealots have surplus energy is axiomatic; how that energy can be properly handled and which causes ought to be sanctioned worried James considerably. No surprise here. James took pains to weigh whether the consequences of the strenuous mood were unequivocally progressive.

Accordingly, beyond his physiological and psychological explorations, James investigated the ability of ethical ideals and religious beliefs to prompt "energy-releasing" overreaching. James's essays dealing with the impact of ethical imperatives are "The Experience of Activity," "Great Men and Their Environment," and "The Moral Philosopher and the Moral Life." His analyses of the catalytic effect of religion appeared in "A Suggestion About Mysticism" and "Conversion" and "The Value of Saintliness" in *The Varieties of Religious Experience.* The fundamental tenet of James's pragmatism is that the truth and validity of ideas rests upon their consequences; James was certain that not all forms of strenuousness were life enhancing and progressive. And it is precisely at this point in the philosopher-politician dialogue that James rises to offer criticism of Roosevelt's aggressive foreign policy with his "Address on the Philippine Question," along with several letters to the *Harvard Crimson* and the *Boston Evening Transcript.* James continues this analysis in his most widely noted and influential popular lecture, "The Moral Equivalent of War." Because this address contains James's astute assessment of the catalysts and consequences of the strenuous mood in its most romantic and dangerous form, war, it deserves a close reading.

James was the last speaker (following, among others, Booker T. Washington and Jane Addams) at a "Peace Banquet" as part of a farewell to the delegates of a Boston peace convention in 1904. His listeners were disappointed with his realism—pessimism, in the minds of many—for James told his fellow delegates, "Our permanent enemy is the noted bellicosity of human nature" (1982, 121). He argued that not only was the fighting disposition ingrained in human nature, but "the plain truth is that people *want* war. They want it anyhow; for itself; and apart from each and every possible consequence. It is the final bouquet of life's fireworks" (122). If the warring instincts could not be eradicated, the solution was to "foster rival excitements and invent new outlets for heroic energy" (123).

A half-dozen years later (1910), James returned to his proposal as he sought to flesh out "The Moral Equivalent of War." His premises are the same: humans have inherited a "pure pugnacity" (1982, 163), and though irrational and horrible, war brings with it such levels of energy, excitement, and reward that "war-taxes are the only ones men never hesitate to pay, as the budgets of all nations show" (163). James next tallies the costs and benefits, both literal and figurative, of war: First, he boldly acknowledges that war's virtues—"fidelity, cohesiveness, tenacity, heroism, conscience, education, inventiveness, economy, wealth, physical health and vigor" (167)—are genuine. Second, he concedes that war as "the supreme theater of human strenuousness" (168) is unmatched in making heroism ordinary and extra effort commonplace. Third, he foresees that a world deprived of an option of settling nations' destinies "quickly, thrillingly, and tragically by force" (168) will become a flabby, insipid, and degenerate "cattleyard of a planet" (166). James's calculating and shocking conclusion—"taking human nature as a whole, wars are its best protection against its weaker and more cowardly self, and [so, perhaps] . . . mankind cannot afford to adopt a peace-economy" (168)—appears to endorse war and align him with the militarists.

Instead, James's strategy was to force his fellow pacifists to appreciate the attractiveness of war and to own up to its benefits. He challenges them, insisting that "so long as anti-militarists propose no substitutes for the disciplinary function of war, no *moral equivalent* of war, analogous, as one might say, to the mechanical equivalent of heat" (169), they will fail. He continues, "I do not believe that peace either ought to be or will be permanent on this globe, unless the states pacifically organized preserve some of the old elements of army-discipline" (170). Though his concrete proposals for equivalents of war—enlisting young men into a peacetime militia "against *nature*" (171), drafting the "luxurious class . . . our gilded youths" (171–72) to work in coal and iron mines and on fishing fleets, and building bridges, roads, and skyscrapers—are short on details, we shall see that his language bristles with the rhetoric Theodore Roosevelt made his stock in trade: manly virtues, hardiness, valor, pride, discipline, energy, seriousness, self-forgetfulness, and excitement—"human nature at its highest dynamic" (166). Having conceded the potency and attractiveness of war, James returns to his considered opinion that the strenuous mood can more usefully respond to nonlethal and noncontagious stimuli: "The marital type of character can be bred without war. Strenuous honor and disinterestedness abound elsewhere" (172). As we now turn to Roosevelt, we will postpone, for the moment, James's contention that there are uniformly positive forms of energy and activism and that higher forms of strenuousness can, accordingly, be made attractive and efficacious.

ROOSEVELT

Although James craved the toughness, resolve, energy, and decisiveness he associated with the strenuous life, Roosevelt's activities in both the private and public spheres remain paradigms of strenuousness. Roosevelt's transformation of himself from an asthmatic and nearsighted weakling into a rugged, self-confident outdoorsman is well known. Details of Roosevelt's matter-of-fact, but nonetheless astonishing, account of his embrace of a life of hardness and action are spelled out in *Ranch Life and the Hunting Trail* (1888) and *Hunting Trips of a Ranchman* (1885).

Roosevelt's personal gains from going west were as much physical as moral, and so his initial efforts to characterize the strenuous life tended to conflate the two. "For cowboy work there is a need of special traits and special training. . . . It is no place for men who lack the ruder, coarser virtues and physical qualities" (1926, 1:279). With regard to the latter, cowboy life brings one ruddy health, vigor, and stamina: ranching "is superbly health-giving, and is full of excitement and adventure, calling for the exhibition of pluck, self-reliance, hardihood, dashing horsemanship; and of all forms of physical labor the easiest and pleasantest is to sit in the saddle" (1:340).

More carefully delineated "cowboy virtues" embody invaluable ethical traits: teamwork, helpfulness, self-reliance, candor, "consideration and politeness. . . . Meanness, cowardice, and dishonesty are not tolerated. There is a high regard for truthfulness and keeping one's word, intense contempt for

any kind of hypocrisy, and a hearty dislike for a man who shirks his work"
(1:325). All in all, these are "the stern, manly qualities that are invaluable to a
nation (1:326). Three additional points are of note. First, these indispensable
and manly "cowboy virtues" are on the wane in cultured and refined eastern
society. Second, with Turner-thesis nostalgia about the vanishing of the frontier, he remarks that "we who have felt the charm of the life . . . will not only
regret its passing for our own sakes, but must also feel real sorrow that those
who come after us are not to see, as we have seen, what is perhaps the pleasantest, healthiest, and most exciting phase of American existence" (1:292–93).
Third, beyond regret and sorrow, Roosevelt notes a troublesome irony:
"Brave, hospitable, hardy, and adventurous, [the frontiersman and cowboy]
is the grim pioneer of our race; he prepares the way for the civilization from
before whose face he must himself disappear" (1:369). Roosevelt's diagnosis
is that vigorous frontiersmen are unwittingly undermining themselves. Their
very success in taming the frontier is removing the main catalyst of the manly
virtues that are fading or absent from the civilization by ironically creating
a setting inhospitable to their very lives. And so, to the extent that manly
virtues, lately endangered, are still needed by civilization, a conscious and
concerted effort must be made to carve out arenas of hardiness and energy
and to create opportunities for risk and test.

Roosevelt's remedy was first enunciated in a speech, "The Strenuous Life,"
given before the Hamilton Club in Chicago on April 10, 1899. This speech
became the opening chapter (followed by thirty-two related essays) of a book
by the same title. Roosevelt begins by expressing his fear of the debilitating
effects of a genial life of "slothful ease" (1926, 13:319), explaining that he is
eager "to preach, not the doctrine of ignoble ease, but the doctrine of the
strenuous life, the life of toil and effort, of labor and strife; to preach that the
highest form of success which comes, not to the man who desires mere easy
peace, but to the man who does not shrink from danger, from hardship, or
from bitter toil, and who out of these wins the splendid ultimate triumph"
(13:319). Roosevelt's examination begins on the personal level, arguing that in
any life worth living and worthy of human excellence, men will not fear work
and women will not shrink from the pains of childbirth and the demands of
motherhood. However, he quickly transmutes personal virtues and traits into
matters of national character and the responsibilities of a rich and powerful
nation: "The timid man, the lazy man, the man who distrusts his county, the
over-civilized man, who has lost the great fighting, masterful virtues, the
ignorant man, and the man of dull mind, whose soul is incapable of feeling

the mighty lift that thrills 'stern men with empires in their brains'—all these, of course, shrink from seeing the nation undertake its new duties" (13:323). Specifically, building an adequate navy and maintaining a strong army were the "new duties" Roosevelt had in mind. Perhaps not surprisingly, given the time and the audience, the rest of the speech deals with isolationism, the Philippines question, and other international affairs. Nonetheless, in a speech and then later a chapter offered as a treatise on "the strenuous life," very little can be found on what is meant by such a life, why it is valuable, and how it is to be cultivated. Roosevelt's concluding paragraph returns to strenuousness in the lives of individual citizens, but it is clear that America's international posture has never been far from the center of his attention: "I preach to you, then, my countrymen, that our country calls not for the life of ease but for the life of strenuous endeavor. . . . Above all, let us shrink from no strife, moral or physical, within or without the nation, provided we are certain that the strife is justified, for it is only through strife, through hard and dangerous endeavor, that we shall ultimately win the goal of true international greatness" (13:331).

Several recurrent themes in the remaining essays of *The Strenuous Life* deserve notice. Like many others of his generation, Roosevelt worries that modern life offers limited opportunities for risk and adventure, and far too few truly stimulating situations.[2] In a moving and effective 1901 address to Vermont Civil War veterans, "Brotherhood and Heroic Virtues," Roosevelt laments, "In our modern life there are only a few occupations where risk has to be feared, and there are so many occupations where no exhausting labor has to be faced; and there are plenty of us who can be benefited by a little actual experience with the rough side of things. It was a good thing, a very good thing, to have a great mass of our people learn what it was to face death and endure toil together, and all on an exact level" (1926, 13:463). Beyond war's benefits, in this volume on strenuousness, Roosevelt recommends two Jamesian-like surrogates for combat: sports and camping. Several essays and speeches advocate a national commitment to athletics, especially team sports. Citing a need to develop moral and physical courage, Roosevelt finds sports indispensable in both areas: "Athletics are good, especially in their rougher forms, because they tend to develop such courage. They are good also because they encourage a true democratic spirit." For Roosevelt a "combination of bodily vigor and moral quality" is the invaluable byproduct of athletic prowess (13:561). Also, in a suggestion remarkably similar to James's recommendation to confront reality on its own terms in nature, Roosevelt advocates that city boys spend extended periods camping:

> The hunter and mountaineer lead healthier lives—in time of need they would make better soldiers—than the trained athlete. . . . There is no large city from which it is impossible to reach a tract of perfectly wild, wooded, or mountainous land within forty-eight hours; and any two young men who can get a month's holiday in August or September cannot use it to better advantage than by tramping on foot, pack on back, over such a tract. Let them go alone, a season or two will teach them much woodcraft, and will enormously increase their stock of health, hardihood, and self-reliance. (13:584)

Roosevelt regularly returned to the bully pulpit to encourage his fellow citizens to embrace the challenges that would make their lives real, earnest, satisfying, and successful. He delineated vices and virtues proper for both sexes as well as the gender-specific arenas. A number of addresses extol the manly virtues of work and courage in danger (read "in war") and the womanly virtues of domesticity and motherhood; the embarrassment of weak and flabby unmanly and unwomanly failures is noted too:

> When men fear work or fear righteous war, when women fear motherhood, they tremble on the brink of doom; and well it is that they should vanish from the earth, where they are fit subjects for the scorn of all men and women who are themselves strong and brave and high-minded. (13:321)

> The willfully idle man, like the willfully barren woman, has no place in a sane, healthy and vigorous community. Moreover, the gross and hideous selfishness for which each stands defeats even its own miserable aims. Exactly as infinitely the happiest woman is she who has born and brought up many healthy children, so infinitely the happiest man is he who has toiled hard and successfully in his life-work. (13:470)

Throughout these essays Roosevelt's most persistent admonition is "Act instead of criticize." The close of his 1907 address "Athletics, Scholarship and Public Service" is typical: "In short, you college men, be doers rather than critics of the deeds that others do" (15:494).

Roosevelt's sometimes unfocused and overenthusiastic proposals for manliness and his tendency to translate the strenuous life into involvement in
international conflicts had to be criticized, and his consistent undervaluing of
other opportunities for increased energy needed to be countered. Roosevelt's
construal of an attractive, valuable, and popular turn-of-the-century American ideal has serious blind spots. Of course, William James had long noticed
such weaknesses in Roosevelt's thinking. For example, on March 4, 1899,
his letter to the *Boston Evening Transcript* expressed the worry that national
leaders, Roosevelt prominent among them, failed to appreciate the Filipinos
as people, treating them instead "as if they were a painted picture, an amount
of mere matter in our way." And then, just five days after Roosevelt gave his
"The Strenuous Life" address, James's thoughtful and lengthy response was
published in the April 15, 1899, *Springfield Republican:*

> Shall Governor Roosevelt be allowed to crow all over our national
> barnyard and hear no equally shrill voice lifted in reply? . . . Although
> in middle life . . . and in a situation of responsibility concrete enough,
> he is still mentally in the *Sturm und Drang* period of early adolescence,
> treats human affairs, when he makes speeches about them, from the
> sole point of view of the organic excitement and difficulty they may
> bring, gushes over war as the ideal condition of human society, for the
> manly strenuousness which it involves, and treats peace as a condition
> of blubberlike and swollen ignobility, fit only for huckstering weaklings,
> dwelling in gray twilight and heedless of the higher life. Not a word of
> the cause,—one foe is as good as another, for aught he tells us; not a
> word of the conditions of success. . . . He swamps everything together
> in one flood of abstract bellicose emotion.

For James, the key is Roosevelt's blindness to "the higher life." That is, his
analysis overlooks how ethical insight ought to be cultivated, how moral
stamina can be increased, and how sensitivity to the moral (and extra-moral)
can be bolstered so that enlightened ethical agents will respond appropriately
in emergency situations. What Roosevelt skips over, William James stresses.
Indeed, James argues that the strenuous mood supplies the moral adrenaline

needed to measure up to all sorts of extraordinary situations, including many that have nothing to do with war: "The most characteristically and peculiarly moral judgment that a man is called upon to make are in unprecedented cases and lonely emergencies, where no popular rhetorical maxims can avail, and the hidden oracle alone can speak; and it speaks often in favor of conduct quite unusual, and suicidal as far as gaining popular approbation goes" (1981, 1265).

Several Nietzschean elements in Roosevelt's saber-rattling and subtle but unmistakable might-makes-right ethic are evident. James's insights on the power of religion and morality to release higher moral energy, and his position on the moral saint as an antidote and corrective to an amoral strongman, provide a powerful critical framework.

James argues that the moral companionship of God is *generally* the stimulus that promotes exemplary moral actions. Belief in God opens the wider perspective and "the more imperative ideals now begin to speak with an altogether new objectivity and significance, and to utter the penetrating, shattering, tragically challenging note of appeal" (1979, 160). Belief in God, James finds, unleashes energy and the courage to endure the uncomfortable path. In fact, James suggests that with no other reasons to believe in God, "Men would postulate one simply as a pretext for living hard, and getting out of the game of existence its keenest possibilities of zest" (161). However, playing the game too hard and taking too many chances can be risky, even dangerous.

Would a saint, or even a very religious person, be equipped to survive in a world fraught with risks and dangers? It depends, James responds, on what is meant by survival. Though saints may be ill equipped for basic survival, they are wonderfully suited for fit survival. However, since fit survival involves humans at our best, the religious among us have the richest, highest sort of value. In other words, sainthood as the choicest fruit of religion adapts its possessors to the ideal human society.

Ultimately, James's assessment of religion appeals to "an imaginary society in which there should be no aggressiveness, but only sympathy and fairness—any small community of true friends now realizes such a society. Abstractly considered, such a society on a large scale would be the millennium, for every good thing might be realized there with no expense of friction. To such a millennial society the saint would be entirely adapted" (1985, 298).

James continues, "Herbert Spencer tells us that the perfect man's conduct will appear perfect only when the environment is perfect: to no inferior environment is it suitably adapted" (284). Therefore a saint's prophetic and challenging behavior will not always be understood or appreciated in conventional society, though her grace and gifts will be richly celebrated in the best society. (Note that in current society, the strenuous mood is required of the saint; in the highest society, the saint, like the rest of us in ordinary life, can enjoy the genial mood.) Therefore, the value of religion and the contribution of the saint are to improve human society; "The saint may waste his tenderness and be the dupe and victim of his charitable fever, but the general function of his charity in social evolution is vital and essential . . . [so his actions] are slow leavens of a better order" (285–87). In sum, James boldly welcomes the energizing force of religion, especially the catalytic power of the saint, and he regards the strenuous mood as the chief benefit of religion. The saint, James contends, is an unqualified success once one understands that he is "magnificently adapted to the larger environments of history" (299).[3]

Another promising approach offering a corrective to Roosevelt's less-than-disciplined endorsement of activism can be found in the writings of James's colleague at Harvard, Josiah Royce. Recall the conclusion of Roosevelt's "The Strenuous Life": "Above all, let us shrink from no strife, moral or physical, within or without the nation, *provided we are certain that the strife is justified*" (1926, 13:331, emphasis added). Paramount among Royce's philosophical goals was the articulation of a structure and principles to appraise the worthiness of causes. In a dozen compactly argued volumes, Royce utilized the existence and well-being of genuine communities as the background condition for delineating the hallmarks of positive (rather than predatory) causes worthy of our loyalty. Royce argues that in a genuine community, love of another is expanded into the love of the community itself, and loyalty to a cause is transformed into loyalty to loyalty. Royce offers very concrete advice: find a cause worthy of strenuousness and devote your life to it.[4]

The twelve volumes of *The Correspondence of William James* make it very clear that James's championing of the strenuous mood was a form of will to believe in which his hopes for an active life were a fervent faith that he hoped would become father to fact. Nervous prostration and other assorted psychological and psychic ills made him crave the toughness, resolve, and decisiveness that he associated with strenuousness. The intense and high-pitched life that James examined in "The Energies of Men" and "The Powers of Men" was one he wanted for himself, but it was not the life he lived. Hardiness and high excitement were also the subjects of countless juvenile letters to his brother Henry, his parents, and his boyhood friends.

But even if, unlike Roosevelt, James was only a want-to-be man of action, he was nonetheless adept at diagnosing both strongman excesses and the sources of a failure of nerve to move beyond conventional morality to the supererogatory. Hence, Roosevelt and James (and Royce), in interesting and challenging ways, offer insights into the strenuous mood, its catalysts and consequences as well as its risks and rewards.

I began by referring to a common agenda that confronted turn-of-the-(last)-century American intellectual leaders—in this case a philosopher and a president. While I regard such a shared cultural endowment as obvious, finding smoking-gun textual confirmations is reassuring. The protagonist of Jack London's *The Sea-Wolf* is Humphrey Van Weyden, a high-society playboy rescued from a sinking ferryboat who becomes a hardened sailor on the sealing ship *Ghost*. In the final chapters London describes how Humphrey, with minimal help from his landlubber fiancée, Maude, implausibly rehabilitates the wrecked and gutted *Ghost*. When he tells her that he is certain that the foremast that he has heroically hoisted and refitted will work, she asks, "Do you know Dr. Jordan's final test of truth?" And then she eloquently pragmaticizes, "'Can we make it work? Can we trust our lives to it?' is the test" (London 1904, 755). Her source, Donald Pizer (1982) points out, was an article by David Starr Jordan, "The Stability of Truth," which appeared in *Popular Science Monthly* in March of 1897.[5] Clearly London read this monthly journal, but how about James and the other pragmatists? Without doubt.

James was a longtime reader and contributor. Three of the articles that would later became chapters of *The Principles of Psychology* were originally published in *Popular Science Monthly,* beginning in 1880. Thereafter, a half dozen of his pieces appeared—significantly, when James sought a wide audience to elucidate and publicize pragmatism, he chose this prestigious journal as a forum for "A Defense of Pragmatism" in 1907.

James died August 26, 1910. In October, when *Popular Science Monthly* reprinted "The Moral Equivalent of War," the editor explained that their gesture was "a tribute to the memory of William James" and claimed that James's "The Moral Equivalent of War" "was written at the suggestion of the editor of the *Popular Science Monthly*" (James 1910, 400). The pages following the reprinted "The Moral Equivalent of War" contained a glowing eulogy that began, "Is there left to us in this land a man so great as William James? If the list of our leaders is scanned, men eminent in philosophy, science, art or letters, in education, law, politics or business, is there a single one to be placed beside him? He excelled in so many ways, in science, in philosophy, in letters, as a teacher, as a leader in good and lost causes, before all as a man—kind and generous beyond measure, of remarkable individuality and distinction." Near the end of the eulogy, the editor notes that the term "pragmatism" "was first used by James's friend, Charles S. Peirce, in this journal" (Eulogy, 1910, 413), referring to Peirce's pair of articles "Illustrations in the Logic of Science: "The Fixation of Belief" and "How to Make Our Ideas Clear."[6] These seminal statements of pragmatism were published in *Popular Science Monthly* in 1877, only five years after the monthly was founded.

In summary, the James-Roosevelt dialogue on strenuousness illustrates how the country's most popular philosopher and its most influential politician were members of the same community of inquirers on pressing national issues. Yet anther illustration comes by way of correspondence between Josiah Royce and the just-discussed David Starr Jordan.

The two exchanged letters when Jordan tried to recruit Royce to join the initial cohort of Stanford faculty in 1891; Royce declined. Eight years later, on May 1, 1899, Royce concludes a letter to Jordan with ethical commentary on American foreign policy: "I rejoice to see what stand you take as to Philippine business, and I wish that I could see how to take part in the fight effectively myself,—the fight I mean against militarism" (1970, 389). The critiques that the Stanford president and the Harvard philosopher offered regarding the Roosevelt administration's international posture nicely underscore my contention that American intellectuals of the early twentieth century welcomed the opportunity to shape a consensus on the national agenda.

NOTES

This chapter is a slightly revised version of "Public Policy and Philosophical Critique: The William James and Theodore Roosevelt Dialogue on Strenuousness" that appeared in *Transactions of the C. S. Peirce Society* 38 (2001): 161–77.

1. For more student reminiscences of James as a teacher, see Simon (1996).

2. See, for example, the studies by Lutz (1991) and Townsend (1996) about this worry.

3. See chapters 10 and 14 for more on religion and the strenuous mood.

4. See chapter 16 for more detail on Royce's requirements for a cause worthy of one's loyalty. For James, one such cause was the Anti-Imperialist League. Interestingly James and Mark Twain were vice presidents of the Anti-Imperialist League—James from 1904 to 1910 and Twain from 1901 to 1910. For more on the efforts of James, Twain, and the League to curb Roosevelt's jingoism and America's fascination with territorial expansion, see my "Twain on War and William James on Peace: Shoring up the Platform of the Anti-Imperialistic Leauge" in *Mark Twain Studies* 2.

5. Jordan's exact words are, "The final test of scientific truth is this: Can we make it

work? Can we trust our life to it?" (1897, 646). Jordan's truth-testing maxims made a lasting impression on London. In his October 11, 1912, letter to Charles Woodruff, he writes, "After all, as Dr. Jordan put it a long time ago, that is the test of truth. Does it work? Will you trust your life to it?" (London 1988, 1091).

6. Incidentally the term "pragmatism" does not appear in either of these articles by Peirce though the maxim that later came to be called "the pragmatic maxim" did. I am indebted to one of the readers of the manuscript for bringing to my attention the error made by the editor of *Popular Science Monthly.*

WORKS CITED

Dooley, Patrick K. 2006. "Twain on War and James on Peace: Shoring up the Platform of the Anti-Imperialist League." *Mark Twain Studies* 2:54–57.

Eulogy for William James. 1910. *Popular Science Monthly* 77:413–14.

James, William. 1890. *The Principles of Psychology.* Edited by Frederick H. Burkhardt and Fredson Bowers. *The Works of William James.* Cambridge, MA: Harvard University Press, 1981.

———. Letter to the editor. 1899. *Boston Evening Transcript,* March 4. Quoted in Perry, *The Thought and Character of William James,* 311.

———. Letter to the editor. 1899. *Springfield Republican,* April 15. Quoted in Perry, *The Thought and Character of William James,* 311.

———. 1902. *The Varieties of Religious Experience.* Edited by Frederick H. Burkhardt and Fredson Bowers. *The Works of William James.* Cambridge, MA: Harvard University Press, 1985.

———. 1910. "The Moral Equivalent of War." *Popular Science Monthly* 77:400–14.

———. 1897. *The Will to Believe.* Edited by Frederick H. Burkhardt and Fredson Bowers. *The Works of William James.* Cambridge, MA: Harvard University Press, 1979.

———. 1982. *Essays in Religion and Morality.* Edited by Frederick H. Burkhardt and Fredson Bowers. *The Works of William James.* Cambridge, MA: Harvard University Press.

Jordan, David. 1897. "The Stability of Truth." *Popular Science Monthly* 50:646.

London, Jack. 1904. *The Sea-Wolf.* In *Jack London: Novel and Stories.* Edited by Donald Pizer. New York: Library of America, 1982.

———. 1988. *The Letters of Jack London.* Edited by Earle Labor, Robert C. Leitz III, Robert C. Leitz I, and Milo Shepard. 3 vols. Stanford, CA: Stanford University Press.

Lutz, Tom. 1991. *American Nervousness, 1903: An Anecdotal History.* Ithaca, NY: Cornell University Press.

Mussolini, Benito. 1933. "The Doctrine of Fascism." In *Social and Political Philosophy: Readings from Plato to Gandhi.* Edited by John Somerville and Ronald E. Santoni, 424–40. New York: Doubleday, 1963.

Perry, Ralph Barton. 1935. *The Thought and Character of William James.* Vol. 2. Boston: Little Brown.

Pizer, Donald. 1982. "Note on the Texts." In *Jack London: Novel and Stories,* 997–98.

Roosevelt, Theodore. 1926. *The Works of Theodore Roosevelt.* National Edition. Edited by Herman Hagedorn. 20 vols. New York: Charles Scribner's Sons.

Royce, Josiah. 1970. *The Letters of Josiah Royce.* Edited by John Clendenning. Chicago: University of Chicago Press.

Simon, Linda. 1996. *William James Remembered.* Lincoln: University of Nebraska Press.

Townsend, Kim. 1996. *Manhood at Harvard: William James and Others.* New York: W. W. Norton.

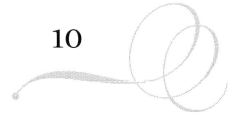

10

The Strenuous Mood

London's *The Sea-Wolf* and James on
Saints and Strongmen

> *What excites and interests the looker-on at life, what the ro-*
> *mances and the statues celebrate and grim civil monuments*
> *remind us of, is the everlasting battle of the powers of light with*
> *those of darkness; with heroism, reduced to its bare chance, yet*
> *ever and anon snatching victory from the jaws of death. What*
> *our human emotions seem to require is the sight of the struggle*
> *going on—the element of precipitousness, so to call it, of strength*
> *and strenuousness, intensity and danger.*
> *—William James*

Among the ideas most identified with William James are his characterizations of the genial and strenuous moods. Here, however, James was as much a follower as a leader, for a number of his contemporaries also explored strenuousness. For example, Stephen Crane had a lifelong preoccupation with courage and all sorts of heroism. Theodore Roosevelt's influential essay "The Strenuous Life" extolled the benefits of a "life of toil, effort, labor and strife" and its ability to transform "timid . . . lazy . . . over-civilized man" (1926, 13:319, 323). Jack London, too, especially in *The Sea-Wolf,* celebrated life in extremis.

America's most popular philosopher and her best-selling novelist were both fascinated with the strenuous life. My interest is in each one's examination of the catalytic ability of challenges, stress, emergency, and high-risk situations to elevate human conduct. I will argue that beyond merely elevating human conduct, James and London celebrated the strenuous mood's ability to cultivate truly exceptional human conduct.

Throughout his moral, philosophical, and religious thought, William James examined the modes and moods of human conduct. In particular, he sought to understand how (and why) humans could elevate their energy levels and increase their normal range of actions.

After a brief look at James's understanding of the physical and psychological mechanisms of a high-energy life, we will turn to London's dramatization of the strenuous life in *The Sea-Wolf.* The third task will be to test how James's attention to the religious and moral dimensions of a life of risk critically confronts London's sometimes runaway muscular and macho heroes.

As already examined in the previous chapter, in his exploration of the strenuous mood in "The Energies of Men" (and its sequel, "The Powers of Men"), James begins with an appeal to the startling experience of "second wind." He goes on to argue that with the proper discipline and regimen, humans ought to be able to routinely raise the pitch of their lives. In both articles James investigates how we can increase our "energy-budget" (1906, 132) so that our everyday "vital equilibrium" (1907, 149) might be at a consistently higher level. James argues that "we live subject to inhibition by degrees of fatigue which we have come only from habit to obey. Most of us may learn to push the barrier farther off, and to live in perfect comfort on much higher levels of power" (1906, 133). As we shall now see, while both James and Jack London are intrigued by strenuousness as such, James also urges a cautionary note as he wonders whether risk and stress *necessarily* produce better lives. And so while the novelist may well confine himself to describing life at a high pitch, the philosopher's responsibility extends to a critique of some of the forms of strenuousness.

The Sea-Wolf, Jack London's longest and most ambitious novel, examines the struggles of Humphrey Van Weyden, an effete, overcivilized, even sissified gentleman author rescued from a ferryboat sunk in the San Francisco Bay by "the schooner *Ghost,* bound seal-hunting to Japan" (1904, 491). Captain Wolf Larsen refuses to change his course, so Humphrey is pressed into service as a sailor. The microworld of the *Ghost,* "a new and elemental environment" (511) to which Humphrey must adapt, is a world so brutal and bestial (and bloody) that the serialization of London's novel in *Century* required significant editorial attention. Donald Pizer, editor of the Library of America volume *Jack London: Novels and Stories,* explains: "*The Sea-Wolf* underwent significant changes at the hands of the *Century* editors, who indicated profanity by dashes, cut a number of philosophical passages as well as those of explicit brutality, and made many word changes" (1982, 997).[1]

How Humphrey manages to muster the will and stamina necessary to survive his many strenuous trials London does not make very clear. Apparently London was more interested in what environmental adaptations Humphrey must make and, crucially, which character modifications he must resist. With regard to this last point, it is not clear whether Humphrey's impressive and sometimes misguided moral fiber is the result of cowardice or "a courage of cowardice" (1904, 549).

The American realists were interested in *both* muscular and moral courage, as demonstrated by Crane in *The Red Badge of Courage* and Frank Norris in *A Man's Woman*. In London's *The Sea-Wolf*, clearly Humphrey's taxing nautical ordeal gives him muscular courage; interestingly, his moral courage is a matter of sustaining a morality *imported* from civilization into "this miniature floating world" (506), "a mote, a speck" (524) that is the *Ghost*.

London treats Humphrey Van Weyden's growth into physical manhood at great length. The citified, soft author used to comfort and supported by a generous inheritance rises through the ranks as cabin boy, then cook's helper, then able-bodied sailor, and eventually mate of the *Ghost*. "Fantastic as the situation was,—a landlubber second in command,—I was, nevertheless, carrying it off well; and during that time I was proud of myself" (597). Gradually Humphrey assumes important duties, even supervising the handling of the sealskins: "It was my task to tally the pelts as they came aboard from the boats, to oversee the skinning and afterward the cleansing of the decks and bringing things shipshape again. . . . It developed what little executive ability I possessed, and I was aware of a toughening or hardening which I was undergoing and which could not be anything but wholesome for 'Sissy' Van Weyden" (603).

After Maude Brewster is rescued and comes aboard, Larsen's introduction of Humphrey stresses how far he has come: "'Not that he is much to speak of now,' Wolf Larsen went on, 'but he has improved wonderfully. You should have seen him when he came on board. A more scrawny, pitiful specimen of humanity one could hardly conceive'" (631–32). The presence of Maude leads Humphrey to take a closer look at himself: his beard, his rough clothing, the dagger at his belt, and especially his hands. The condition of his hands, frequently described, becomes a measure of his virility.[2] Early on he is bothered by the condition of his fingernails and the grime ingrained in his hands (528); later, while proud of his "splendid condition . . . my muscles are growing harder and increasing in size" (562), he is still bothered by his hands. "They have a parboiled appearance, are afflicted with hang-nails, while the nails are broken and discolored, and the edges of the quick seem to be assuming a fungoid sort of growth" (562). Still later, though happy with his physical fitness and his successes as both sailor and mate, he continues to lament the condition of his hands: "The knuckles were skinned and inflamed clear across, the fingers swollen, the nails rimmed with black" (633).

For London, Humphrey's hands symbolize his struggles. While he must adapt physically to the harsh and brutal world at sea, he is leery of regressing, sinking to the level of the other sailors, or even worse, the level of the seal hunters. Humphrey's worry about his hands signifies an important remnant of civilization he struggles to retain.

London also skillfully uses two metaphors relating to balance and legs to underscore Humphrey's problem. At his initial interview Humphrey explains what his work is. "I am a gentleman. . . . I have worked, I do work" (499). "'Who feeds you,' was his next question. 'I have an income'" (499). Larsen's retort is the first of many references to legs. "Who earned it? Eh? I thought so. Your father. You stand on dead men's legs. You've never had any of your own" (500). Eventually Humphrey earns his sea legs, observing, "I grew to love the heave and roll of the *Ghost* under my feet" (597). Even Larsen compliments him: "'Bravo!' he cried. 'You do me proud, Hump! You've found your legs with a vengeance. You're quite an individual. You were unfortunate in having your life cast in easy places, but you're developing, and I like you the better for it'" (624). Beyond physical toughening, Humphrey's getting his sea legs involves learning how to cook, to sail, and to navigate; he becomes ship medic and he earns the respect of the rest of the crew, since "unlike any one else in the ship's company, I now found myself with no quarrels on my *hands* and in the good graces of all" (579, emphasis added).

But above all, London's discussion of equilibrium and balance captures Humphrey's bend-but-don't-break behavior. Luckily he is not bothered by seasickness, and as already noted, he learns to keep his balance at sea. His moral equilibrium is another matter. Though worried that his muscular toughening will coarsen him, he retains sensitivity to the brutality on the *Ghost*. When Harrison, a young sailor sent aloft to the halyards, freezes some eighty feet above the deck, no thought is given to rescuing him. Instead, the crew gathers to witness his eventual fall. "All hands were on deck now, and all eyes were aloft, where a human life was at grapples with death" (531). The cheapness of life weighs heavily on Humphrey. "Life had always seemed a peculiarly sacred thing, but here it counted for nothing, was a cipher in the arithmetic of commerce" (531). Gradually the crew loses interest in the terrified and trembling sailor; they go to eat: "At six o'clock, when I served supper, going on deck to get some food from the galley, I saw Harrison, still in the same position. The conversation at the table was of other things. Nobody seemed interested in the wantonly imperiled life" (532–33). The Larsen-Humphrey dinner conversation provides London with the opportunity to introduce his most effective metaphor:

> "You were looking squeamish this afternoon," he began. "What was the matter?"
> . . . I answered, "It was because of the brutal treatment of that boy."
> He gave a short laugh. "Like seasickness, I suppose. Some men are subject to it, and others are not."
> "Not so," I objected.
> "Just so," he went on. "The earth is full of brutality as the sea is full of motion. And some men are made sick by the one, and some by the other. That's the only reason." (533)

The question of whether Humphrey's moral sensitivity is a matter of his natural constitution or was learned in society leads to London's account of the strenuous mood and moral courage. How well Humphrey's imported and, as Larsen correctly describes it, "conventional morality" measures up is a matter of some confusion for London. Interestingly, it is mainly nonmoral factors that conspire to keep Humphrey faithful to his moral code.

Though Humphrey worries a great deal about losing his moral integrity, his usual strategy is to stay clear of Larsen. While prudent, this strategy pragmatically amounts to hand-wringing while Larsen continues to brutalize, recklessly endanger, and even murder his crew members. But unlike Johnson and Leach, who confront Larsen and lose their lives, the extent of Humphrey's involvement amounts to ethical commentary with occasional cheerleading from the moral sidelines. When Johnson confronts Larsen, Larsen asks Humphrey, "'What do you think of him, Hump? . . .' 'I think that he is a better man than you are,' I answered, impelled, somehow, with a desire to draw upon myself a portion of the wrath I felt was about to break upon his head" (569).

Even Humphrey can only partially accept his own rationalization of his "courage of cowardice" (549):

What else was I to do? Force, nothing but force obtained on this brute-ship. Moral suasion was a thing unknown. . . .

So I thought it out at the time, feeling the need for vindication and desiring to be at peace with my conscience. But this vindication did not satisfy. Nor to this day can I permit my manhood to look back upon those events and feel entirely exonerated. (516)

Perhaps, at least early on, Humphrey is too hard on himself; his hands-off posture makes a good deal of sense. However, as his physical powers and skill as a sailor develop, he needs to rethink his moral involvement. And to some extent he does—but his second strategy is ethically unambitious. He decides to bide his time for the right moment and place to escape.

Throughout the last third of the novel, the moral issue of whether or not killing Larsen would be justifiable homicide becomes an increasingly important theme for London. London has Humphrey clearly state the ethical issue: "As for Wolf Larsen and myself, we got along fairly well; though I could not quite rid myself of the idea that right conduct, for me, lay in killing him" (617). Several grounds—self-defense, greater good, and lesser evil—would render this homicide justifiable. Additionally, London had earlier (following the long passage in which Humphrey rationalizes his "cowardly courage") articulated the extraordinary emergency conditions that placed normal moral imperatives in abeyance: "The situation [on the *Ghost*] was something that really exceeded rational formulas for conduct" (516).

Donald Pizer (1965) has persuasively argued that the protagonist in Crane's *Maggie* is condemned by her adherence to an inappropriate middle-class morality. Analogously, Humphrey is captive to an imported, conventional, civilized morality. Humphrey repeatedly ponders killing Larsen. Surely this would not be murder. When he is twice moved to act upon his moral indignation, a variety of factors thwart him. My point is that an array of nonmoral considerations—fear, weakness, luck, and twice the pleading of Maude—effectively detains Humphrey from doing what he morally ought to do.

It is important to stress that nonmoral incentives are at work here. Early on he is too weak and too unskilled to act. Later, even with sufficient weapons, know-how, and opportunity, both failure of nerve and happenstance intervene. Once, for example, Humphrey reports,

So unnerved was I by the thought of impending violence to Leach and Johnson that my reason must have left me. I know that I slipped down into the steerage in a daze, and that I was just beginning the ascent to the deck, a loaded shot-gun in my hands, when I heard the startled cry

"There's five men in that boat!"

... Then my knees gave from under me and I sank down, myself again, but overcome by shock at knowledge of what I had so nearly done. Also, I was very thankful as I put the gun away and slipped back on deck. (619)

Beyond fear and luck, Leach talks Humphrey out of his plan to kill Larsen. "I think yer square, Mr. Van Weyden. But stay where you are and keep yer mouth shut. Say nothin' but saw wood" (600). Later, even as Humphrey rescues Maude from Larsen's clutches by stabbing him on the shoulder, she stops him from finishing the job.

But Maude had seen my first blow, and she cried, "Don't! Please don't."

I dropped my arm for a moment, and a moment only. Again the knife was raised, and Wolf Larsen would have surely died had she not stepped between. Her arms were around me, her hair was brushing my face. My pulse rushed up in an unwonted manner, yet my range mounted with it. She looked me bravely in the eyes.

"For my sake," she begged. (679–80)

Curiously, one properly moral reason blocks Humphrey from a justifiable homicide—a promise. When it is obvious the days of Leach and Johnson are numbered, Larsen brokers an agreement.

"Do you believe in promises?" he asked. "Are they sacred things?"

"Of course," I answered.

"Then here's a compact," he went on, consummate actor that he was. "If I promise not to lay my hands upon Leach and Johnson, will you promise, in turn, not to attempt to kill me?" ...

"Is it a go?" he asked impatiently.

"A go," I answered. (624–25)

However, the compact has been broken in two ways: Larsen has already murdered both sailors, and promises would be nullified by the extraordinary crisis situation that has developed.

And so while *The Sea-Wolf* skillfully dramatizes Humphrey's physical empowerment, London fumbled his account of moral growth. Indeed, little if any ethical development occurs. Put another way, how Humphrey's imported morality holds sway and why it does not adapt (as did his other behavior) are left unexplained. Thus, unlike Norris's *A Man's Woman*, which perceptively examines both muscular and moral heroism, only the former is convincingly handled in *The Sea-Wolf.* Put yet a third way, James's initial accounts in "The Powers of Men" refer to "an unusual necessity [that] forces us to press onward" (1907, 132). London's *The Sea-Wolf* amply illustrates how danger and physical challenges raise energy levels and risk thresholds. James, however, goes further as he explores how morality and religion can both release and rein in strenuousness.

As a matter of fact, James's frequent meditations on how we humans can elevate our energies and improve our welfare—how strenuousness can become a near-routine part of our lives—appear in many of his essays ranging over several years. For example, in *The Varieties of Religious Experience*, he comments on the mechanisms that bring us to a new pitch of life, whereupon "with the annulling of these customary inhibitions [of lives of ease and comfort], ranges of new energy are set free, and life seems cast upon a higher plane of power" (1902, 291). Or in *The Principles of Psychology*, he searches for hypotheses and empirical evidence that will convincingly explain how "in consequence of some outer experience or some inexplicable inward charge, *we suddenly pass from the ease and careless to the sober and strenuous mood*" (1890, 1140).

A detailed examination of James's speculations will carry us too far afield. Instead, what will be helpful is a sketch of the stages and direction of James's analysis as he moves through the psychological, ethical, and religious dimensions of strenuousness. And, as we shall see, from the end point of his explorations of exceptional humans—saints—James is well equipped to offer both a critique and an antidote to the strongman, Wolf Larsen, and to the Nietzschean code of might makes right in London's *The Sea-Wolf.*[3]

James begins by arguing that while pleasure and pain are generally regarded as the springs of human actions, "important as is the influence of pleasures and pain upon our movements, they are far from being our only stimuli" (1890, 1156). Further, and analogously, though fear and danger are believed to be the usual spurs of exceptional conduct, James contends that devotion to a wide range of causes—personal, social, moral, and religious—contains sufficient impulsive force to motivate actions above and beyond the ordinary. The common denominator of these enabling beliefs is "the *urgency, namely, with which it is able to compel attention and dominate in consciousness*" (1164).

James's approach to heroism, then, goes beyond the muscular to the moral and religious. While Wolf Larsen is clearly a strongman, James celebrates the "strong-willed man" who "hears the still small voice unflinchingly, and who, when the death-bringing consideration comes, looks at its face, consents to its presence, clings to it, affirms it, and hold it fast, in spite of the host of exciting mental images which rise in revolt against it and would expel it from the mind. Sustained in this way by a resolute effort of attention, the difficult object erelong begins to call up its own congeners and associates and ends by challenging the disposition of the man's consciousness altogether. . . . This strain of the attention is the fundamental act of will" (1168). James is here appealing to his account of voluntary action: the actions for which we are morally responsible are produced by the resolute holding of a motor idea before one's consciousness and saying yes to the consequences that follow.

In addition to habit, practice, and moral training, James argues that belief in God is perhaps the surest way to embrace a heroic, strenuous life: "Our religious life lies more, our practical life lies less, than it is used to, on the perilous edge. . . . Thus not only our morality but our religion, so far as the latter is deliberate, depend on the effort which we can make. '*Will you or won't you have it so?*' is the most probing questions we are ever asked; we are asked it every hour of the day, and about the largest as well as the smallest, the most theoretical as well as the most practical things" (1181–82).

So far James's account has argued that higher ideals (both moral and religious) are as effective, perhaps more so, than the death-and-danger environment of the *Ghost* in releasing the energy that leads ordinary people to overstep ordinary boundaries. Besides motivating humans to pursue a better life, James contends that religion's most exuberant adherents, saints, offer us a vision of human society at its best, communities vibrant with a maximum of variety and a minimum of friction, "Because the best fruits of religious experience are the best things that history has to show. They have always been esteemed so; here if anywhere is the *genuinely strenuous life*" (1902, 210, emphasis added). As vanguards of a better future, religious saints extend biological survival of the fittest to "the survival of the humanly fittest" (266). For James, then, sainthood both instantiates the viability of a "genuinely" strenuous life and also provides a paradigm of undiluted altruism, a radical "helpfulness in general human affairs" (1890, 283).

In his chapters in *The Varieties of Religious Experience* on "Saintliness" and "The Value of Saintliness," James does not shrink from displaying the sometimes "distinctly pathological" (1902, 249) behaviors as well the "childish, contemptible or immoral" (264) traits and "all sorts of holy excesses, fanaticism or theopathic absorption, self-torment, prudery, scrupulosity, gullibility and morbid inability to meet the world" (294) of some saints. Ultimately, though his final pragmatic assessment of sainthood is a resoundingly positive verdict:

> Genuine saints find in the elevated excitement with which their faith endows them an authority and impressiveness which makes them irresistible in situations where men of shallower nature cannot get on at all without the use of worldly prudence. This practical proof that worldly wisdom may be safely transcended is the saint's magic gift to mankind. Not only does his vision of a better world console us for the generally prevailing prose and barrenness; but even when on the whole we have to confess him ill adapted, he makes some converts and the environment gets better for his ministry. (286–87)

Even so, how would James's "genuine" saints fare on the *Ghost*? Not well, surely, but that is not the final measure: "The saint may waste his tenderness and be dupe and victim of his charitable fever, but the general function of his charity in social evolution is vital and essential . . . [and his actions] are slow leavens of a better order" (285–87).

As noted earlier, James was every bit as intrigued as London with living at the extreme, but he was also interested in assessing the various manifestations of and the ultimate value of strenuousness. James's pragmatic evaluation of the strongman and the saint as exemplars of the strenuous life appeals to a framework that evaluates success in term of environmental adaptation. But as it turns out, James's criterion of ends and means is success in the *very long* run—"The whole feud revolves essentially upon two pivots: 'Shall the seen world or the unseen world be our chief sphere of adaptation? and must our means of adapting to this seen world be aggressiveness or non-resistance?'" (297). Humphrey adapts and survives in the "red of tooth and claw" world of the *Ghost,* and James's gentle saints would certainly perish. James, however, offers one last consideration: "The saint is therefore abstractly a higher type of man than the 'strong man,' because he is adapted to the highest society conceivable, whether that society ever be concretely possible or not. The strongman would immediately tend by presence to make that society deteriorate. It would become inferior in everything save in a certain kind of bellicose excitement, dear to men as they now are" (298).[4]

And so while Jack London routinely savored the excitement of a strenuous life, William James, due to a variety of physical, psychological, and psychic ailments, was mostly a want-to-be man of action. James, however deprived of firsthand experience he was, is still adept at diagnosing both strongman excesses and the sources of a failure of nerve to move beyond conventional morality to actions above and beyond the call of ordinary ethical duties. Hence, James and London, in interesting and challenging ways, offer refinement and insight into the strenuous mood, both its catalysts and its consequences.

NOTES

This chapter is slightly recast version of "The Strenuous Mood: William James's 'Energies in Men' and Jack London's *The Sea-Wolf*" that appeared in *American Literary Realism* 33 (2001): 152–62.

1. Also see Pizer (1982) for more on the syndicated and book versions of *The Sea-Wolf*.

2. See Campbell for an illuminating discussion of the "motif of hands" (1997, 87) in Frank Norris and Harold Frederic.

3. Although this chapter is on James and London, it is important to acknowledge London's remarkable and intense interest in Nietzsche. He told several correspondents, including Charmian Kittredge, that he had read a great deal of Nietzsche in 1904—the year *The Sea-Wolf* was published. In fact, in September 1904 he wrote his future (second) wife, "Have been getting hold of some of Neitzsche [sic]. I'll turn you loose first on his *Geneology of Morals*—and after that, something you'll like—*Thus Spake Zarathustra*" (1988, 446). In 1906 he wrote Frederic Bamford, "Personally I like Nietzsche tremendously, but I cannot go all the way with him" (584). In 1912 he told George P. Brett, "I, as you know, am in the opposite intellectual camp from that of Nietzsche. Yet no man in my own camp stirs me as does Nietzsche or as does De Casseres" (1072), and then later the same year he wrote directly to De Casseres, saying, "The bunch of manuscripts you sent me was great. . . . By 'St. Nietzsche,' they're the real stuff!" (1084). Hamilton notes that London's library contained annotated copies of five of Nietzsche's works: *The Case of Wagner, The Twilight of the Idols, Nietzsche Contra Wagner* (all 1896), *The Dawn of Day* (1903), and *A Genealogy of Morals* (1897).

While the influence of Nietzsche upon London is palpable, London's assessment that he had managed to attain a critical distance from the German philosopher is unreliable. In 1915 (eleven years after *The Sea-Wolf* appeared) in three separate letters he explicitly reports both admiration for and disagreement with Nietzsche—to H. E.

Kelsey (April 3): "Please read my *Sea-Wolf* and my *Martin Eden*—both novels being indictments of the superman philosophy of Nietzsche and of modern German ideas" (1439); to J. H. Greer (August 4): "I have been more stimulated by Nietzsche than by any other writer in the world. At the same time I have been an intellectual enemy to Nietzsche. Both *Martin Eden* and *The Sea Wolf* were indictments by me of the Nietzschean philosophy of the super-man—of course both such indictments were based on the vital lie of life" (1485); and to Mary Austin (November 5): "I have again and again written books that failed to get across. Long years ago, at the very beginning of my writing career, I attacked Nietzsche and his super-man idea. That was in *The Sea Wolf*. Lots of people read *The Sea Wolf*, no one discovered that it was an attack upon the super-man philosophy" (1513).

Accordingly then, count me among the readers of Jack London who *do not* see *The Sea-Wolf* as "an attack upon the super-man philosophy," at least a successful attack. As noted earlier, whereas London skillfully dramatizes Humphrey's muscular heroism, London fails to come to grips with a moral heroism that might have effectively checkmated superman Wolf Larsen.

4. See chapter 13 for more on James's pairing of religion and the strenuous mood.

WORKS CITED

Campbell, Donna M. 1997. "Frederic, Norris, and the Fear of Effeminacy." In *Resisting Regionalism: Gender and Naturalism in American Fiction, 1885–1915*, 75–108. Athens: Ohio University Press.

Hamilton, David Mike. 1986. *"The Tools of My Trade": The Annotated Books in Jack London's Library*. Seattle: University of Washington Press.

James, William. 1890. *The Principles of Psychology*. Edited by Frederick H. Burkhardt, Fredson Bowers, and Ignas K. Skrupskelis. *The Works of William James*. Cambridge, MA: Harvard University Press, 1981.

———. 1899. "What Makes a Life Significant." *Talks to Teachers*. Edited by Frederick H. Burkhardt, Fredson Bowers, and Ignas K. Skrupskelis. *The Works of William James*. Cambridge, MA: Harvard University Press, 1983.

———. 1902. *The Varieties of Religious Experience*. Edited by Frederick H. Burkhardt, Fredson Bowers, and Ignas K. Skrupskelis. *The Works of William James*. Cambridge, MA: Harvard University Press, 1985.

———. 1906. "The Energies of Men." In *Essays in Religion and Morality*. Edited by Frederick H. Burkhardt, Fredson Bowers, and Ignas K. Skrupskelis. *The Works of William James*. Cambridge, MA: Harvard University Press, 1982.

———. 1907. "The Powers of Men." In *Essays in Religion and Morality*. Edited by Frederick H. Burkhardt, Fredson Bowers, and Ignas K. Skrupskelis. *The Works of William James*. Cambridge, MA: Harvard University Press, 1982.

———. 1897. *The Will to Believe*. Edited by Frederick H. Burkhardt, Fredson Bowers, and Ignas K. Skrupskelis. *The Works of William James*. Cambridge, MA: Harvard University Press, 1979.

London, Jack. 1904. *The Sea-Wolf.* In *Jack London: Novels and Stories.* Edited by Donald Pizer. New York: Library of America, 1982.

———. 1988. *The Letters of Jack London.* Edited by Earle Labor, Robert C. Leitz III, Robert C. Leitz I, and Milo Shepard. 3 vols. Stanford, CA: Stanford University Press.

Pizer, Donald. 1965. "Stephen Crane's *Maggie* and American Naturalism." *Criticism* 7:168–75.

———. 1982. "A Note on the Texts." In *Jack London: Novels and Stories*, 997–98.

Roosevelt, Theodore. 1926. *The Works of Theodore Roosevelt.* National Edition. Edited by Herman Hagedorn. Vol. 13. New York: Charles Scribner's Sons.

11

London's "South of the Slot" and James's "The Divided Self"

> *"I am a hopeless materialist."*
> —*Jack London to Ralph Keeler*

When Jack London developed his materialistic philosophy, especially as he worked out, in his philosophy of psychology, positions on the nature of consciousness, the role of habit, and the relative impact of inherited and acquired traits, his mentor was William James, the popular proponent of the distinctively American philosophy of pragmatism. London's celebrated short story "South of the Slot" exhibits pervasive Jamesian influences. Though, as we shall see, there are ample links between London and James, David Starr Jordan was a significant intellectual intermediary between them.

On September 7, 1915, just fourteen months before his untimely death, Jack London wrote to John M. Wright that in his new Pantheon, he was "inscribing names such as David Starr Jordan, as Herbert Spencer, as Huxley, as Darwin" (1988, 1498). The common denominators among these thinkers are that they are materialists and evolutionists. The first thinker, David Starr Jordan, though not readily recognized today, was a well-known and influential American intellectual at the end of the twentieth century. He was a mainstay in Jack London's self-directed education. In his July 29, 1899, letter to Cloudesley Johns, London notes: "I am glad you took Jordan in the right way. He is, to a certain extent, a hero of mine. He is so clean, and broad, and wholesome" (1988, 99). Jordan (1851–1931) was a biologist educated at Cornell who became a zoology professor at Butler University and then entered Indiana University's School of Medicine. He became president of Indiana University at age thirty-four and thereafter the first president and later chancellor of Stanford University. He was a national and international leader of the Peace Society prior to World War I. Among his other notable duties, he was called as an expert witness on the theory of evolution at the 1925 Scopes trial in Tennessee.

The editors of London's letters note that London "met Jordan in 1892, when he took Jordan's university extension course at Oakland on evolution" (London 1988, 74). Jordan clearly made a lasting impression on this sixteen-year-old Bay Area student. Years later, a number of London's letters would mention hearing Jordan lecture, for instance, at the Oakland Section of the Socialist Party and at the Ruskin Club of Oakland. Moreover, there is little doubt that London paid close attention to Jordan's books and essays, especially his two-part article "The Stability of Truth," which appeared in the 1896 March and April issues of *Popular Science Monthly*. Jordan's article was a printed version of his president's address to the California Science Association meeting in Oakland in December 1895. Early on in his address, Jordan gives a textbook account of the pragmatic theories of meaning and truth—that the meaning of ideas must be stated in terms of patterns of conduct, and the truth of ideas is ultimately discovered by way of experiential (that is, scientific) procedures. He then states, "The final test of scientific truth is this: Can we make it work? Can we trust our lives to it?" (1897, 646).[1] Jordan goes on to explain that while philosophy and science have traditionally been viewed as contrary and competing approaches, on the pragmatic account they are complementary and cooperating modes of inquiry. Continuing his discussion of pragmatic philosophy in the next paragraph, Jordan notes that "Dr. William James defines metaphysics as "the persistent attempt to think clearly" (647).[2]

In his July 12, 1914, letter to Charles James, London (asked by James to comment on his own philosophical position) begins by noting that when he discusses philosophy, he never gets angry, although "it has been my inevitable experience that metaphysicians get angry with me." Perhaps, he explains, this is because while they think of themselves as "members of a school of thinking or reasoning," he strictly adheres to a "definition of metaphysics, which is the accepted definition of metaphysics in the world today" (1988, 1351)—presumably the Jamesian persistent-attempt-to-think-clearly view. Returning to London's philosophical position, in several letters he consistently reiterates his allegiance to metaphysical materialism: he is, he says, "a materialistic monist" (603); a "positive scientific thinker" (1339); "a hard, positive, scientific philosopher" (1517). More expansively he explains, "It is my conclusion that for as long as I live, I shall be heavily ballasted with this material world in which I live, and of which it seems that I am a very material part" (1445). Further, even though the last novel published during his lifetime, *The Star Rover*, celebrated spiritualism and immortality, London adamantly insists, "In *The Star Rover* I merely took the right of the fiction writer to exploit reincarnation. Again, I repeat, I do not believe in reincarnation at all. . . . Neither am I a believer in immortality. I believe that when I die I am dead, I mean I am dead for all time and forever" (1504, 1502).

London's clearest and most significant delineation of his materialist position can be found in his account of his philosophy of psychology. Especially challenging for materialists are problems concerned with the genesis of our belief in personal identity, our sense of uniqueness, and our awareness of self-consciousness and providing convincing mechanisms to explicate character formation and ethical development. On these difficult philosophical/psychological issues, note the sophistication of London's thinking in two letters, the first to Henry Mean Bland on August 23, 1906, in which he writes, "As a state of consciousness, arising out of the aggregation of matter that constitutes me, I believe in the soul. But in the immortal soul I do not believe" (1988, 60), and the second to Ralph Kaspar on June 25, 1914, in which London states: "I see the soul as nothing else than the sum of the activities of the organism plus personal habits, memories, and the experiences of the organism, plus inherited habits, memories, experiences, of the organism. *I believe that when I am dead, I am dead. I believe that with my death I am just as much obliterated as the last mosquito you or I smashed*" (1337). Let us now explore, in detail, how James's psychology provided London with a philosophical anthropology upon whose cogent theoretical scaffolding he ably constructed the intriguing plot of his popular and well-regarded "South of the Slot."

Such an influence is no surprise given James's inescapable presence in the American cultural scene at the turn of the (last) century. His hugely successful two-volume, 1,200-page *The Principles of Psychology* (1890) was in so much demand that James capitalized upon its popularity by taking scissors and paste to his full-length analysis to produce a one-volume condensation entitled *Psychology: Briefer Course* (1892). (Until the mid-1940s, James's works were the standard introductory texts in basic psychology courses. Both texts were used; the first text was referred to as "James," and the second as "Jimmie.")

In what follows I explore how a tandem reading of James's theoretical framework and London's dramatic descriptions yields a shared position on character development. It seems clear that London's view on character formation is especially influenced by the "Habit" section of *The Principles of*

Psychology, and his view of character change follows closely James's accounts of gradual and sudden personality alteration in *The Varieties of Religious Experience* (1902). In both these treatments James aims to sort out inherent versus acquired character traits—James dubs the first "brain-born" and the second "back-stairs" generated.

For James and, I will argue, for London, in the standard case of character formation, routine and habits make us what we are. The most popular and influential section of James's *The Principles of Psychology* was chapter 4: "Habit." It had first appeared in the February 1887 *Popular Science Monthly*,[3] and then for several years after the publication of *The Principles of Psychology*, the YMCA and other groups reprinted and distributed "Habit" in pamphlet form. James's fine summary of his chapter, written in his own hand in his personal copy at the head of the "Habit" chapter in the *Briefer Course*, is "Sow an action, and you reap a habit; sow a habit and you reap a character; sow a character and you reap a destiny" (Perry 1948, 196).

According to James's account, a high degree of conscious choice and explicit awareness of one's actions are indispensable for the first stages of habit formation. Gradually, however, the need for willful decisions gives way to habitual actions, so that we are soon armed with behaviors that are rote and largely unconscious:

> Habit is thus the enormous fly-wheel of society, its most precious conservative agent. It alone is what keeps us all within the bounds of ordinance, and saves the children of fortune from the envious uprisings of the poor. It alone prevents the hardest and most repulsive walks of life from being deserted by those brought up to tread therein. It keeps the fisherman and the deck-hand at sea through the winter; it holds the miner in his darkness, and nails the countryman to his log-cabin and his lonely farm through all the months of snow; it protects us from the invasion by the natives of the desert and the frozen zone. (1890, 121)

James's theory that conscious choices become habit suggests a hypothesis to be tested: Does London also hold that deliberately chosen motivation is the first step that nerves his heroes to embrace the strenuous life? Is it also the case for London that deeply ingrown habits (accompanied by a gradually diminishing conscious awareness of life choices) best explain how and why his heroes continue to endure the ongoing demands of a life lived at high energy and predictable risk? More simply put, does London endorse James's theory

of habit that holds that the gap between motivation and character formation is bridged by way of habit? In the famous "fly-wheel of society" passage
quoted above, James goes on to state that habit "dooms us all to fight out the
battle of life upon the lines of *our nurture or our early choice*" (121, emphasis
added). I think London well understood how a consciously chosen habit and
lifestyle become the "fly-wheel" of one's personality and thereby form the
basis for character formation.

In addition, London was interested in exploring character change, for
even when one's character, wrought by choices, becomes habitual, it still can
be dramatically and even diametrically changed. Such a transformation is
the core of *The Sea-Wolf*—Humphrey must adapt to the strenuous life or he
will die. Or, turning now to "South of the Slot," how does Professor Freddie
Drummond become union organizer Bill Totts? An obvious place to look for
guidance is William James's *The Varieties of Religious Experience*—especially
since London owned a copy which he annotated.[4] Granted, the Freddie-becomes-Bill transformation is not a religious conversion. Still, James's Lecture
8, "The Divided Self, and the Process of Its Unification," Lecture 9, "Conversion," and Lecture 10, "Conversion-Concluded," are helpful.

Clearly, acknowledging the nonreligious nature of the conversion in
"South of the Slot" is important in this joint reading of James and London.
The classical American pragmatists were of one voice on a seamless continuum from the secular to the sacred and from the mundane to the religious.
John Dewey, in his influential *A Common Faith,* is emphatic that the religious
dimension of human experience and culture amounts to a more-of-the-same
ontological continuity, not a discontinuous metaphysical difference in reality.
In *The Varieties of Religious Experience,* James repeatedly reminds his readers
that the psychological mechanisms he sees at work in religious experiences
explain (instead of explain away, à la Freud) the reality and value of this
dimension of human lives. Accepting the medieval Scholastic doctrine that
grace builds on nature, the fundamental premise of James's religious investigations is that the natural-supernatural border is a permeable membrane.
As he puts it, "No chasm exists between the orders of human excellence, but
. . . here as elsewhere, nature shows continuous differences" (1902, 194–5).
Note too James's remarkable contention that susceptibility to marked personality change, whether described as a character transformation or as a
religious conversion, is a stubbornly human phenomenon: "Were we writing
the story of the mind from the purely natural-history point of view, with no
religious interest whatever, we should still have to write down man's liability

to sudden and complete conversion as one of his most curious peculiarities" (188). Throughout his analysis of the divided self and conversion, James's central objective is in offering a general psychological account of personality change. All sorts of variants of "change"—"transformation," "alteration," "modification," "substitution," "transmutation," and of course, "if the change be a religious one, we call it *conversion, especially if it be by crisis or sudden*" (162)—appear in James's pages. His goal is to provide a convincing account, not linguistic rigor: "Whether such language be rigorously exact for the present is of no importance. It is exact enough, if you recognize from your own experience the facts which I seek to designate by it" (162). Equivalently, in reading "South of the Slot," can one recognize the facts that James seeks to illuminate? I submit that James's theoretical framework is a tailor-made fit with London's depiction of the Freddie-becomes-Bill conversion: "The hot place in a man's consciousness, the group of ideas to which he devotes himself, and from which he works, call it *the habitual center of his personal energy* [are supplanted by] ideas, previously peripheral in his consciousness, [that] now take a central place . . . [and] form the habitual centre of his energy" (162). For London, the possibility of such a radical transformation in a deeply divided self was prepared by his protagonist's ability to lead two lives as Freddie Drummond, University of California sociology professor, and as Bill Totts, unskilled laborer. "He made a practice of living in both worlds, and in both worlds he lived signally well" (London 1909, 817).[5]

The personalities and demeanors of Freddie Drummond and Bill Totts are as different as their names. To my ear, the former is florid and somewhat effeminate, the latter spare, even macho.[6] Freddie Drummond, personally and socially inhibited, is a fastidious Apollonian man of reason and control: "He was a very reserved man, and his natural inhibition was large in quantity and steel-like in quality. He had but few friends. He was too undemonstrative, too frigid. He had no vices, nor had anyone ever discovered any temptations. Tobacco he detested, beer he abhorred, and he was never known to drink anything stronger than an occasional light wine with dinner" (820). Bill Totts, on the contrary, is Dionysian, gregarious, passionate, "limbered up," and "graceful" (822). The narrator comments that when Freddie becomes Bill, "The very sound of his voice was changed, and the laugh was loud and hearty, while his loose speech, and occasional oath were as a matter of course on his lips. Also, Bill Totts was a trifle inclined to later hours, and at time, in saloons, to be good-naturedly bellicose with other workmen. Then, too, at Sunday picnics or when coming home from the show, either arm betrayed a practiced familiarity in stealing around girls' waists, while he displayed a wit keen and delightful in the flirtatious badinage that was expected of a good fellow in his class" (822).[7]

Naturally, Bill and Freddie are attracted to very different women. Mary Condon is vibrant and responsive, "a royal-bodied woman, graceful and sinewy as a panther, with amazing black eyes that could fill with fire or laughter-love, as the mood might dictate" (824), while Catherine Van Vorst, like Freddie, college educated and upper class, is "in appearance cold and reserved, aristocratic and wholesomely conservative. . . . Though warm in her way, [she] possessed an inhibition equal to Drummond's" (826).

Before we turn to how London and James describe the process and stages that culminate in so different and such widely divergent selves, it is worth noting that after his first foray into the underworld, the narrator remarks that Freddie is "astonished at his own fluidity" (819). James expresses no surprise on this point; indeed, he remarks how a simple change of clothes and locale can swiftly usher in another self: "The President of the United States [of course, Theodore Roosevelt] when, with paddle, gun, and fishing rod, he goes camping in the wilderness for a vacation, changes his system of ideas from top to bottom. The presidential anxieties have lapsed into the background entirely; the official habits are replaced by the habits of a son of nature, and those who knew the man only as the strenuous magistrate would not 'know him for the same person' if they saw him as the camper" (1902, 160). The temporary shift from statesman to backwoodsman is one thing; the permanent transformation from university sociologist to unskilled laborer is quite another. How are slight and superficial behavioral changes turned into stable and steadfast personality alterations? London explains that Freddie "discovered that he was a good actor and demonstrated the plasticity of his nature" (1909, 819). The London-James consonance could not be closer. In his chapter on habits, as already noted, James argues that habits make the person precisely because our bodies and nerves are plastic:

> *Plasticity*, then, in the wide sense of the word, means the possession of a structure weak enough to yield to an influence, but strong enough not to yield all at once. Each relatively stable phase of equilibrium in such a structure is marked by what we may call a new set of habits. Organic matter, especially nervous tissue, seems endowed with a very extraordinary degree of plasticity of this sort; so we may lay down without hesitation as our first proposition the following, *that the phenomena of*

habit in living beings are due to the plasticity of the organic materials of which their bodies are composed. (1890, 110)[8]

Freddie's good acting at becoming a lower-class worker, including adopting a new dress, diet, and language, actually creates for him one half of his divided self: "Down below he was 'Big' Bill Totts, who could drink and smoke, and slang and fight, and be an all-around favorite. Everybody liked Bill, and more than one working girl made love to him. At first he had been merely a good actor, but as time went on simulation became second nature. He no longer played a part, and he loved sausages, sausages and bacon, than which, in his own proper sphere, were nothing more loathsome in the way of food" (1909, 821). According to London, "As time went on, simulation became second nature" for Freddie; "from doing the thing for the need's sake, he came to doing the thing for the thing's sake" (821).

Early on, the giveaway sign that Freddie was still an apprentice and not yet a journeyman laborer was that "his hands were soft" (818). Though London does not comment that his hands have become toughened and calloused, surely they must have.[9] Physical evidence aside, London is clear that Freddie's regularly acting as Bill has made his second self a clear rival to his original persona: "So thoroughly was Bill Totts himself, so thoroughly a workman, a genuine denizen of South of the Slot, that he was as class-conscious as the average of his kind, and his hatred for a scab even exceeded that of the average loyal union man" (822). Note London's near-perfect replication of the Jamesian language of the process and result whereby role playing and acting eventually usher in genuine emotions: "From acting outraged feelings, Freddie Drummond, in the rôle of his other self, came to experience genuine outrage" (823).

James describes the condition wherein the second self becomes as fully developed as the first as a state of equilibrium, "a case of heterogeneous personality tardily and slowly finding its unity and level" (1902, 154). London tells us "it was while gathering material for 'Women and Work' that Freddie received his first warning of the danger he was in. He was too successful at living in both worlds" (1909, 823).

James's account of the death of the original self and the flourishing of the new self comes by way of a lengthy examination of the conversion crises of Tolstoy and John Bunyan. Analogously for London, the turning point for Freddie is his involvement in the laundry workers' strike with Mary Condon at his side. Thereafter Freddie senses that if he is to hold on to Freddie and not totally become Bill, he must soon "sheet-anchor himself . . . [with] closer ties and relations with his own social nook" (826), so he begins his courtship of Catherine Van Vorst. Nonetheless, again he falls victim to "the lure of the free and open, of the unhampered, irresponsible life South of the Slot" (826–27) when he risks one more sortie into the underworld. This time, however, he realizes that he so relishes his Bill Totts persona that his two identities have come into perfect balance. Accordingly, he becomes aware that "either he must become wholly Bill Totts and be married to Mary Condon, or he must remain wholly Freddie Drummond and be married to Catherine Van Vorst" (827).

Casting his lot with his first self, he makes himself stay North of the Slot, working on his manuscripts, giving lectures, and preparing for his wedding. Months later, when he returns South of the Slot, accompanying his fiancée "to see a Boy's Club, recently instituted by the settlement workers with whom she was interested" (828), he finds himself in the middle of scab drivers and policemen, funded by the Beef Trust, dispatched to break the meat strike. Freddie watches the riot that follows, but "looking out of Freddie Drummond's eyes was Bill Totts" (831). James provides a number of narratives of divided selves in the midst of their conversion crises. London's account of Freddie becoming Bill once and for all could be inserted into James's text without any editing: "Somewhere in his complicated psychology, one Bill Totts was heaving and straining in an effort to come to life. . . . And Freddie Drummond found that he had divided all the will and force of him with Bill Totts, and between them the entity that constituted the pair of them was being wrenched in twain" (831).

In a brief epilogue to his short story, London relates that in the years that followed, labor leader William Totts married Mary Condon, president of the International Glove Workers' Union No. 974. Further, we learn that Totts "called the notorious Cooks and Waiters' Strike, which, before its successful termination, brought out with it scores of other unions, among which, of the more remotely allied, were the Chicken Pickers and the Undertakers" (833). In his chapter "Conversion—Concluded," James discusses "the question of the transience or permanence of these abrupt conversions" (1902, 208)—that is, degree of backsliding. Relying on empirical studies compiled by E. D. Starbuck, James reports that "according to the statements of the subjects themselves, there had been backsliding of some sort in nearly all the cases, 93 per cent. of the women, 77 per cent. of the men. Discussing the returns more minutely, Starbuck finds that only 6 per cent. are relapses from the religious faith which the conversion confirmed, and that the backsliding complained of is in most only a fluctuation in the ardor of sentiment" (209). James expresses confidence in the reliability of Starbuck's surprisingly positive statistics. Through his own research, James finds that the steadfast triumph of the second, newer self was, almost without exception, amply reinforced by "the ecstasy of happiness produced" (206) by each conversion. London agrees. Being Bill Totts brought happiness and fulfillment whereas, even if Freddie Drummond's life had not been unhappy, it offered little more than peaceful and pleasant days.[10]

Given William James's inescapable presence on the American cultural scene and the fact that Jack London owned and annotated at least two of James's books, it is no surprise that reading, in tandem, the most popular philosopher and the most popular novelist in America at the turn of the (last) century opens up fruitful and illuminating avenues of study in both directions. But even if it seems that, with little resistance, the vector of influence flows from James to London, other parallels and prototypes at least need to be considered.

Plausible sources might include Robert Louis Stevenson, Carl Jung, and Sigmund Freud. Surprisingly, London's reading of the two psychoanalysts came late in his life (no earlier than 1912), indeed mostly in 1916, the year just before he died. While Jung's notions of a "shadow self" and the shifting boundaries between our conscious and unconscious personalities provide helpful hints about the processes involved in Freddie Drummond becoming Bill Totts, London's reading of Jung's *Psychology of the Unconscious* was more than a half-dozen years *after* he wrote "South of the Slot."[11]

In the dozens of references to Stevenson in London's letters, the topic that attracts the most attention is commentary on Stevenson's South Seas and Hawaii travel reports, in particular London's eagerness to contrast his own skill and grit as a real sailor in a small vessel with Stevenson's role as a mere passenger on a large boat.[12] London's letters contain no mention of *Dr. Jekyll and Mr. Hyde.* And so while Stevenson's 1886 novella might have inspired London, the Jekyll-Hyde personality oscillations are chemically (not behaviorally) driven; the physical changes are more drastic; and the altered persona's subsequent actions are monstrous, even fatally violent, quite unlike London's college professor's conversion into a blue-collar worker.

Supposing, then, that William James's psychology of habit formation and his treatise on sudden and gradual conversion provided the theoretical momentum for London's characterizations of remarkable character changes, where else in his works might the Jamesian influence show itself? The conversions of his animal characters Buck and White Fang recommend themselves. Whether James's account of dual selves and personality changes will illuminate the reversals/reversions that ultimately culminate in triumphal self-assertions in *Call of the Wild* and *White Fang* is surely a fruitful area for further investigation.[13]

NOTES

This chapter is a slightly modified version of "Jack London's 'South of the Slot' and William James's 'The Divided Self and the Process of Its Unification'" in *Western American Literature* 41 (2006): 346–59.

1. London was clearly impressed with Jordan's algorithms for truth testing. See note 5 in chapter 9 for more on Jordan's influence on London.

2. A definition of metaphysics by William James appears in the concluding chapter, "Epilogue: Psychology and Philosophy," of his *Psychology: Briefer Course*; his actual phrase is "Metaphysics means only an unusually obstinate attempt to think clearly and consistently" (1892, 345).

3. Actually, three of James's essays that first appeared in *Popular Science Monthly* later became chapters in *The Principles of Psychology.* Jordan's two-part article piece, "The Stability of Truth," already discussed, is only one example of *Popular Science Monthly*'s enthusiastic campaign on behalf of the then-emerging school of classical American pragmatism. I discuss James's relationship with *Popular Science Monthly* at greater length in chapter 9.

4. Hamilton reports that London owned and annotated two books by William James, *The Varieties of Religious Experience* and *The Will to Believe.* Of the former, Hamilton notes that "London marked many pages in this book" (1986, 171) and that he has one of his characters in *John Barleycorn* try to read *Varieties.* And he has another character in *Mutiny of the Elsinore* briefly glance at a few pages of *The Will to Believe.*

5. See Gair (1993) for a lengthy account of a whole range of dualities that Drummond and Totts confront.

6. Additionally, Charles Crow (personal communication) has helpfully suggested that "the name 'Freddie' is Cal Berkley slang for fraternity boy. Thus, inevitably, a youthful, neatly dressed professor named Frederic(k) would be called 'Freddie,' as was Crews in the fifties and sixties (and perhaps still), Drummond in his earlier era."

7. "South of the Slot," initially appearing as the lead article in the May 22, 1909, issue of the *Saturday Evening Post,* was augmented by three striking illustrations by W. J Aylard. On the opening page, readers are presented with images of Freddie Drummond—cool and dapper in his tuxedo and white tie, wearing dress shoes and with well-combed hair—and, across the page, of Bill Totts—agitated and robust, shod in work boots, with disheveled hair and a heavy shirt open at the chest. Not only did "South of the Slot" attract lively interest as a short story, but London and Walter Nichols over several years collaborated on a dramatized version of the story. See 883n3 in *The Letters of Jack London* for details on several drafts of their play script.

8. See my "Correct Habits and Moral Character: John Dewey and Traditional

Education" for more on plasticity and habits in the psychologies of William James and John Dewey.

9. See my "The Strenuous Mood: William James' 'Energies in Men' and Jack London's *The Sea-Wolf*" for more on London's attention to the conditions of his characters' hands.

10. Reesman makes the interesting observation that Bill Totts is actually Drummond's true self, thereby providing further illustration of "London's characteristic notion that finding one's true self promotes the cause of justice" (1999, 87).

11. See McClintock's definitive essay on the influence of Jung on the group of short stories that London wrote in 1916. Incidentally, McClintock comments that in his early use of a wandering hero undertaking a difficult journey that makes him confront danger and death, London refers to "the highest summit of life. "This Jungian phrase," McClintock notes, "as well as concept, was anticipated in London's fictions years before as a basic irony in many of his stories: the act of killing creates an ecstasy which 'marks the summit of life,' he wrote in *The Call of the Wild*" (1970, 337).

12. Hamilton notes that only three annotated books by Stevenson were in London's library: *In the South Seas* (1888), *The Schooner* Equator (1889), and *The Letters of Robert Louis Stevenson* (1911).

13. I am indebted to Sanford Marovitz, who offered these suggestions in response to the initial version of this chapter, presented at the Jack London Society Seventh Biennial Symposium, May 22, 2004, in Santa Rosa, California.

WORKS CITED

Dooley, Patrick K. 1991. "Correct Habits and Moral Character: John Dewey and Traditional Education." *Journal of Thought* 26:31–45.

———. 2001. "The Strenuous Mood: William James' 'Energies in Men' and Jack London's *The Sea-Wolf*." *American Literary Realism* 33:252–62.

Gair, Christopher. 1993. "Hegemony, Metaphor, and Structural Difference: The 'Strange Dualism' of 'South of the Slot.'" *Arizona Quarterly* 49:73–97.

Hamilton, David Mike. 1986. *"Tools of My Trade": The Annotated Books in Jack London's Library.* Seattle: University of Washington Press.

James, William. 1890. *The Principles of Psychology.* Edited by Fredson Bowers and Ignas Skrupskelis. *The Works of William James.* Cambridge, MA: Harvard University Press, 1981.

———. 1892. *Psychology: Briefer Course.* Edited by Fredson Bowers and Ignas Skrupskelis. *The Works of William James.* Cambridge, MA: Harvard University Press, 1984.

———. 1902. *The Varieties of Religious Experience.* Edited by Frederick H. Burkhardt, Fredson Bowers, and Ignas K. Skrupskelis. *The Works of William James.* Cambridge, MA: Harvard University Press, 1985.

———. 1910. "The Moral Equivalent of War." *Popular Science Monthly* 77:400–410.

Jordan, David. 1897. "The Stability of Truth." Pt. 1. *Popular Science Monthly* 50 (March): 642–54.

London, Jack. 1904. *The Sea-Wolf.* In *Jack London: Novels and Stories.* Edited by Donald Pizer. New York: Library of America, 1982.

———. 1909. "South of the Slot." In Pizer, ed., *Jack London: Novels and Stories.*

———. 1988. *The Letters of Jack London.* Edited by Earle Labor, Robert C. Leitz III, Robert C. Leitz I, and Milo Shepard. 3 vols. Stanford, CA: Stanford University Press.

McClintock, James I. 1970. "Jack London's Use of Carl Jung's *Psychology of the Unconscious.*" *American Literature* 42:336–347.

Perry, Ralph Barton. 1948. *The Thought and Character of William James: Briefer Version.* Cambridge, MA: Harvard University Press.

Reesman, Jeanne Campbell. 1999. *Jack London: A Study of the Short Fiction.* New York: Twayne.

12

Muscular and Moral Heroism in Norris's *A Man's Woman*

Is it nothing that you have given the world an example of hero-
ism? You have your code; let me have mine.
—*Frank Norris*

Frank Norris viewed novel writing as a calling. A vocation as a novelist, he argued, both engaged one in serious ethical discussion and required social involvement. His manifesto on the topic appeared in a 1902 article for the *Critic,* "The Responsibilities of the Novelist." Norris is not bashful about the importance of his craft, observing that "the novel is the great expression of modern life" (1986b, 1206).[1] The novelist, he notes, is comparable to the cathedral architects of the Middle Ages and the great painters of the Renaissance: "To-day is the day of the novel" (1207). "The People have a right to the Truth" (1210), he continues, and as the prophets of the age, novelists have a duty to proclaim it: "The Pulpit, the Press, the Novel—these indisputably are the great moulders of Public opinion and Public morals, to-day. But the Pulpit speaks but once a week; the Press is read with lightning haste and the morning news is wastepaper by noon. But the novel goes into the home to stay. It is read word for word, is talked about, discussed; its influence penetrates every chink and corner of the family" (1209–10).

Though few writers would welcome measurement against such an apologetic, Norris performs well in the arena of moral suasion. He has a good grasp of moral discourse, he states ethical quandaries clearly, and he has a gift for value-conflict dramatization. For instance, in the graphic lifeboat scene of

Vandover and the Brute, Norris effectively illustrates that an incident that most people regarded as murder was, in truth, a case of justifiable homicide.

Vandover's return trip to San Francisco aboard the *Mazatlan* turns into disaster as the ship drifts onto the reef and capsizes. After helping women and children into a lifeboat, Vandover and a few other men climb aboard. Too many, it turns out, are onboard. "The lifeboat had been built to hold thirty-five people; more than forty had crowded into it, and it needed all prudence and care to keep it afloat in the heavy seas that were running" (1986b, 101). One more passenger is desperate to climb into the boat. "A little Jew" jumps off the foundering *Mazatlan* and grabs a lifeboat oar. From the lifeboat "there was a cry, 'Draw him in!' but the engineer refused . . . 'It's too late!' . . . 'One more and we are swamped'" (102). Vandover and the others in the boat plead, "You can't let him drown." . . . "Take him in anyhow; we must risk it" (102). The engineer is clear, however, about his nautical duties and resolute about his moral responsibilities: "'Risk hell!' thundered the engineer. 'Look here, you!' he cried to Vandover and the rest. 'I'm in command here and am responsible for the lives of all of you. It's a matter of his life or ours; one life or forty. One more and we are swamped. Let go there!'" (102). Vandover and the others are soon persuaded that the engineer is correct. The frantic man goes hand-over-hand along the oar until he grabs on the gunwale of the boat. As a result "the Jew was hindering the progress of the boat and at every moment it threatened to turn broad on to the seas" (103). The man will not release his hands, so the engineer beats his hands off with a broken oar, and he drowns.

After several hours at sea in an open boat, Vandover and company are picked up by a small schooner. The next day, after a night onboard the ship, he awakes and finds it difficult to reconstruct what has happened. Slowly it comes back to him, especially "the drowning of the little Jew of the plush cap with ear-laps. He shuddered and grew sick again for a minute, telling himself that he would never forget that scene" (107).

After the rescued are transferred to a Cape Horner, Vandover eventually reaches the San Francisco docks early on a Sunday morning. He stops at one of his haunts, the Imperial, to have breakfast. Meeting the night waiter Toby, he explains his shabby appearance: "I was in a wreck down the coast" (110). Toby eagerly informs him that twenty-three had perished at sea and that "the papers have been full of it" (110). One survivor of note, he goes on, "was a little Jew named Brann, a diamond expert; he jumped overboard and——" (110). Vandover interrupts, "Don't. . . . I saw him drown—it was sickening"

(110). Norris lets the story make its own ethical point; forgoing editorial comment, he writes: "'Were *you* in that boat?' exclaimed Toby. 'Well, wait till I tell you; the authorities here are right after that first engineer with a sharp stick, and some of the passengers, too, for not taking him in. A woman in one of the other boats saw it all and gave the whole thing away. A thing like that is regular murder, you know'" (110).

No; it was justifiable homicide. Norris ignores the allegation; no rebuttal is issued, and "Vandover shut his teeth against answering" (110).[2] The scene of the lifeboat of the *Mazatlan* is truly memorable; still, it is short and Norris's ethical commentary is brief, even cryptic. However, his *A Man's Woman* contains extended and detailed ethical analysis, and in it can be found Norris's most perceptive ethical insights. Although a close reading reveals that Norris occasionally mislabels what he has carefully and vividly described, his grasp of ethical nuances and moral dilemmas is exceptional.[3] Of special note is his attention to differences between ordinary and extraordinary moral actions, his awareness of the relationship of acts of duty and those of heroism, and his treatment of conduct required by moral law as distinguished from optional and heroic supererogatory actions that are above and beyond the call of obligation.

A Man's Woman has not been highly regarded by critics. Donald Pizer calls it "tedious" and "his worst novel" (1966, 86, 109). Warren French observes that "most of the novel is devoted to . . . two of the most thoroughly obnoxious characters ever to be treated sympathetically in fiction" (1962, 132). Most commentators have had similar opinions.[4] Apparently Norris himself was unhappy with his novel, terming it "a kind of theatrical sort with a lot of niggling analysis" (1986a, 93). He was, it seems, eager to wrap it up and became careless with details at the end. For instance, although at a half-dozen points we are given detailed descriptions of the ugly face[5] of the main character, Ward Bennett, in the last chapters Norris casually adds that Bennett "tugged at his mustache" (1986b, 267)—apparently just grown—and that he had only "one good eye" (233). This is news, too.

Most readers of *A Man's Woman* place it several notches beneath Norris's best works, commonly believed to be *McTeague, The Octopus, The Pit,* and even *Vandover.*[6] While I understand this assessment, I will argue that in *A Man's Woman,* Norris's sensitivity to the ethical dimension of human experience is far more obvious than in any of his other works. For instance, at several points in the novel, the help and the harm of what Plato dubbed "the noble lie" are traced.[7] Near the end of the grim arctic section, Bennett lies to his devoted friend Richard Ferriss[8] that he still has plenty of tobacco left: "I tell you I have eight-tenths of a kilo left" (1986b, 18). This is surely a minor and understandable fib. A day or so later, Bennett presses Ferriss to find out if Lloyd Searight had ever expressed a serious interest in Bennett. Ferriss, torn between "the woman he loved . . . and his best friend," is puzzled. "Must he tell Bennett the truth?" (41). Norris's examination of the morality of lying deftly applies the act-versus-rule utilitarianism distinction worked out by John Stuart Mill. Ferriss understands that it is not lying in general but a particular lie that is the issue. "Why not tell his friend that which he wanted to hear, even if it were not the truth?" (42). Since it is inevitable that they both will be dead within twenty-four hours, no other consequences are morally considerable. "Consequences? But there were to be *no* consequences. This was the end" (42). And so Ferriss, "trying to invent the most plausible lie" (42–43), tells Bennett that Lloyd loves him and that she had pleaded with Ferriss, "You must bring him back to me. Remember, he is everything to me—everything in the world" (43).

But they do not die. Three whalers are sighted. As they prepare to be rescued, Ferriss tries to correct his well-intentioned fabrication.

> "Listen! . . . What I told you—a while ago—about Lloyd—I thought— it's all a mistake, don't you understand—"
>
> Bennett was not listening. (46)

As it turns out, serious consequences flowing from lies told by Ferriss (and later by Lloyd) complicate the lives of the main characters in the novel.

Norris's ethical sensibilities are evident in his clarity about the need to respond to ethical duty in the face of competing human sympathies.[9] When Ferriss takes ill, Bennett stays at his side. Dr. Pitts states the morality-sympathy tension facing Bennett: "Mr. Ferriss is no danger, and you will do him more harm by staying than by going" (89). Convinced that leaving his friend is morally sound, Bennett later explains to Lloyd, "I could not have left him if I was not sure that I was doing him harm by staying" (106). Sadly, this is one of the few moments of ethical lucidity for Bennett; in the central moral conflict in the novel, he is either unable to understand or unwilling to do what is morally required. Put another way, Bennett doggedly, tenaciously, even obsessively pursues what he believes he has to do, ignoring all the while what he morally ought to do. Turning now to heroism in *A Man's Woman*, Norris's examination of matters beyond ordinary moral obligation covers several types of heroism.[10]

THE MUSCULAR PSEUDO-HEROISM OF BENNETT

Celebrated in the press as "one of the world's great men" (1986b, 172), Bennett is widely known and admired for his arctic quests. Though the crew of his expedition responds to him mostly out of fear, "once more Bennett's discipline prevailed. His iron hand shut down upon his men, more than ever resistless. Obediently they turned their faces to the southward. The march was resumed" (33). Genuine admiration is a factor, too. Adler, the sailing master, is especially worshipful: "To Adler's mind it would have been a privilege and an honour to have died for Bennett. Why, he was his chief, his king, his god, his master, who could do no wrong. Bennett could have slain him where he stood and Adler would still have trusted him" (202). Even Lloyd is inspired to a life of worldly engagement by the example of Bennett, for "he had been her inspiration; he had made her want to be brave and strong and determined, and it was because of him that the greater things of the world interested her" (171). All this notwithstanding, Bennett's behavior is reducible to brute strength and reflexes. Against nature, with the ice, snow, and cold as the enemy, Bennett is well armed. But his awesome determination is simple and single minded to the point of blindness:

> He himself did the work of three. On that vast frame of bone and muscle, fatigue seemed to leave no trace. Upon that inexorable bestial determination difficulties beyond belief left no mark. Not one of the twelve men under his command fighting the stubborn ice with tooth and nail who was not galvanized with his tremendous energy. It was as though a spur was in their flanks, a lash upon their backs. Their minds, their wills, their efforts, their physical strength to the last ounce and pennyweight belonged indissolubly to him. For the time being they were his slaves, his serfs, his beasts of burden, his draught animals, no better than the dogs straining in the traces beside them. (13)

Frequently Ferriss is described as Bennett's "dearest friend." Ferriss understands Bennett; he realizes that he will use and even abuse others to further his own interests. "Bennett was not a man to ask concessions, to catch at small favors. What he wanted he took with an iron hand, without ruth and without scruple" (40–41). Powerful desires and instincts, not reason and deliberation, animate Bennett. When Bennett rescues Lloyd from her excited and panicked horse by braining the beast with his geologist's hammer, she is both awed and sickened by his actions: "But the savagery of the whole affair stuck in Lloyd's imagination. There was primitiveness, a certain hideous simplicity in the way Bennett had met the situation that filled her with wonder and with even a little terror and mistrust of him" (105).

Bennett is at home in the arctic; he is adapted, as Norris puts it, to "his own field of action" (260).[11] His temperament and skills are ideal for the eat, march, and sleep routine of his band of arctic explorers but, understandably, his behavior, intelligence, and sensibilities fail him in more sophisticated settings. Force is the only tactic he understands; he believes it appropriate for any situation. Larger than life, is he therefore a hero and his exploits heroic? Only in an extended and unimportant sense. His quest is clearly an optional action; it is not continuous with any sort of moral imperative. His motivations are not ethical—fame and a national pride bordering on jingoism are his central concerns. There is, however, an odd sense in which, given his abilities and temperament, he does have a personal, though surely not a moral, duty to challenge the arctic. As Adler, his sailing master, puts it, reaching the North Pole is "his work, that's what he's cut out for" (237). Further, again using Adler as his spokesperson, Norris explains that personal fulfillment and national pride are paramount in Bennett's resuming his "work": "The danger don't figure; what he'd have to go through with don't figure; the chances of life or death don't figure; nothing in the world don't figure. *It's his work*; God A'mighty cut him out for that, and he's got to do it" (238).

Therefore, only in the qualified sense that Bennett ought to do what he is suited for is his life as an explorer a response to any sort of "duty." However, since it is not clear that there is a general moral obligation to explore the surface of the globe, the added goal involved in going beyond exploration—to actually reach the North Pole—would be a heroic act only in a loose and colloquial sense. Thus understood, Bennett exemplifies neither morality nor heroism; Lloyd Searight, however, embodies both.

THE MORAL AND HEROIC LLOYD SEARIGHT

Norris's extended (severely overextended, in the view of many commentators) treatment of Lloyd's life carefully scrutinizes three moral matters: caring for a patient with a highly infectious disease, setting the record straight about why she left her patient, and discontinuing her lifework as she defers to her husband's career. I will argue that Lloyd has a moral obligation with regard to the first two matters; her deference to her husband is, as Norris properly puts it, "in the nature of heroic subjugation" (241). The third matter is properly and technically heroic, above and beyond the call of moral duty. It is an action extending the ordinary moral obligation involved in the vows made to one's spouse. (Note that Norris's idiosyncratic view is that while it is morally acceptable, albeit heroic, for a wife to abandon her career for her spouse's sake, it would be immoral for the husband to reciprocate. Nearly a century later, it is clear that there is no basis for this moral asymmetry. Given Victorian culture and Norris's peculiar view of the proper role of women to facilitate the development of men, his assignment of different rights and responsibilities for men and women is understandable, even if no longer persuasive.[12])

Norris at one time thought of giving *A Man's Woman* the title of *The Heroine*.[13] Not only does Lloyd become a genuine moral heroine, but she is clearheaded and astute about ethics. Though independently wealthy, she has embarked upon a career of public service. She has a hunger to do so: "Lloyd was animated by no great philanthropy, no vast love of humanity in her work; only she wanted, with all her soul she wanted, to count in the general economy of things; to choose a work and do it . . . [and] supported by her own stubborn energy and her immense wealth, she felt that she was doing. . . . No matter how lofty the thoughts, how brilliant the talk, how beautiful the literature—for her, first, last, and always, were acts . . . concrete, substantial, material acts" (57).

The other nurses are not aware of it, but she is the founder and main benefactor of the nursing agency. Still, like all the rest, she responds whenever she is "next on call" (50). Her part in the novel begins with the announcement of a possible epidemic of typhoid fever. Except for a newly graduated young English woman, none of the Searight agency nurses have any hesitation to come to the aid of any patient, whatever the illness. "Nothing could have been stronger than the *esprit de corps* of this group of young women, whose lives were devoted to an unending battle with disease" (51). Norris stresses that such a response is a matter of professional and moral duty—there is nothing of the supererogatory involved here. That is, while laypersons need not endanger themselves—indeed, doing so might be foolish and immoral at worst, and heroic at best—professionals have to step into the breach. Precisely because policemen, soldiers, firemen, doctors, and nurses are suitably equipped by training, special resources, and know-how, they incur ethical obligations beyond the scope of ordinary moral duties. Norris was obviously keenly aware of this; as a result, *A Man's Woman* is among the first and best examinations of moral and professional ethics in American literature.

Lloyd is called to attend at a "very bad case of typhoid fever in a little sub-urb of the City, called Medford. It was not her turn to go, but the physicians in charge of this case, as some time happened, had asked especially for her" (115). And so she packs her nurse's bag. Despite the fact that the case had already caused the death of one nurse and infected another, Lloyd responds without the slightest hesitancy. "Of course, I am going to take it. Did you ever hear of a nurse doing otherwise?" (115).

How dangerous is the case? Clearly it is not a certain-death situation. The first nurse (a male, by the way) was careless. Dr. Pitts observes that it "killed off my first nurse out of hand. . . . [He] took no care of himself; ate his meals in the sickroom against my wishes" (127). The second nurse, one of Lloyd's colleagues, is in serious but not critical condition. Lloyd correctly sizes up the situation, unlike her fiancé, Bennett, who is convinced that entering the sickroom is signing one's own death certificate. Bennett believes Lloyd has come to nurse "at peril of her life" (123); neither of the professionals, Dr. Pitts nor Nurse Searight, sees it that way. Evidence of the trustworthiness of the health professionals' opinion is the fact that Dr. Pitts has routinely allowed his housekeeper into the sickroom to spell him while he takes meals and rest periods.

The climactic scene in the novel is the confrontation between Bennett and Lloyd about caring for a typhoid fever victim. In more than two-dozen pages devoted to the nurse-explorer struggle, every conceivable aspect is explored: the matter of her professional ethics, the fact that her nursing skills minimize the danger, and the fact that the patient is Richard Ferriss, a close friend of both Bennett and Lloyd. On this last point Norris comments that Lloyd is not surprised to find Bennett at Dr. Pitts's home. "Bennett had, no doubt, heard of Ferriss's desperate illness. Small wonder he was excited when the life of his dearest friend was threatened" (133). But his only interest, it turns out, is to block her from tending to an infectious patient—he is not yet aware that the patient is his friend Ferriss. Bennett pleads with her, "I've come out here to ask you, to beg you, you understand, to leave this house, where you are fool-ishly risking your life" (133).

Lloyd responds that it is her obligation and that she is not risking her life: "This is my profession. . . . I am here because it is my duty to be here" (134). On and on, page after page, Lloyd tries to reason with Bennett. "Come, if we are to quarrel, let us quarrel upon reasonable grounds. It does not follow that I risk my life by staying" (137). While Bennett is too much the mental and moral midget to appreciate her arguments, I wish to note that Lloyd puts forward a clear and compelling case—Norris knew whereof he spoke when it came to moral theory.

Lloyd's case begins with her duty to practice her profession, and she continues with it by stressing that it is a matter of personal conviction and ethical right. She then moves to a consideration of her relationship with Bennett: though she loves him, she is not his subordinate; further, if he should prevent her from performing her duty, she could no longer love him or respect herself. "Admitting, for the moment, that you could induce me to shirk my duty, how should I love you for it? Ask yourself that. . . . Be the man I thought you were. You have your code, let me have mine. . . . How could you still love me if you knew I had failed in my duty?" (137–38).

She will not give up; he will not be persuaded. During a pause in their struggle, Norris interjects that though her strength was beginning to wane, "her courage was unshaken" (141). And then she accidentally divulges that the patient is Ferriss. "Do you know how sick he is? Do you understand that he is lying at the point of death at this very moment, and that the longer I stay away from him the more his life is in peril? Has he not rights as well as I; has he not a right to live? It is not only my own humiliation that is at stake, it is the life of your dearest friend, the man who stood by you, and helped you, and who suffered the same hardships and privations as yourself" (141). This information about the identity of the patient gives Lloyd a second wind. On and on the debate goes. Unfortunately, Bennett is thick and blind. Even the appeal to another sort of moral obligation, the moral duty to come to the aid of one's friend, makes no dent in Bennett's resolve: "Right or wrong, the conviction that Lloyd was terribly imperiling her life by remaining at her patient's bedside had sunk into his mind and was not be eradicated. It was a terror that had gripped him close and that could not be reasoned away. But Ferriss? What of him? Now it had brusquely transpired that his life, too, hung in the balance. How to decide?" (142).

The complexities and nuances are too much for Bennett, because for him "only two alternatives presented themselves, the death of Ferriss or the death of Lloyd. He could see no compromise, could imagine no escape. . . . His mind was made up" (143). Norris explains that the explorer's world is one of clear choices, simple options, and moral absolutes. But away from that world, Bennett can handle neither variations nor novel situations nor competing ethical imperatives: "He had lost the faculty . . . of dealing with complicated situations. . . . For him a thing was absolutely right or absolutely wrong, and between the two there was no gradation" (144).[14] At length Lloyd appeals to

Bennett on the basis of the friendship shared with Ferriss. But he is deaf to this as well as all other lines of reasoning.

One last consideration remains: their marriage plans. Though he seems to understand when she states, "Believe me, . . . you will kill my love for you if you persist" (151), he will not acknowledge the fact that if he breaks her, he will also destroy their love. Bennett's brain circuits are so overloaded that he has suffered a mental meltdown. Now with McTeague-like intelligence, "persistently, perversely, Bennett stopped his ears to every consideration, to every argument. She wished to hazard her life. That was all he understood" (151). Eventually the debate does end. When critical actions are required, Bennett acts instinctively. The housekeeper calls, "Nurse—Miss Searight . . . quick—there is something wrong" (151); he blocks the door.[15] A few minutes later, the housekeeper again calls, and again he stands in the way. The conflict finally over, Bennett takes Lloyd to the railway station and wires for another nurse to be sent from the nursing agency.

On the train back to the city, Lloyd tries to come to grips with her moral and professional duties.[16] Bennett had broken her to the point that she begins to think it was her fault. "She had failed; the mistake had been made" (154). As Lloyd misremembers it, "She had proved false to her trust at a moment of danger" (159). Turning things completely around, for a brief period, she begins to agree with Bennett that attending to an infectious patient is an heroic, not moral, act—perhaps, as Bennett claimed, tending to Ferriss was an optional instead of a required action. If that were the case, Bennett should be blamed for his callousness, for "instead of appreciating her *heroism* he had forced her to become a coward in the eyes of the world" (171, emphasis added).

Another moral concern vies for her attention. What should she tell her nursing companions? "She was returning to the house after abandoning her post. What was she to say to them, the other women of her profession?" (159). Unsure if she can even face them, she nonetheless resolves to return to the institute. She has no other choice. "Beside her nurse's bag, her satchel was the only baggage she had at that moment, and she knew there was but little money in her purse" (160). Her motivation for returning, Norris acutely notes, has little to do with ethics: "It was all the more humiliating because she knew that her impelling motive was not one of duty. There was nothing lofty in the matter—nothing self-sacrificing. She went back because she had to go back. Little material necessities, almost ludicrous in their pettiness, forced her on" (162).

As it turns out, she does not have to explain herself. Lloyd is told that a second nurse has been sent for, but that request was countermanded because

Ferriss had died. Further, they believe "that Lloyd had left the case *after,* and not before, [Ferriss's death] had occurred" (167). Lloyd lets the confusion stand. Norris comments that she has "flinched and faltered at the crucial moment" (167). Due to a failure of nerve to come clean about what happened, she has "truly been the coward" (167). Whereas she believes "in her heart of hearts she had been true to herself and to her trust" (167) in her attempt to fulfill her duty as a nurse, on the matter of truth telling she takes the path of least resistance. "This deception which had been thrust upon her at the moment of her return to the house, . . . was so easy to play" (167). But easy or not, she knows the deception is "a hideous and unspeakable hypocrisy" (167).

Norris next examines Lloyd's duty to tell the truth about the facts concerning her role, or lack of one, in Ferriss's death. For a period she is passive; she begs off telling any details. When asked how he had died, she blurts out, "It was a haemorrhage" (169). With that comment, instead of merely refraining from telling the truth, she has lied. Therein she has compromised her honor and her downward counterconversion is launched; "to her knowledge she had never deliberately lied before" (177), and she had always believed that it would be difficult for her—so difficult "that she would have bungled, hesitated, stammered" (177). Surprisingly, lying is effortless, and she manages it convincingly. With her moral gyroscope temporarily knocked off balance, she senses she is on the verge of a fundamental character change. "It argued some sudden collapse of her whole system of morals, some fundamental disarrangement of the entire machine" (177).

She resolves to halt her moral backslide and to restore her integrity: "The idea 'I ought' persisted and persisted and persisted. She could and she ought. There was no excuse for her, and no sooner had she thrust aside the shifting mass of sophistries under which she had striven to conceal them, no sooner had she let in the light, than these two conceptions of Duty and Will began suddenly to grow" (179). Also then clarity about her conduct at Medford returns to her. She had not failed in her duty, "No, she was not subdued" (180). Still, there is the matter of truth telling. She appreciates that her response to the truth-telling moral imperative will be a stern, character-defining moment. It is now up to her alone—no one else can help or hinder: "Here was the greater fight, here was the higher test. Here was the ultimate, supreme crisis of all, and here, at last, come what might, she would not, would not, would not fail" (180).

She confesses to the assembled nurses at supper, "Do you all understand—perfectly? I left my patient at the moment of crisis, and with no one with him but a servant. And he died that same afternoon" (186). But in a short time the nurses discovered the truth: Lloyd had not abandoned her patient but had been blocked from the exercise of her duty by Bennett.

Lloyd's resolve to recapture her character brings her peace of mind: "Perhaps she had at last begun to feel the good effects of the trial by fire which she had voluntarily undergone—to know a certain happiness that now there was no longer any deceit in her heart" (189). Beyond that, and more significantly, her hatred of Bennett also disappears: "In driving deceit from her it would appear that she had also driven out hatred, that the one could not stay so soon as the other had departed" (190). Her integrity restored, she is in a position to help Bennett regain physical and moral soundness.

But next Bennett is infected with the deadly typhoid. Too weak to prevent her from nursing him back to health, he is cared for by Lloyd and Dr. Pitts. After a prolonged convalescence, Bennett's strength returns, their love is rekindled, and they are married and he resolves to give up his career.

The two of them write a book describing the failed arctic expedition. Their joint authorship serves as a catharsis. "He, Bennett, too, like Lloyd, was at that time endeavoring to free himself from a false position, and through the medium of confession stand in his true colours in the eyes of his associates. Unconsciously they were both working out their salvation along the same lines" (240–41). The confessional purgation facilitates the emergence of another self for both. She fully recaptures the integrity of her former self, but his new self is a radical departure from the old, bold Bennett. "Bennett had come forth from the ordeal chastened, softened, and humbled. . . . Ambition was numb and lifeless within him" (241). To the disgust of his former sailing master, Adler, the new Bennett is fast becoming an ordinary man. Adler pleads with Lloyd to intervene: "Don't let him chuck; don't let him get soft. Make him be a Man and not a professor" (238).

Norris's view of the proper roles for men and women, especially the duties of a man's woman, now asserts itself as Lloyd is asked to respond to a novel moral imperative. She ought, Norris suggests, to heroically abandon her career so that Bennett might regain his: "Here widened the difference between the man and the woman. Lloyd's discontinuance of her lifework had been in the nature of heroic subjugation of self. Bennett's abandonment of his career was hardly better than weakness. In one it had been renunciation; in the other surrender. In the end, and after all was over, it was the woman who remained stronger" (241–42).

In the sense that she responds heroically, she is truly the stronger one. Norris is clear, too, that Bennett's "heroism" is far different from Lloyd's genuine heroism. His work needs only adrenaline and physical strength: "The battle must be fought again. That horrible, grisly Enemy far up there to the north . . . must be defied again. The monster that defended the great prize, the object of so many fruitless quests must be once more attacked" (244). But Lloyd's moral stance requires self-abnegation and selfless devotion. Her role, correctly described by Norris, is heroic: a life of "steadfast unselfishness, renunciation, patience, the *heroism greater than all others*" (244, emphasis added). [17]

So we leave them, him on a new and better ship fitted to conquer the arctic, her waving good-bye from the deck of the tugboat that escorted the expedition out of the harbor. Her, the exemplar of both moral and truly heroic behavior; him, capable of only a muscular pseudoheroism motivated by vanity, egoism, fame, and the sort of patriotism that inspired the *Apollo* mission to the moon and lead many Americans to regard Neil Armstrong as a hero. The "heroism" of the first men on the moon was of the same stripe as Bennett's. Though both accomplishments were extraordinary, neither was an action of genuinely moral heroism. Norris knew the difference, and *A Man's Woman* deserves attention for its probing examination of ordinary ethical obligations as well as its dramatic depiction of both muscular and moral exploits above and beyond the call of duty.

Notes

This chapter is a substantially revised version of "Muscular and Moral Heroism in Frank Norris's *A Man's Woman*" in *Excavatio: International Studies Related to Emile Zola and Naturalism* 8 (1996): 100–117.

1. Commenting on Norris's essay, Pizer observes, "In a larger sphere than the problem of mass culture, Norris appeals for the fully committed writer—for the writer conscious of the social involvement of art and of its function as an instrument of social control and improvement" (1964a, 83).

2. Norris's "no comment" strategy is apparently what he had in mind in his essay "The Novel with a 'Purpose,'" where he wrote, "The novel with a purpose is, one contends, a preaching novel. But it preaches by telling things and showing things" (1986b, 1197). See McElrath (1992, 68–69) for a slightly different reading on why this was not an instance of murder. When I wrote McElrath, asking him to amplify his analysis, he sent this helpful comment:

> You are the second person, now, who has written me about my interpretation of the disposition of the engineer of chapter 9. I was simply describing what seems to be implied by Toby's statement to Van in chapter 10 (page 150 in the

first edition). "Well, wait till I tell you; the authorities here are right after that first engineer with a sharp stick, and some passengers, too, for not taking him in. . . . A thing like that is regular murder, you know." I was assuming that Toby was correct: that the legal authorities would prosecute the engineer for "regular murder," a capital crime. That is, I interpret Norris as making the point that Van's society would view the situation in terms of absolute moral/legal distinctions; it would think in black-white terms the way its product, Van, typically does about good/evil, right/wrong, asexuality/sexuality, and so forth. In short, I saw this as another instance in which Norris makes it clear that Van is not unique in his non-situational way of thinking; rather, his absolutist perspective is typical of Victorian society. Norris has, after all, shown that what the engineer did to Brann was not "regular murder."

That's it, and I guess that I still agree with my 1976 perspective on the implications of the text.

3. Hoffman is one of a handful of commentators who stress the ethical explorations of the novel. Strangely, though, he refers only to the first section of the book, commenting that "*A Man's Woman* . . . is fundamentally a story of moral dilemmas and crises against the adventurous background of survival of the fittest in the Arctic" (1956, 510).

4. Wagenknecht finds it "his only really bad book" (1930, 319); Graham dismisses it as "Norris's worst novel" (1978, 5); and Cooper states it is, "of all Norris's novels, the nearest approach to a failure" (1911, 321). McElrath's is, by far, the most patient and serious examination of *A Man's Woman,* though even he concludes that the work is "Norris's least successful novel" (1992, 90).

5. Every commentator on *A Man's Woman* makes reference to the gigantic size and ugly features of Bennett. The best quips, perhaps, are by Frohock: "Ward Bennett, the explorer, is a McTeague in a Brooks Brothers suit: he even has the same jutting jaw and somewhat Neanderthal brow. . . . [He is an] educated gorilla" (1968, 34, 35).

6. In their reference guide to Norris, Crisler and McElrath comment, "Today it is virtually a universally disliked book. But it was the best-selling work of Norris's career through 1900" (1974, xi). Bixler observes, "It became popular, possibly because of the wide-spread interest in arctic exploration at the turn of the century" (1934, 114).

7. Pizer notes an earlier Norris short story, "Man Proposes," that describes a nearly identical treatment of a "harmless and benevolent lie" (1966, 102).

8. This is an odd name; many commentators routinely misspell "Ferriss" as "Ferris." Lloyd Searight is one of Norris's women with a man's name. Marchand comments, "It is a curious quirk of mind which led Norris to give masculine names to so many of his female characters. Thus beside Lloyd Searight, we have Turner Ravis (*Vandover and the Brute*), Sidney Dyke (*The Octopus*), Page Dearborn (*The Pit*), Jack Doychert ("His Single Blessedness" in *Collected Writings*), Travis Bessimer (*Blix*) and Travis Hallett ("Travis Hallett's Half-back" in *Collected Writings*). Although his own daughter was christened Jeannette, he never called her by any name but 'Billy'" (1942, 108). To which I would add, conversely, in *Vandover and the Brute* we are introduced

to Vandover's drinking buddy Dolly (Dolliver) Haight. Note Hart's comment on Norris's peculiarity with character names: "Although most of Norris' male characters [McTeague and Vandover among them] have no first names, his women always do, and the 'good' women are endowed with both first and last names" (1970, 23).

9. Philosopher Jonathan Bennett's (1994) analysis of Huck Finn is perhaps the best single piece on conflicts between sympathy and moral duty.

10. The technical philosophical term for heroic actions above and beyond the call of duty is "supererogation." See the opening sections of chapter 4 for the conditions that must be satisfied for an act to qualify as supererogatory.

11. Johnson aptly characterizes Bennett as a "virile, morally untrammeled explorer" (1962, 102).

12. Pizer (1964a, 1966) describes this masculine-feminine ethic in detail; see also Dillingham (1968) and Verma (1986). For a good examination of male-female roles during Norris's era, see Kaplan; for a contemporary critique of a woman's "duty" to defer, see Straumanis (1984).

13. A letter of Frank Norris to Grant Richards (June 13, 1899) states, "As to my arrangements for future work I would say I have just finished another novel called *The Heroine* which I presume the D and Mc. Co. will publish as a book as soon as it has been serialized somewhere" (1986, 84).

14. On this precise point, McElrath (1976) stresses Norris's deft handling of Vandover's inability to tolerate ambiguity and nuance.

15. In his comments on this scene, Dillingham notes that Bennett must have three, or four, hands: "The ensuing scene was intended to show the powerful clash of two indomitable wills, but what with Bennett's putting his hands over his ears (and on the door knob at the same time) to shut out Lloyd's pleadings and with the theatrical emphasis upon Bennett's superior will power, the whole thing is ready-made for silent-movie melodrama" (1969, 110).

16. It is clear to me that Lloyd has a strict moral duty to attend at Ferriss's bedside; Pizer is not as convinced. Pizer argues that Lloyd has misunderstood her ethical duties, since she (like Bennett) has become too single minded in her devotion to combating an enemy—in her case, disease. "Her error is to mistake strength for independence, to center herself too exclusively on her own career and her own work. Like Bennett, she has allowed strength to narrow into pride and selfishness" (1966, 106).

17. See Straumanis's interesting examination of the suspicious claim that the same act can be a duty for a woman yet an act of supererogation for a man: "If a woman believes that it is her duty to give up her work in order to stay home to care for her small child, then it seems she is obligated to do something which would be considered supererogation in her husband, were he to do the same thing" (1984, 99). She sees a parallel error in the view that it is the husband's duty to be the breadwinner.

She further argues that in much of Western culture, traditional Judeo-Christian morality posits that "women have a duty to serve, to assist and to be auxiliary to men ... [which amounts to] a requirement to supererogation" (3). Straumanis proposes this as a test for a correct and adequate theory of supererogation: "Nothing can be obligatory for women while it is supererogatory for men (and vice versa, of course)" (11).

WORKS CITED

Bennett, Jonathan. 1994. "The Conscience Huckleberry Finn." *Philosophy* 49:123–34.

Bixler, Paul H. 1934. "Frank Norris's Literary Reputation." *American Literature* 6:109–21.

Cooper, Frederic Taber. 1911. "Frank Norris." In *Some American Story Tellers,* 295–330. New York: Holt.

Cristler, Jesse, and Joseph McElrath Jr. 1974. *Frank Norris: A Reference Guide.* Boston: G. K. Hall.

Dillingham, William. 1968. "Frank Norris and the Genteel Tradition." *Tennessee Studies in Literature* 5:15–24.

———. 1969. *Frank Norris: Instinct and Art.* Lincoln: University of Nebraska Press.

French, Warren. 1962. *Frank Norris.* New York: Twayne.

Frohock, W. M. 1968. *Frank Norris.* Minneapolis: University of Minnesota Press.

Graham, Don. 1978. *The Fiction of Frank Norris: The Aesthetic Context.* Columbia: University of Missouri Press.

Hart, James D. 1970. *A Novelist in the Making.* Cambridge, MA: Harvard University Press.

Hoffman, Charles G. 1956. "Norris and the Responsibility of the Novelist." *South Atlantic Quarterly* 54:505–15.

Johnson, George W. 1962. "The Frontier Behind Frank Norris' *McTeague.*" *Huntington Library Quarterly* 26:91–104.

Kaplan, Amy. 1990. "Romancing the Empire: The Embodiment of American Masculinity in the Popular Historical Novel of the 1890s." *American Literary History* 2:659–90.

Marchand, Ernest. 1942. *Frank Norris: A Study.* Stanford, CA: Stanford University Press.

McElrath, Joseph R. Jr. 1976. "Frank Norris's *Vandover and the Brute:* Narrative Technique and Sociocritical Viewpoint." *Studies in American Fiction* 4:27–43.

———. 1992. *Frank Norris Revisited.* New York: Twayne.

Norris, Frank. 1900. *A Man's Woman.* New York: Doubleday & McClure.

———. 1986a. *Frank Norris: Collected Letters.* Edited by Jesse Cristler. San Francisco: Book Club of California.

———. 1986b. *Frank Norris: Novels and Essays.* Edited by Donald Pizer. New York: Library of America, 1986.

Pizer, Donald, ed. 1964a. *The Literary Criticism of Frank Norris.* Austin: University of Texas Press.

———. 1964b. "The Masculine-Feminine Ethic in Frank Norris' Popular Novels." *Texas Studies in Language and Literature* 6:84–91.

———. 1966. *The Novels of Frank Norris.* Bloomington: Indiana University Press.

Straumanis, Joan. 1984. "Duties to Oneself: An Ethical Bias for Self-Liberation." *Journal of Social Philosophy* 15:1–13.

Verma, S. N. 1986. *Frank Norris: A Literary Legend.* New Delhi: Vikas.

Wagenknecht, Edward. 1930. "Frank Norris in Retrospect." *Virginia Quarterly Review* 6:313–20.

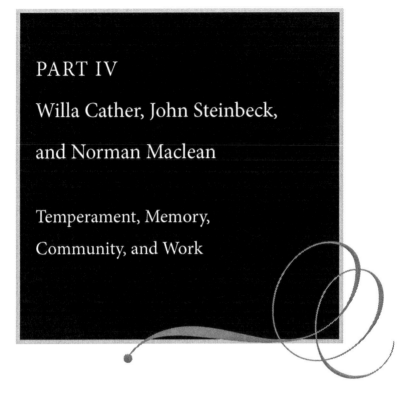

PART IV

Willa Cather, John Steinbeck,

and Norman Maclean

Temperament, Memory,

Community, and Work

13

Philosophical Pragmatism and Theological Temperament

The Religious and the Miraculous in Cather's *Death Comes for the Archbishop*

> *In a theological usage, a miracle is an extraordinary event, perceptible to the senses, produced by God in a religious context as a sign of the supernatural.*
> —New Catholic Encyclopedia

In his seminal and influential *Pragmatism* (1907), William James argues that one's philosophy is a reflection of one's temperament. Through the eyes and hearts of her two missionaries, Jean Latour and Joseph Vaillant, Willa Cather in *Death Comes for the Archbishop* (1927) explores the extent to which religion, too, is a matter of temperament.[1] Although both Cather's protagonists are from the same French province, were seminary schoolmates, took the same theological studies, and began their missionary vocations in Ohio, surely there are enough personality differences to foster divergent temperaments. Latour is a suave, refined intellectual from a scholarly, professional family; Vaillant is a direct, homely plodder, the son of a provincial baker. Cather's New Mexico missionaries are different enough to hold contrary, sometimes incompatible, notions of religion and the religious, especially miracles.

All the late nineteenth-century classical American philosophers—Charles Sanders Peirce, William James, John Dewey, Josiah Royce, George Santayana, George Herbert Mead, and Alfred North Whitehead—were interested in the place of religion in formal philosophy as well as its important cognitive and emotional role in the lives of individuals. Furthermore, the American pragmatists, notably James and Dewey, sought to capture the special qualities of religious experiences and then pragmatically appraise the impact and value of religion for life.[2] I find that Cather's wonderful historical narrative provides a rich resource for both tasks—a phenomenological description of religion and an assessment of its value for life. I here explore the positions of Latour and Vaillant on what counts as religion and the miraculous, and the extent to which edifying and sacred experiences can be rendered tangible, public, and accessible. Further, I investigate whether the reality of religion is reducible to effects in the believer. To what degree are miracles in the eye of the beholder? With regard to religion and miracles, can an objective-reality portion be separated a subjective-reaction aspect? For example, can an ordinary, commonplace event become miraculous in the discerning eye of a devout believer, or must miracles be unusual and improbable happenings that nonbelievers and believers alike find inexplicable? Latour holds the former view of "natural" miracles,[3] while Vaillant leans toward the latter, "unnatural" miracles. Cather's sympathies, it seems to me, are with the Latourian commonplace-event-made-miraculous view.

The book opens with Vicar Apostolic Latour wandering in a desert while crossing his vast diocese on horseback. He is lost. The layer after layer of blunted, pyramidal, conical red hills and round, cone-shaped junipers confuse and disorient him. Seeing a cruciform juniper tree, he dismounts and prays. Though after half an hour he arises refreshed and invigorated, he and his horse and pack mule are still without water. Some time later they stumble upon the small Mexican settlement of Agua Secreta, nourished by cool, sweet water from a hidden spring. The grandfather of the family living there, after welcoming Latour, confidently offers a miraculous religious account of how the bishop has found their village—that the Blessed Virgin brought him here. Cather, however, proposes a simpler ordinary and natural explanation: "Father Latour thought he felt a change in the body of his mare. She lifted her head for the first time in a long while, and seemed to redistribute her weight upon her legs. The pack-mule behaved in a similar matter, and both quickened their pace. Was it possible they scented water?" (1927, 23–24).

Earlier in the day, before his horse and pack mule had perked up, Latour "expected to make a dry camp in the wilderness, and to sleep under a juniper tree" (30) but instead at day's end finds himself in a featherbed, hydrated and well fed. Looking back upon the day's events, he reflects on how differently he and his vicar understand religious events: "If Father Vaillant were here, he would say, 'A miracle'; that the Holy Mother, to whom [Latour] had addressed himself before the cruciform tree, had led him hither. And it was a miracle, Father Latour knew that. But his dear Joseph must always have the miracle very direct and spectacular, not with Nature, but against it. He would almost be able to tell the colour of the mantle Our Lady wore when She took the mare by the bridle path yonder among the junipers and led her out of the pathless sand-hills, as the angel led the ass on the Flight into Egypt" (30).[4] That something can be both a natural event and a miracle requires a theology of religious discernment; philosophically, the Latourian-Cather position instantiates John Dewey's metaphysical view of the continuity of the secular and the sacred. That is, religious events are of a piece with ordinary ones; the religious aspect of an event is not a displacement or substitution of the commonplace, but an enrichment, an extension, and an unnoticed dimension of the ordinary. In the classical Scholastic terminology of St. Thomas Aquinas, the supernatural does not subvert or replace the natural but builds upon it.[5]

Judging how and in which instances the religious infuses the ordinary requires good vision or spiritual acuity, if you will. On this matter, Cather symbolically helps her reader gauge Vaillant's religious outlook. In a detailed description of him in the third chapter of the opening book, Cather points up several of his unattractive physical features, emphasizing "his eyes [which] were near-sighted, of such a pale, watery blue as to be unimpressive" (40). In "On the Lonely Road to Mora," Cather has the bishop lead his half-blind vicar: Father Latour rides first, sitting straight upon his mule, with his chin lowered just enough to keep the drive of rain out of his eyes. Father Vaillant follows, "unable to see much,—in weather like this his glasses were of no use, and he had taken them off" (68). Not only does Vaillant need glasses to see ordinary, mundane things, but he needs corrective spiritual lenses to see sacred and miraculous events. His kind of myopia demands that miracles be spectacular and highly unusual, like the availability of wintertime roses to fill Brother Juan Diego's *tilma* and the subsequent creation of a portrait of Our Lady of Guadeloupe upon it. Note that during old Padre Escolástico Herrera's account of the miraculous portrait, Cather comments that Vaillant "was deeply stirred . . . *wiping his glasses,* which were clouded by his strong feelings" (53, emphasis added). Although Latour heard Padre Herrera's account at the same time, he stoically offers a rational account of what is miraculous about the *tilma* turned holy painting. "Where there is great love there are always miracles," Latour explains. "One might say that an apparition is human vision corrected by divine love. I do not see you as you really are, Joseph, I see you through my affection for you. The Miracles of the Church seem to me to rest not so much on the faces or voices or healing power coming suddenly near to us from afar off, but upon our perceptions made finer, so that for a moment our eyes can see and our ears can hear what is there about us always" (53–54).

Somewhat ironically, Latour's rational and scientific worldview provides room for most events to become potentially miraculous. For the nearsighted, prescientific, and mystical Valliant, miracles are hardly complicated affairs— exceptional events just *are* miraculous. However, Latour holds that uncommon and even puzzling events may be merely natural. When the vicar descends a deep and steep canyon to make a sick call at the settlement of Arroyo Rondo, it looks to him as if the villagers have miraculously made water run up hill. In the second and third editions of *Death Comes for the Archbishop*, now adopted for the Willa Cather Scholarly Edition, Cather clarified her description, explaining that there was a network of box troughs so that the water "rushed into an open ditch with such tumult that it had all the *appearance* of water running up hill" (175, emphasis added). That is, Cather's later version of the text changes a Vaillantian exceptional-therefore-miraculous event into a Latourian uncommon and surprising but nevertheless natural occurrence.

Bishop Latour attempts to teach Vaillant how to discern which natural events are miraculous.[6] However, it turns out to be a complex and subtle matter to discriminate between the truly mundane and the ordinary qua miracle. There are two revealing discussions between the bishop and his vicar on this issue. The first concerns the discovery of the yellow rock formation from which the stone for the great cathedral will be quarried. Latour initially views this event as no more than happenstance: "The Bishop sat down on a boulder, still looking up at the cliff. 'It is the stone I have always wanted, and I found it quite by chance. I was coming back from Isleta. I had been to see Padre Jesus when he was dying. I had never come by this trail, but when I reached Santo Domingo I found the road so washed by a heavy rain that I turned back and decided to try this way home. I rode up here from the west in late afternoon; this hill confronted me as it confronts us now, and I knew instantly that it was my Cathedral" (252–53). Vaillant, however, sees the sacred in Latour's journey: "Oh, such things are never accidents, Jean" (253). Latour does not disagree, accepting Vaillant's religious interpretation in this case, but when their conversation turns to building the cathedral, Vaillant "wiped he glasses" (253). One wonders why Cather had Vaillant do this—he seems to have seen the nature of the discovery more clearly than Latour.

After Latour has recalled Vaillant back to Santa Fe from his parish in Tucson, a letter requesting a priest for the mining area of Colorado arrives from the bishop of Leavenworth. Vaillant sees his recall and reassignment as a miracle. "I often think, Jean, how you were an unconscious agent in the hands of Providence when you recalled me from Tucson. I seem to be doing the most important work of my life there, and you recalled me for no reason at all, apparently. You did not know why, and I did not know why. . . . When the call came, I was here to answer it—by a miracle, indeed" (264). In this instance, Latour refuses Vaillant's interpretation, suggesting to his vicar that he has overread the evidence. Though Vaillant does not know the reason, Latour does. Privy to his own motivations that have desacralized his summons of Vaillant and thereby reduced it to a mundane, human event, he explains: "Miracles are all very well, Joseph, but I see none here. I sent for you because I felt the need of your companionship. I used my authority as a Bishop to gratify my personal wish. That was selfish, if you will, but surely natural enough. We are countrymen, and are bound by early memories. And that two friends, having come together, should part and go their separate ways—that is natural, too. No, I don't think we need any miracle to explain all this" (264–65).

Despite Latour's attempts to correct Vaillant's spiritual vision, significant theological differences—due, I think, to temperament—remain between the bishop and his vicar. For example, whereas Latour is able to appreciate worthwhile consequences quite independently of their cause, Vaillant tends to believe that salutary results have to have a wholesome source. For instance, the vicar is very bothered by the fact that he is so busy with the functions of his priestly duties that he has little time for personal devotions to the Blessed Virgin. Accordingly, when Vaillant is brought back to Santa Fe with malarial fever, he sees his "Month of Mary" convalescence chiefly in terms of personal piety: "This was a very happy season for Father Vaillant. For years he had not been able to properly observe this month which in his boyhood he had selected to be the holy month of the year for him. . . . But here there was no time for such things. Last year, in May, he had been on his way to the Hopi Indians, riding thirty miles a day, *marrying, baptizing, confessing as he went,* making camp in the sand-hills at night" (211, emphasis added). Cather explains that Vaillant was frustrated that the exercise of his public and official duties as a missionary had compromised his private prayer life because his personal "devotions had been constantly interrupted by practical considerations" (211). While "riding thirty miles a day and making camp in the sand-hills at night" are, to be sure, "practical considerations," "marrying, baptizing, [and] confessing" are religious matters central to the life of a missionary. Vaillant obviously sees his personal holiness as a necessary condition for the creation of genuine religious experiences for his parishioners. Latour, however, has less trouble separating a clergyman's private life from his public liturgical roles. Interestingly, in an extended description of Latour's most moving and memorable religious experience, "December Night"—the very next chapter after Vaillant's "The Month of May"—we learn that through the exercise of his *official* priestly duties, counseling and praying with and hearing Old Sada's confession, Latour experiences emotional nourishment and spiritual refreshment after a prolonged period of aridity.

Now let us turn to the interesting case of Padre Martínez. For the theologies of both Latour and Vaillant, Padre Martínez presents a troublesome test case of the nature and value of religion. Despite his scandalous personal life, his wealth and social standing, and his political influence, qua priest Martínez is a powerful, even charismatic religious force.[7] On the first evening of his first official visit to Taos, the wealthiest and second-largest parish in his diocese, Latour confronts the undisciplined, disordered, private personality of Antonio Jóse Martínez. Then the next morning, he experiences the public and official Padre Martínez during a memorable High Mass:

> The building was clean and in good repair, the congregation large and devout. The delicate lace, snowy linen, and burnished brass on the altar told of a devoted Altar Guild. The boys who served at the altar wore rich smocks of handmade lace over their scarlet cassocks. The Bishop had never heard the Mass more impressively sung than by Father Martínez. The man had a beautiful baritone voice, and he drew from some well of emotional power. Nothing in the service was slighted, every phrase and gesture had its full value. At the moment of the Elevation the dark priest seemed to give his whole force, his swarthy body and all its blood, to that lifting-up. . . . He had an altogether compelling personality, a disturbing, mysterious magnetic power. (157)

The padre's understanding of religion, akin to the Latourian view, is able to separate results from causes. When Latour visits Martínez at Taos, their dinner conversation turns to priestly celibacy. Martínez, appealing to the revered Church Father St. Augustine, opposes celibacy on the ground that a practice "against nature" (153) cannot be holy—his argument is the flip side of Latour's with-nature account of "natural" miracles. Martínez then suggests that Latour has a blindness analogous to Vaillant's inability to discern the miraculous in the ordinary. Martínez, knowing that Latour is familiar with these passages from Augustine, faults him with not having read the relevant passages sympathetically and thereby perceptively: "You have probably read them with a sealed mind. Celibate priests lose their perceptions" (153).

Embedded in Latour's theology of discerning the miraculous in the commonplace is a pragmatic theory of valuation. That is, the import, even the wholesomeness of an outcome, can be evaluated independently of how or why it is produced. Surely, then, Latour cannot be too surprised that the personally lax and impious Martínez can be an effective and potent instrument in the production of genuine religious fervor in his congregation. When Latour leaves Taos and Martínez and returns to Santa Fe, Vaillant is waiting for him, eager for a report on the renegade pastor and what the bishop will do with him. Latour announces his decision to his vicar: "For the present, I shall do nothing to change the curious situation in Taos. It is not expedient to interfere. The church is strong, the people are devout. No matter what the conduct of the priest has been, he has built up a strong organization, and his people are devotedly loyal to him" (164). Note the word "expedient," a mainstay of the American pragmatists. Note, too, Latour's reasons for not interfering—the congregation is devout and the church is strong. In effect, Latour acknowledges that the unified community that Martínez presides over is not bogus but is actually a genuinely religious congregation. Vaillant, however, cannot see the desert for the cactus because he cannot separate irreligious (or nonreligious) causes from religious effects: "'But Jean,' Father Joseph broke out in agitation, 'the man's life is an open scandal, and one hears of it everywhere'" (165). A cynical reading of Latour's follow-up argument would point out that the reasons for his temporary hands-off policy are more political than religious: "I do not wish to lose the parish of Taos in order to punish its priest, my friend. I have no priest strong enough to put in his place" (165–66). Latour's wider political/practical/religious framework for episcopal decision making is beyond Vaillant, who begs off the discussion. "'You are doubtless right,' said Father Joseph. 'I am often too hasty in my judgments'" (166). Interestingly, the narrator concludes this scene by telling us that "Father Vaillant took off his glasses" (166).

On a related issue, when one's theology permits (as in the case of Latour) an assessment of religion's results somewhat independently of causes (and sources), a missionary's confrontation with an indigenous or an imported but firmly established religion is mollified. Throughout the book, Latour is more open, tolerant, respectful, and catholic than is Vaillant of both native

Indian and also Mexican Catholic religiosity. Commenting on a conversation between Latour and his young Indian guide, Jacinto, Cather brings up the difficult incommensurability of language, culture, and religion: "The Bishop seldom questioned Jacinto about his thoughts or beliefs. He didn't think it polite, and he believed it to be useless. There was no way in which he could transfer his own memories of European civilization into the Indian mind, and he was quite willing to believe that behind Jacinto there was a long tradition, a story of experience, which no language could translate for him" (97). Obviously the Vatican appreciates the tolerance and realism that make Latour better suited for an episcopal office. Whereas Vaillant energetically seeks converts, whom he wants to literally turn around, Latour's patent and pragmatic diocesan leadership is geared to a slower but more effective evolution of beliefs.

The differences of expectation and method between Latour and Vaillant are aptly symbolized in Cather's horticultural metaphors. References to gardening, planting, and growing abound in *Death Comes for the Archbishop*. Whereas the more idealistic and dogmatic Vaillant wants to plant or transplant a French version of Catholicism to New Mexico, the more accommodating and pragmatic Latour seeks to join a new scion onto an already-thriving indigenous or a vigorously acclimated root. Rather than uproot and replace the Indian and Mexican religions, Latour labors to graft an imported, genial religion upon a culture that already has a lively appreciation of the sacred (as well as the presacred and the natural). Before he goes to New Mexico, the bishop's favorite gardening activities are with his vineyards on the shores of Lake Erie; in his retirement, he trains his housekeeper Fructosa (who could not notice that name!) and Tranquilino how to prune and nurture fruit orchards. The ultimate message, then, of Cather's well-regarded historical narrative is that for both orchards and dioceses, it is the quality, the fruitfulness, and the hardiness of the harvest that are the measures of its success. From a philosophical point of view, a past-looking, place-linked, static outlook gives way to a pragmatic process and future-oriented posture in Cather's narrative. Indeed, it is the former that chiefly distinguishes the Indian and Mexican culture and religion that Latour found in New Mexico from the American culture and Catholic religion he sought to graft upon the minds and souls of his parishioners.[8]

It seems to me that Cather missed a wonderful opportunity to symbolize the different temperaments, and therefore theologies, of Latour and Vaillant with regard to religiosity and, especially, the miraculous. In the first chapter of book 2, "The White Mules," Father Vaillant shames rancho owner Manuel Lujon out of his prize pair of cream-colored mules, Contento and Angelica.

Thereafter Cather has Vaillant ride Contento, and Latour, Angelica. She has the wrong missionary on the wrong mount—it is the discerning and farsighted Latour who is content, while the nearsighted and sometimes impetuous Vaillant is the one who needs the guidance of an angel!

NOTES

This chapter is a slightly revised version of "Philosophical Pragmatism and Theological Temperament: The Religious and the Miraculous in Willa Cather's *Death Comes for the Archbishop,*" *Literature and Belief* 22 (2002): 123–37.

1. On the question of James's influence on Cather, Curtin (1975) points out that Cather was managing editor of *McClure's* when it published James's famous essay "The Moral Equivalent of War" in 1910. Incidentally, those familiar with Cather's works need not be reminded, but others ought to know, that her most celebrated short story, "Paul's Case," is subtitled "A Study in Temperament." The different temperaments of Latour and Valliant are also evident in their styles as missionaries; see my "Is Proselytizing Indigenous People an Act of Violence? Willa Cather's Missionaries in *Shadows on the Rock* and *Death Comes for the Archbishop.*"

2. For James on this issue, see "Reflex Action and Theism" and "Pragmatism and Religion." For Dewey, see "Religion Versus the Religious" and "Experience, Nature and Art." For another examination of pragmatism and religion in Harold Frederic, see chapter 8.

3. See Arnold for an insightful examination of "Latour, who instinctively sees the sacred possibility in the physical" (1988, 41), and Rosowski, who argues that "Cather wrote of a highly developed power of symbolization which provides meaning to the most ordinary acts and the most disparate objects" (1986, 172).

4. Murphy's (1999) valuable explanatory notes for the Willa Cather Scholarly Edition of *Death Comes for the Archbishop* locate and explicate the section of *The Catholic Encyclopedia* that Cather mined for her treatment of the with-nature/against-nature controversy regarding miracles.

5. See the account of grace building upon nature in Aquinas's the *Summa Theologia: Prima Secundae Pars,* Question 109, "The Need of Grace," and Question 110, "The Nature of Grace." Consult Appendix 8, "Natural and Supernatural," in the Blackfriars edition of the *Summa* for a helpful summary of Aquinas's view on the "harmony of nature and grace, reason and faith" (1964, 1:99).

Dewey's characteristic way of putting the matter is to stress the continuity between ordinary and aesthetic experiences, and between the secular and the sacred. See, for example, his "The Human Abode of the Religious Function."

6. In the prologue set in Rome, when Bishop Ferrand urges the cardinals of the Vatican Propagation of the Faith to appoint Latour to the newly created Vicarate of New Mexico, the host of the dinner, Cardinal de Allande, asks him "if your French priest [Jean Marie Latour] had a *discerning* eye" (14, emphasis added).

7. The historical sources for Cather's narrative are Twitchell (1911) and Howlett (1908). Howlett paints Martínez as a rogue and political rebel, to which Cather adds lechery and unpriestly pursuit of money and property to further darken the portrait. It is now generally agreed that the actual Martínez was politically powerful and is now esteemed by Hispanic New Mexican historians. Perhaps the best short statement of the case against Cather's Martínez is made by Martínez y Alira (1991); see Mares (1988) for a collection of articles that offer a detailed examination of historical facts gathered to refute Cather's alleged misrepresentation. Since Cather changed the names of Bishop Lamy to Latour and Vicar Machebeuf to Vaillant, it is puzzling, given the literary license she took with Martínez's life and character, that she did not change his name too.

8. See also Urgo (1995) for an illuminating discussion of mobility and futurity in the American mind-set versus place-and-past rootedness in the Navajo.

WORKS CITED

Arnold, Marilyn. 1988. "The Integrating Vision of Bishop Latour in Willa Cather's *Death Comes for the Archbishop.*" *Literature and Belief* 8:39–57.

Cather, Willa. 1927. *Death Comes for the Archbishop.* Edited by John J. Murphy and Charles Mignon. The Willa Cather Scholarly Edition. Lincoln: University of Nebraska Press, 1999.

Curtin, William M. 1975. "Willa Cather and *The Varieties of Religious Experience.*" *Renascence* 27:115–23.

Dewey, John. 1934a. "The Human Abode of the Religious Function." In *A Common Faith,* 59–87. New Haven, CT: Yale University Press, 1976.

———. 1934b. "Religion Versus the Religious." In *A Common Faith,* 1–28. New Haven, CT: Yale University Press, 1976.

———. 1938. "Experience, Nature and Art." In *Experience and Nature,* 354–93. New York: Dover, 1958.

Dooley, Patrick K. 2007. "Is Proselytizing Indigenous People an Act of Violence? Willa Cather's Missionaries in *Shadows on the Rock* and *Death Comes for the Archbishop.*" *Cithera* 46:25–34.

Howlett, William J. 1908. *Life of the Right Reverend Joseph P. Machebeuf.* Pueblo, CO: Franklin.

James, William. 1897. "Reflex Action and Theism." In *The Will to Believe.* Edited by Frederick H. Burkhardt, Fredson Bowers, and Ignas K. Skrupskelis. *The Works of William James.* Cambridge, MA: Harvard University Press, 1979.

———. 1907. "Pragmatism and Religion." In *Pragmatism.* Edited by Frederick Burkhardt, Fredson Bowers, and Ignas K. Skrupskelis. *The Works of William James.* Cambridge, MA: Harvard University Press, 1975.

Mares, E. A., ed. 1988. *Padre Martinez: New Perspectives from Taos.* Taos, NM: Millicent Rogers Museum.

Martínez y Alira, Jerome J. 1991. "The Apotheosis of Bishop Lamy: Local Faith Perspectives." *Willa Cather Pioneer Memorial Newsletter* 35:19–22.

Murphy, John J. 1999. "Explanatory Notes." In Cather, *Death Comes for the Archbishop*, 350–403.

Pater, T. G. 2003. "Miracles (Theology of)." In *The New Catholic Encyclopedia, Second Edition* 9:664–70. Detroit: Thompson-Gale.

Rosowski, Susan J. 1986. *The Voyage Perilous: Willa Cather's Romanticism*. Lincoln: University of Nebraska Press.

Thomas Aquinas. 1964. *Summa Theologia: Prima Secundae Pars*. Blackfriars edition. New York: McGraw-Hill.

Twitchell, Ralph Emerson. 1911. *Leading Facts of New Mexico History*. Cedar Rapids, IA: Torch.

Urgo, Joseph R. 1995. *Willa Cather and the Myth of the American Migration*. Urbana: University of Illinois Press.

14

Cather's Phenomenology of Memory and James's "Specious Present"

"One day is with the Lord as a thousand years, and a thousand years as one day."
—2 Peter 3:8

They held the funeral on the second day, with the town coming to look at Miss Emily beneath a mass of bought flowers, with the crayon face of her father musing profoundly above the bier and the ladies sibilant and macabre; and the very old men—some in their brushed Confederate uniforms—on the porch and the lawn, talking of Miss Emily as if she had been a contemporary of theirs believing that they had danced with her and courted her perhaps, confusing time with its mathematical progression, as the old do, to whom all the past is not a diminishing road but, instead, a huge meadow which no winter ever quite touches, divided from them now by the narrow bottle-neck of the most recent decade of years.
—William Faulkner

Several years ago I was a visiting professor of English and philosophy at the United States Air Force Academy at Colorado Springs. When I told one of my English department colleagues that my family and I were planning to visit Taos, Santa Fe, and Mesa Verde, he suggested that I read Willa Cather's *Death Comes for the Archbishop,* and so I did. About the same time, my brother called and said that if I wanted to say good-bye to our father before it was too late I had better come home to Bismarck, North Dakota, soon. And so I did.

It was a bittersweet visit. My father's condition had progressed to the point that his grasp of the present and past was jumbled and he seemed to sleep most of the time. For the weekend I was home, he sometimes knew I was his son but other times, especially late in the evening, he thought I was either his brother or his father. However, each time I came into the house he knew it was me, but often he so quickly lost track of my comings and goings that it seemed to him that I had made several fresh, new visits that had each involved a trip from Colorado.

My younger brother who had called me home found all of this very sad; but somehow to me it was not—partly because I had just finished *Death Comes for the Archbishop.* What stood out above all else was the last book, wherein Bishop Latour lies in the study with his eyes closed and—notice Cather's carefully chosen verb—"the Bishop was *living* his life" (297, emphasis added). At the time, that section of her wonderful book most impressed me. Later when I reread the book in connection with research for essays dealing with Cather's treatment of pragmatic religion and her environmentalism, I found considerable value in many themes of her rich narrative.[1]

What I find compelling about Cather's statement that Latour is *living* his life—not reliving or remembering it—is how perfectly her account dramatizes William James's contention that humans' awareness of time requires the consciousness of a "specious present." The most influential aspect of the "Sense of Time" and "Memory" chapters of William James's *The Principles of Psychology* was his contention that our consciousness of the now is not an awareness of an evanescent moment on the heels of a vanishing past awaiting a future, but that our sense of the present is an elastic and extended "saddle" of awareness that contains both pulses of the past and inchoate expectations of the future. With regard to the elasticity of the present, one's consciousness can embrace, *as the present,* a second, minute, hour, day, year, or scores of years.

In her rich phenomenology of memory, Willa Cather perceptively displays, via the recollecting consciousness of her characters, how their "past" lives are present and remain vividly alive. In effect, then, Cather can be seen as perceptively utilizing, extending, and embellishing James's specious present. She accomplishes this whenever she allows us to be privy to the consciousness of her characters as they enjoy continuing to live (instead of reliving) the defining events of their lives.

Given the pervasive extent of memory and remembering in Cather's oeuvre, this chapter will be a first step in what I believe to be a very fruitful approach to her works. Accordingly, at this stage I will limit my examination to the fertile and haunting recollections of Bishop Latour in the final sections of *Death Comes for the Archbishop.*

Regarding the influence of James upon Cather, in the June 1905 *McClure's* the lead article was James's tribute "A Knight-Errant of the Intellectual Life: Thomas Davidson." The issue also contained the first printing of Cather's "Paul's Case: A Study in Temperament." Five years later, when Cather was managing editor, *McClure's* published James's famous essay "The Moral Equivalent of War."[2] In her *Willa Cather: A Memoir,* Elizabeth Sergeant recalls that Cather had said "she had no use for Freud[;] Tolstoy and William James provided all the psychology she needed" (1953, 37). Even though further research may reveal other James-Cather connections, given James's inescapable presence in the American cultural scene at the turn of the (last) century, it would be a greater surprise if Cather had *not* been influenced by James. Still, even absent extensive documentable evidence of James's direct influence upon Cather, the important point is that reading them in tandem is mutually illuminating.

After taking a look at James's account of the specious present to provide a theoretical framework, we will see the extent to which Cather's description of how death comes for the archbishop perceptively explores the contours of a human being's consciousness of time.

William James's "Specious Present"

The hugely and widely seminal image in James's *The Principles of Psychology* was his stream-of-consciousness metaphor. James posits that our awareness of time, of ourselves, and of our surroundings is both continuous and changing as our mind shifts its attention across the waxing and waning pulses of consciousness. James's chapters on time and memory explore how both *passing away* and *permanence* are necessary to account for our internal perception of time. Since overlapping pulses (instead of beads on a string) best illustrate our stream of consciousness, James hypothesizes, "*The knowledge of some other part of the stream, past or future, near or remote, is always mixed with our knowledge of the present thing.* . . . Part of the complexity is the echo of the objects just past, and, in a less degree, perhaps, the foretaste of those just present to arrive. Objects fade out of consciousness slowly . . . the lingerings of the past dropping successively away, and the incomings of the future making up the lost. These lingerings of old objects, these incomings of new, are the germs of memory and expectation, the retrospective and prospective sense of time" (1890, 571). Since a moment-to-moment awareness of an instantaneous present will not support the reality of our conscious experience or, as he puts it, "the practically cognized present is no knife-edge" (573), James postulates the need for a broader sense of a "specious" present:[3] "The only fact of our immediate experience is what has been well called 'the specious' present, a sort of saddle-back of time with a certain length of its own, on which we sit perched, and from which we look in two directions into time. The unit of composition of our perception of time is a *duration,* with a bow and a stern, as it were—a rearward- and a forward-looking end" (1892, 245).

How expansive the specious present may be in terms of objectively measurable time (seconds, minutes, hours), and how elastic our subjective awareness of a present moment (episode, event, or even a lifetime), is a function of selective attention. This is, in turn, a function of intelligence. And so, James contends, "We have every reason to think that creatures may possibly differ enormously in the amounts of duration which they intuitively feel, and in the fineness of the events that may fill it" (601).

By an appeal to an ingenious thought experiment (he has his readers first imagine superslow motion and then time-lapse photography), James contrasts two extremes: short-lived creatures able to make ultrafine discriminations, and long-lived ones able to notice only very obvious changes:

Suppose we were able, within the length of a second, to note 10,000 events distinctly, instead of the barely 10, as now; if our life were then destined to hold the same number of impressions, it might be 100 times as short. We should live less than a month, and personally know nothing of the change of seasons. If born in winter, we should believe in summer as we now believe in the heats of the Carboniferous era. The motions of organic beings would be so slow to our senses as to be inferred, not seen. The sun would stand still in the sky, the moon be almost free of change, and so on. But now reverse the hypothesis and suppose a being to get only one 1000th part of the sensations that we get in a given time, and consequently to live 1000 times as long. Winters and summers will be to him like quarters of an hour. Mushrooms and the swifter-growing plants will shoot into being so rapidly as to appear instantaneous creations; annual shrubs will rise and fall from the earth like restlessly boiling-water springs; the motions of animals will be as invisible as are to us the movements of bullets and cannon-balls; the sun will scour through the sky like a meteor, leaving a fiery trail behind him, etc. That such imaginary cases (barring superhuman longevity) may be realized somewhere in the animal kingdom, it would be rash to deny. (601)

James does not speculate about divine consciousness, but it seems to me illuminating to suggest that given God's infinite knowledge and His eternal awareness, His specious present would embrace all of time. Moreover, given His infinite power, His discriminating attention would be able to speed up or slow down change, so for Him it would indeed be the case that "one day is with the Lord as a thousand years, and a thousand years as one day." Given James's psychological framework, let us now turn to Cather's description of human beings' sense of the present.

CATHER'S RICH PHENOMENOLOGY OF MEMORY IN *DEATH COMES FOR THE ARCHBISHOP*

To set the stage for her description of the elastic time-consciousness of Bishop Latour, wherein his impending death has him confront his whole life, Cather provides an account of the last parting of Latour and Vaillant. (Although Vaillant had been Latour's longtime vicar in the diocese of Santa Fe, by this time in the narrative he has been called to be the bishop of a newly organized diocese in Denver.) After each has blessed the other, she notes in the final sentence of the penultimate chapter: "They embraced each other for the past—for the future" (1927, 275).

The final chapter of the book opens with the news of Vaillant's death by quoting a letter from Latour to Vaillant's sister: "Since your brother was called to his reward . . . I feel nearer to him than before. . . . Meanwhile, I am enjoying to the full that period of reflection which is the happiest conclusion to a life of action" (276). Note again Cather's inspired word choice. She does not refer to his retirement years as a period for recollection or remembering, but rather as a period for *reflection*.[4] "Reflection" connotes neither dredging up past memories nor imagining future activities but suggests heightened attention, deliberate scrutiny, and a keen awareness of a present and ongoing task. Such a fine-grained self-examination requires precise nuances that are responding to subtle cues. Perhaps that is why, to the surprise of everyone in the archbishop's household, when Latour returns to his study to prepare for his death he reverts to using his native language: "From that moment on, he spoke only French" (281). A short time later the narrator comments that in his last days Latour avails himself of "the light and elastic mesh of the French tongue" (289).

As Latour gradually widens the margins of his consciousness, as he brightens and deepens in "the shallow light of the present" (305), he begins the process of "living over his life" (297). His reflections are aided by a strict daily regimen. "After his *déjeuner* the old Archbishop made pretense of sleeping. He requested not to be disturbed until dinner-time, and those long hours of solitude were precious to him" (296). His study is dark and quiet. In the midst of this repose he finds that sounds—"church bells . . . and the whistle of a locomotive" (205)—and smells—the "particular quality in the air of new countries . . . that lightness, that dry aromatic odour" (287–88)—are especially evocative of memories.[5] Although Cather offers a striking image of the release of his memories—"something soft and wild and free, something that whispered to the ear on the pillow, lightened the heart, softly, softly picked the lock, slid the bolt, and released the prisoned spirit of the man into the wind, into the blue and gold, into the morning, into the morning!" (288)—it is not precisely remembering that Latour is busy with. As a matter of fact, each morning for all his thirty years in New Mexico, "He always awoke as a young man; not until he rose and began to shave did he realize that he was growing older. His first consciousness was a sense of the light dry wind . . . that made one's body feel light and one's heart cry, 'To-day, to-day,' like a child's" (287).

Given that the bishop of Santa Fe's typical morning sense of himself is as a young man, it is natural that, with regard to Vaillant, Latour's mind is dominated by a vivid consciousness of their early days, when they were seminary students or young missionaries in Ohio, or their first days in New Mexico. It is also not surprising, then, that when Latour goes to Vaillant's funeral, "He could see Joseph clearly as he could see Bernard [his young seminarian aid] but always as he was when they first came to New Mexico. It was not sentiment; that was the picture of Father Joseph that his memory produced for him, and it did not produce any other" (302).

Accordingly, I would suggest that when Cather speaks of Latour's "memory," she is referring to a complex combination of memory and present consciousness that is strictly analogous to what James finds available in the specious present: "He observed that there was no longer any perspective in his memories" (305). (This quasi-seamless sense of past/present/future is mirrored in the physical structure of book 9 of *Death Comes for the Archbishop*. While it, like the previous eight books, is divided into chapters, the chapters in book 9 are simply numbered; the chapters in all the other books are numbered and also given titles.[6]) In other words, for him the ordinary sense of time passing though days, weeks, and years has disappeared: "He was soon to have done with calendared time, and it had already ceased to count for him" (305).

The philosophical and psychological climax of Cather's phenomenological exegesis of Latour's reflections is a precise and powerful description of the reality of human self-awareness. "He sat in the middle of his own consciousness; none of his former states of mind were lost or outgrown. They were all within reach of his hand, and all comprehensible" (305).

What consumes Latour's energy during his remaining days are his reflections on the whole sweep of the continuous and overlapping pulses of thought in his stream of consciousness. His attention is given over to an examination of his life experiences. James (along with the other classical American pragmatists, Dewey is insistent among them) argues that what is philosophically problematic and thereby in need of investigation are not thoughts or things, not subjects or objects, not appearance or reality. Instead, what begs for scrutiny and analysis are the *experiences* of human beings.[7] These experiences are neither "in here" nor "out there." Instead, our experiences are both at once because our knowing is the product of an active and interactive transaction (or negotiation) between object and subject, thing and thought, appearance and reality. In service to needs and in response to desires, by its selective attention, our consciousness constitutes our worlds of experience. Likewise, as death comes for the archbishop, his intense and expansive awareness ranges over all the experiences of his whole life: "Sometimes, when Magdalena or Bernard [his cook and housekeeper] came in and asked him a question, it took him several seconds to bring himself back to the present. He could see they thought his mind was failing; but it was only extraordinarily active in some other part of the great picture of his life—some part of which they knew nothing" (305).

Count James among those who would applaud Cather's firm grip on the phenomena of the perception of time and memory. Concisely summarized, Cather explains that as Latour "sat in the middle of his consciousnesses [when] there was no longer any perspective in his memories," his awareness was bathed "in the shallow light of the present" (305). I believe James would only quibble with the last phrase, which he would amend to "in the *penetrating* light of the *specious* present."[8]

NOTES

This chapter is a slightly revised version of "Willa Cather's Phenomenology of Memory and William James's 'Specious Present,'" *Philosophy Today* 50.4 (2006): 23–34.

1. See chapter 13 and my "Biocentric, Homocentric and Theocentric Environmentalism in *My Ántonia, O'Pioneers!,* and *Death Comes for the Archbishop.*"

2. Although Skaggs posits a direct Willa Cather–William James link via Cather's friendship with her *McClure's* colleague Viola Rosboro, in that case the connection is with *The Varieties of Religious Experience* instead of *The Principles of Psychology.* Incidentally, later in her essay Skaggs offers a much darker interpretation of Latour's final days of reflection: "What Cather does in her finale [book 9 of *Death Comes for the Archbishop*] is to depict a mind growing senile, calcified, and therefore impractical and impolitic. . . . Latour spends his last days self-absorbed, recalling his own past, which has become his surrounding present" (2002, 116, 118). For more on Cather's degree of familiarity with James, especially the James-Lange theory of emotions, see her "Literary Notes," originally published in 1901 when she was guest editor of the *Courier.*

3. In his *The Principles of Psychology,* James credits Mr. E. R. Clay with the idea of the specious present. Myers, the widely respected commentator on James's psychology, notes that "James borrowed this term from an obscure Irish-American writer, E. R. Clay, who coined it in his book *The Alternative* (1882)" (1986, 519). In addition, Myers offers this opinion on the importance and influence of James's account of the specious present: "The concept of the specious present is a basic consideration for almost all subsequent discussions of time, and though James may not have invented the concept, no one is more responsible than he for its sturdy popularity. The ideal of the specious present helps clarify 'the present moment' and the past-present-future distinction within the *now.* It suggests how an immediately past event can be said to be presently apprehended, when it would be odd to say that it is remembered; or how an event coming to be is in a way both future and present" (160).

The *Webster's Third New International Dictionary* definition of "specious present" is concise and helpful: "the time span of immediate consciousness; interval within which what is earlier may be distinguished from what is later though both are directly present to consciousness."

See also McDermott's entry on the "specious present" in *The Cambridge Dictionary of Philosophy.* Note especially his insightful conclusion: "The datum of the present . . . is perpetually elusive, for as we have our experience, now, it is always bathed retrospectively and prospectively. Contrary to common sense, no single experience ever is had by our consciousness utterly alone, single and without relations, for and aft" (1999, 868).

4. Prompted by a request from the editor of the *Commonweal* to explain how she came to write *Death Comes for the Archbishop,* Cather responded with a November 23, 1927, letter that begins by describing her first trip to the Southwest. Note her final phrase! "When I first went to the Southwest some fifteen years ago, I stayed there for a considerable period of time. It was then much harder to get about than today. There were no automobile roads and no hotels off the main lines of railroad. One had to

travel by wagon and carry a camp outfit. One traveled slowly, *and had plenty of time for reflection*" (1999, 373, emphasis added).

5. In her perceptive analysis of how Cather handles time (and space) in *Death Comes for the Archbishop,* Williams notes Latour's sensitivity to sounds, especially "the tolling of the Angelus bells." She continues, "Although Latour's thoughts are linear—from distant to recent past—they are triggered by the sound of the bell all at once and experienced synchronously. The synchronous experience of time becomes central to the novel; the novel works to represent time and space, history and tradition, in non-linear ways" (1999, 81).

6. My observation here was sparked by Woodress's comment that book 9 is "not divided into chapters" (1987, 399); this is not the case, however. In addition, Woodress does not go the next step of seeing the nearly seamless format of book 9 as a symbol of the time continuity we normally experience.

In one of the earliest reviews of *Death Comes to the Archbishop,* September 11, 1927, in the *New York Herald Tribune,* West aptly captures how, in his last days, Latour's consciousness of time is that of a seamless continuum: "He has now the excess of experience which comes to old age; since no more action is required from him, there is no particular reason why his attention should be focused on the present. So as he lies in his bed in the study in Santa Fe where he had begun his work forty years before, *all the events of his life exist contemporaneously, in his head,* his childish days in Clermont and on the coast of the Mediterranean, his youth in the seminary in Rome, his travels among the deserts and the mesas, the Mexican and the Indians" (1927, 318, emphasis added).

7. Also notice how Cather stresses "experience": "During those last weeks of the Bishop's life he thought very little about death; it was the Past he was leaving. The future would take care of itself. But he had an intellectual curiosity about dying; about the changes that took place in a man's belief and scale of values. More and more life seemed to him an *experience of the Ego,* in no sense the Ego itself" (304, emphasis added).

8. I went to Bismarck on November 8, 1996. My father was one of the kindest persons I have ever known, and it would be difficult to imagine a more supportive and generous parent, but he was not emotional or demonstrative. However, when I woke him up when I had to leave on November 11 and I hugged him, he held on very tightly and did not want to let go. He died three weeks later on December 4; my brother and my father's caretakers said he had a good, peaceful death. In memoriam, Kiaran L. Dooley, 1908–96.

WORKS CITED

Cather, Willa. 1927. *Death Comes for the Archbishop.* Edited by John J. Murphy and Charles Mignon. The Willa Cather Scholarly Edition. Lincoln: University of Nebraska Press, 1999.

———. 1901. "Literary Notes." In *The World and the Parish: Willa Cather's Articles and Reviews, 1893–1902.* Edited by William M. Curtin. Vol. 1. Lincoln: University of Nebraska Press, 1970.

———. 1927. "On *Death Comes for the Archbishop.*" In Cather, *Death Comes for the Archbishop.*

Dooley, Patrick K. 2002. "Biocentric, Homocentric and Theocentric Environmentalism in *My Ántonia, O'Pioneers!,* and *Death Comes for the Archbishop.*" *Cather Studies* 5:48–56.

Faulkner, William. 1952. "A Rose for Emily." In *Collected Stories of William Faulkner.* New York: Random House.

James, William. 1890. *The Principles of Psychology.* Edited by Frederick H. Burkhardt, Fredson Bowers, and Ignas K. Skrupskelis. *The Works of William James.* Cambridge, MA: Harvard University Press, 1981.

———. 1892. *Psychology: Briefer Course.* The Works of William James. Edited by Frederick H. Burkhardt, Fredson Bowers, and Ignas K. Skrupskelis. Cambridge, MA: Harvard University Press, 1984.

McDermott, John. 1999. "Specious Present." In *The Cambridge Dictionary of Philosophy.* Edited by Robert Audi. Cambridge: Cambridge University Press.

Myers, Gerald E. 1986. *William James: His Life and Thought.* New Haven, CT: Yale University Press.

Sergeant, Elizabeth. 1953. *Willa Cather: A Memoir.* Lincoln: University of Nebraska Press.

Skaggs, Merrill Maguire. 2002. "*Death Comes for the Archbishop:* Willa Cather's Varieties of Religious Experience." In *Willa Cather and the Culture of Belief,* edited by John J. Murphy, 101–21. Provo, UT: Brigham Young University Press.

West, Rebecca. 1927. "Miss Cather's Business as an Artist." *New York Herald Tribune Books,* September 11:1, 5–6. Reprinted in *Willa Cather: The Contemporary Reviews,* edited by Margaret O'Connor, 317–20. New York: Cambridge University Press, 2001.

Williams, Deborah Lindsay. 1999. "Losing Nothing, Comprehending Everything: Learning to Read Both the Old World and the New in *Death Comes for the Archbishop.*" *Cather Studies* 4:80–96.

Woodress, James. 1987. *Willa Cather: A Literary Life.* Lincoln: University of Nebraska Press.

15

Tools, Work, and Machines in Cather's *One of Ours*

With prosperity came a kind of carelessness [and] a coming gen-
eration which tries to cheat its aesthetic sense by buying things
instead of making anything.
   — Willa Cather

Willa Cather won the Pulitzer Prize of 1923 for *One of Ours,* which had been published the previous year. Though it was her best-selling book in her life-time, critics were less sure of its merits. Of the three-dozen reviews noted in Marilyn Arnold's *Willa Cather: A Reference Guide* that appeared in 1922 and 1923, more than half panned it. The most frequent argument was that Cather should have ended the novel after book 3, just before Claude Wheeler departs for France to join the Allied cause in World War I. But even the reviewers who saluted the firsthand, experience-funded realism of the Nebraska sec-tions of the book found much to criticize about her phlegmatic protagonist and lower-case hero, Claude.

   While scoffing at Claude as an unassertive bungler or pitying him as a fool is expected (and it is often hard to disagree with either characteriza-tion), I wish to offer an apologia on his behalf: his difficulties are traceable to being born a generation late and not being the eldest sibling. As for my first claim, I will show how Cather portrays him as adept with the hand tools and mule- and horse-powered equipment that first-generation homesteaders used. Conversely, he is ill at ease with the mechanized and gasoline-powered implements that his father readily buys and that his older brother sells. With regard to my second point, though assiduously courted by his older brother,

Gladys Farmer more than anyone else appreciates Claude's gifts and aptitudes, telling him, "I don't think I shall ever marry Bayliss . . . because you are the member of the family I have always admired" (1922, 345).

In the opening scene Cather hints at how we might better understand Claude. He is washing "the little Ford" so he and his brother can go to town in style to watch the circus that has come to Frankfort. His father, however, has him drive the mules and wagon, taking not only his brother Ralph but also the Wheeler's two rough and crude hired men, along with a load of foul-smelling cowhides. Claude see this deflating change of plans as "his father's idea of a joke" (14); other commentators point to this incident as the first indication of Nat Wheeler's dominating, bullying personality.[1] My reading suggests, cruel joke though it is, that it shows that Nat Wheeler senses that his middle son is best suited to animal-powered equipment.

In town, Claude meets his friend Ernest Havel for a picnic lunch before the circus. Luxuriating at one of the bends of Lovely Creek, Claude "felt that he had now closed the door on his disagreeable morning" (22). Note Cather's idyllic scene of human-nature harmony: "The horses stood with their heads over the wagon-box, munching on their oats. The stream trickled by under the willow roots with a cool, persuasive sound. Claude and Ernest lay in the shade, their coats under their heads, talking very little" (22). Soon, however, this idyllic scene has, like Hawthorne's, its own "machine in the garden" discord: "Occasionally a motor dashed along the road toward town, and a cloud of dust and a smell of gasoline blew in over the creek bottom; but for the most part the silence of the warm, lazy summer noon was undisturbed" (23). I suspect that Claude, but not Ernest, is aware (if only subconsciously) of this mechanized intrusion.

After the circus, Leonard Dawson gives Claude a ride home in his car. Claude "was glad enough to turn the mules over to Ralph, who didn't mind the hired men as much as he did" (25). Leonard, the oldest son of the Wheeler's neighbor, is twenty-five years old to Claude's nineteen. Though Leonard is thus a half-dozen years closer to the horse-and-mule homesteading generation, Cather notes that, unlike Claude, Leonard is readily attuned to the mechanized postpioneer age: "At sunset the car was speeding over a fine stretch of smooth road across the level county that lay between Frankfort and the rougher land along Lovely Creek. Leonard's attention was largely given up to admiring the faultless behaviour of his engine" (26).

And so, unlike his father and brothers and the friends his age, Claude is not comfortable with gasoline-powered equipment. Instead, his best moments, free of interference from other humans or intrusions from machine noise, occur when he retreats to the tree claim, where he can study the stars, or when he walks in the pastures, hearing and seeing the wind in the long prairie grass, or when he gathers corn in early autumn. Harvest scenes are especially telling.

From Cather we learn that, nearing the harvest season "after Ralph left [to tend the ranch in Colorado,] Claude had the place to himself again, and work went on as usual. The stock did well, and there were no vexatious interruptions" (113). The ordinary practice would be for Claude and his hired man, Dan, to harvest the corn together. But he sends Dan "to shuck on the north quarter, and he [Claude} worked on the south" (114). Claude prefers to work alone, for, in the absence of other humans and/or machines, he finds peace, instead of being lonely.

> That afternoon Claude suddenly stopped flinging white ears into the wagon besides him. It was about five o'clock, the yellowest hour of the autumn day. He stood lost in a forest of light, dry rustling corn leaves, quite hidden away from the world. Taking off his husking-gloves, he wiped the sweat from his face, climbed up to the wagon box, and lay down on the ivory-coloured corn. The horses cautiously advanced a step or two, and munched with great content at ears they tore from the stalks with their teeth.
>
> Claude lay still, his arms under his head, looking up at the hard, polished blue sky, watching the flocks of crows go over from the fields where they fed on shattered grain, to their nests in the trees along Lovely Creek. . . .
>
> He sprang down into the gold light to finish his load. Warm silence nestled over the cornfield. Sometimes a light breeze rose for a moment and rattled the stiff, dry leaves, and he himself made a great rustling and cracking as he tore the husks from the ears. (115–16)

Claude and animals populate a world wherein only their sounds and those of nature can be heard. Moreover, and this I think is Cather's deeper contention, this is precisely the world that early homesteaders found in Nebraska.

Claude identifies with the first and second waves of homesteaders.[2] Because they lacked the power to dominate nature, these homesteaders sought ways and means of harmoniously harnessing natural forces by (for example) damming up Lovely Creek to power a grist and flour mill. Even as a youngster, Claude had been attracted to such "natural" machines. "Best of all he liked going in where the water-wheel hung dripping in its dark cave, and quivering streaks of sunlight came in through the cracks to play on the green slime and the spotted jewel-weed growing in the shale" (167–68). To Claude's eye the waterwheel fits its environment; for Cather, a water-powered mill symbolizes an earlier generation's patient and modest alteration of nature. Accordingly, while Jason Royce earlier had been content to let nature set his work and rest schedule, later he mechanically bypasses the natural cycles so he can run his mill when he and his customers want it: "Jason Royce must have kept his mill going out of sentiment, for there was not much money in it now. But milling had been his first business, and he had not found many things in life to be sentimental about. Sometimes one still came upon him in dusty miller's clothes, giving his man a day off. He had long ago ceased to depend on the risings and fallings of Lovely Creek for his power, and had put in a gasoline engine. The old dam now lay 'like a holler tooth,' as one of his men said, grown up with weeds and willow bush" (168).

Further along in the story, when Claude asks Jason for his daughter Enid's hand in marriage, the old miller makes it clear that he has long noticed and liked Claude's affinity with earlier, more nature-friendly times: "You took my fancy when you were a little shaver, and I used to let you in to see the water-wheel. When I gave up water-power and put in an engine, I said to myself, 'There's just one fellow in the country will be sorry to see the old wheel go, and that's Claude Wheeler'" (203). How the solitude-preferring, old-ways-are-the-better-ways Claude has been moved to court Enid takes us to the crucial horse-and-mule versus gasoline-powered machine clash in *One of Ours*.

Cather crafts an interestingly indirect narration of the accident that injures Claude and paves the way for a courtship that leads to a disastrous marriage. We readers are allowed to overhear Leonard Dawson (a witness to the incident) telling Ernest Havel what happened:

> It was the queerest thing I ever saw. He was out with the team of mules and a heavy plough, working the road in that deep cut between their place and mine. The gasoline motor truck came along, making more noise that usual, maybe. But those mules know a motor truck, and what they did was pure cussedness. They began to rear and plunge in that deep cut. I was working my corn over in the field and shouted to the gasoline man to stop, but he didn't hear me. Claude jumped for the critters' heads and got 'em by the bits, but that time he was all tangled up in the lines. Those damned mules lifted him up off his feet and started to

run.... They carried him right along, swinging in the air, and finally ran
him into the barbed-wire fence and cut his face and neck up. (189–90)

Perhaps we need to remind ourselves of the historical situation to glean
Cather's subtle commentary on how the old ways gave way to the new. From
the late 1910s, when *One of Ours* is set, until the mid-1920s (several years after
Cather was writing the book), the vast majority of Americans lived on farms,
where they were largely eager to trade in their horses and mules for gasoline-
powered machinery as soon as they could afford to do so. Yet in these decades
of transition, most Americans (like Cather's characters) typically had no
objection to still using horses and mules: Ernest Havel is cultivating his corn
with a team of horses when he hears of Claude's accident, and Claude's father
prefers "the rattling buckboard in which, though he kept two automobiles, he
still drove about the country" (15). Claude (and Mahailey—more about her
shortly), however, would just as soon have only the old ways. They have little
confidence in and do not welcome the new, "improved," easier ways.

In the scene immediately preceding the runaway-mule accident (caused, I
stress, by the noise of a "gasoline motor truck"), Claude and Enid have driven
to Hastings to shop—he, for summer clothes; she, for spiritual advice from
the unctuous Brother Arthur Weldon. Cather begins the scene by telling why
they both enjoyed frequent drives around the area that summer: "The advantage of this form of companionship was that it did not put too great a strain
upon one's conversational powers. Enid could be admirably silent, and she
was never embarrassed by either silence or speech. She was cool and sure of
herself under any circumstances, and that was one reason why she drove a car
so well,—much better than Claude, indeed" (177). Next we find out that this
trip to Hastings is quite a haul, "about seventy miles to the northeast" (177).

When they are about to leave Hastings, Claude "called Enid's attention to
a mass of thunderheads in the west" (183). Characteristically cautious, Claude
suggests that they stay at the hotel. (Later Mrs. Wheeler says that she had
hoped they would have the sense to do just that!) Enid will not hear of it, so
they start back, certain to run into heavy rain and impassable muddy roads.
Less than twenty miles from home, they stop to put on tire chains and to
cover the packages in the backseat of their open coupé. After a scary spinout
in deep mud, "Enid sat calm and motionless" (184). Claude then suggests
they spend the night at a nearby farmhouse. But the Rices, Enid observes, are
not clean people and have a lot of children. "Better be crowded than dead,"
retorts Claude. "It's too dangerous, Enid. I don't like the responsibility. Your

father would blame me for taking such a chance" (185). Enid's solution is for her to take over the driving: "Do you mind letting me drive for a while? There are only three bad hills left, and I think I can slide down them sideways; I've often tried it" (185). And so, slipping and skidding, they finally arrive at the Wheeler farmstead. "'It was Enid who got us home,' Claude told [his mother]. 'She's a dreadfully foolhardy girl, and somebody ought to shake her, but she's a fine driver'" (186).

Later that evening as Enid is going up to the Wheeler's guest room, she walks near Claude's chair:

> "Have you forgiven me?" she asked teasingly.
> "What made you so pig-headed? Did you want to frighten me? or to show me how well you could drive?"
> "Neither. I wanted to get home. Good-night." (187)

Neither, to be sure. What she wanted to do was to begin dictating the terms of their relationship. Thereafter, we learn that "*Enid* decided that *she* would be married in the first week of June" (246, emphasis added). On their wedding night on the way to Denver, she shuts him out of their Pullman car stateroom. It is also clear that their marriage is never consummated. Note especially Cather's comment that for Enid: "Everything about a man's embrace was distasteful . . . ; something inflicted upon women, like the pain of childbirth—for Eve's transgression, perhaps" (281).[3] Still later, she abandons Claude, their new house, and Nebraska to go to China to nurse Caroline, her ill older missionary sister. Though there are many levels of incompatibility between Claude and Enid, my point is that in their trip to Hastings his cautious temperament and mechanical insecurity and her confidence with machines and independence (recall the just-noted comment that "she was cool and sure of herself under any circumstances") foretell a fragile marriage waiting to disintegrate (177).

Flawed though Claude is, he has considerable talent. As we have so far seen, his capabilities are well-suited for, even prized by, the pioneer generation of homesteaders.

First of all, Claude is a hard worker—quite unlike his father: "In the early days [Mr. Wheeler] had homesteaded and bought and leased enough land to make him rich. Now he had only to rent it out to good farmers who liked to work—he didn't, and of that he made no secret" (17). And Claude is unlike his younger brother, who buys every new gadget on the market (today we would call Ralph an equipment junkie). Note Mrs. Evangeline Wheeler's view of her two youngest sons: "Claude had always worked hard when he was at home, and made a good field hand, while Ralph had never done much but tinker with machinery and run errands in his car" (105). Cather also details how Ralph lavishly outfits himself to manage the ranch his father purchased in Yucca County, Colorado. For example, Ralph thinks that a new phonograph is one the of things he needs to properly equip his ranch and new home. "He wanted one of the latest make, put out under the name of a great American inventor" (103). And also unlike Claude, his older brother engages in work that is bookish and urban, since "it was because Bayliss was quick at figures and undersized for a farmer that his father sent him to town to learn the implement business" (127).

Accordingly, Cather is clear that as a pioneer Claude would have been a steady, frugal, conservative, respectful steward of the land. The sharpest contrast between Claude and his father and siblings can be seen in their attitudes about tools. Claude is partial to hand tools, even broken ones. He is loath to discard what he is used to and what has served him well, so he makes himself an expert at repair—a skill much prized by Mahailey: "If the leg of the kitchen table got wobbly, she knew he would put in new screws for her. When she broke a handle off her rolling-pin, he put on another, and he fitted a haft to her favorite butcher-knife after everyone else said it must be thrown away. These objects, after they were mended, acquired a new value in her eyes, and she liked to work with them" (38).[4] However, Ralph's ethos is whim and throwaway. As a consequence, the Wheeler cellar is full of his purchases: "Mysterious objects stood about in the grey twilight; electric batteries, old bicycles and typewriters, a machine for making cement fence-posts, a vulcanizer, a stereopticon with a broken lens. The mechanical toys Ralph could not operate successfully as well as those he had got tired of, were stored away here. . . . Nearly every time Claude went to the cellar, he made a desperate resolve to clear the place out some day, reflecting bitterly that the money this wreckage cost could have put a boy through college decently" (35). Cather briefly returns to her contrast of the pioneer generation's careful expenditure with the affluent later generation's prodigality in the last three books of *One of Ours*. Mahailey's sense of the havoc of World War I and her view of what Claude may be able to do to help those whose homes have been shattered is predictable. Her parting words to Claude, shaving in the washroom the morning he is to leave, are:

> "You tell 'em over there that I'm awfully sorry about them old women, with their dishes an' their stove all broke up."

"All right, I will." Claude scraped away at this chin.

She lingered. "Maybe you can help 'em mend their things, like you do fur me," she suggested hopefully. (349)

Cather's acute commentary on modern America's careless consumption can also be found in her description of the French reaction to the shiploads of food, equipment, and "useless things" that land with the troops. All this is seen through the eyes of the proprietress of the cheese store, whose inventory is nearly cleaned out by Sergeant Hick and nine soldiers under Lieutenant Claude Wheeler. After the cheese woman charges them two-and-a-half times the market value, we learn her opinion of Claude's soldiers—an opinion, by the way, that Cather wonderfully describes as one that gives her a "moral plank to cling to" (364):

> She liked them well enough, but she did not like to do business with them. If she didn't take their money, the next one would. All the same, fictitious values were distasteful to her, and made everything seem flimsy and unsafe. . . . She laughed aloud. They looked back and waved to her. She replied with a smile that was both friendly and angry. She liked them, but not the legend of waste and prodigality that ran before them—and followed after. It was superfluous and disintegrating in a world of hard facts. (429)[5]

More generally, Cather's characterization of modern America reminds us of the paradox that while hard work produces wealth, affluence can be dangerous and debilitating. Such is clear both in her praise of the gritty strenuousness of pioneer parents and in her chagrin at the relaxed and careless lifestyle of their children and grandchildren: "With prosperity came a kind of callousness; everybody wanted to destroy the old things they used to take pride in. The orchards, which had been nursed and tended so carefully twenty years ago, were now left to die of neglect. It was less trouble to run to town in an automobile and buy fruit than it was to raise it" (144).[6] Beyond valorizing family-centered subsistence homesteading, Cather notes serious deficiencies in monoculture farming geared to specialized cash crops. And beyond her diagnosis of a diminished spiritual and physical tone, Cather decries the bad bargain of bartering wholesome and high-quality products for trendy, shoddy merchandise: "The farmer raised and took to market things with an intrinsic value; wheat and corn as good as could be grown anywhere in the world, hogs and cattle that were the best of their kind. In return he got manufactured articles of poor quality; showy furniture that went to pieces, carpets and draperies that faded, clothes that made a handsome man look like a clown. Most of his money was paid out for machinery—and that, too, went to pieces. A steam thresher didn't last long; a horse outlived three automobiles" (144).

Just as Jason Royce had seen youngster Claude's allegiance to the values of generations past rather than generations future, Gladys Farmer sensed high schooler Claude's work ethic and moral fiber: "Claude was her one hope. Ever since they graduated from high school, all through the four years she had been teaching, she had waited to see him emerge and prove himself. She wanted him to be more successful than Bayliss *and still be Claude*" (212). While only Gladys, Mahailey, and Jason Royce seemed to appreciate Claude's hand-tool skills and his land-use loyalties, nearly everyone notices his body.

He is a fine physical specimen. He is a gifted athlete, especially good at football and track; he also attracts the discriminating eye of the art students at the state university. Miss Peachy Millmore—what a name!—"coaxed him to pose in his track clothes for the life class on Saturday morning, telling him that he had 'a magnificent physique,' a compliment which covered him with confusion. But he posed, of course" (82).[7] Clearly the better pairing—physically, emotionally, and temperamentally—would have been Claude and Gladys, and Enid and Bayliss.[8] It takes Claude longer than most to realize that his marriage is disastrous. But when he finally does, in one of the few assertive moments in his Nebraska life, this realization leads him to caution Gladys that marrying Bayliss would be a serious mistake.

I have argued that Claude Wheeler's best qualities would have made him an ideal self-sufficient first-generation pioneer homesteader. Unfortunately he was born into the third generation of farmers, who are eager to use gasoline-powered equipment to produce abundant cash crops to contribute wealth to the nation's increasingly urban economy. Beyond being unsuited for modern farming, Claude is denied the liberalizing sort of education available at the state university. Though the distaste for the sort of education he receives at Temple is ample, his protests are not; and so for his second year of college, he is sent back to the "struggling denominational college on the outskirts of the state capital" (40).

What sort of summative assessment can be filed on behalf of Claude Wheeler? Even the positive light I have tried to shine on his personality and achievements cannot overcome the dark contours of his passivity and lack of spunk. The self-assessment he offers Gladys just before he leaves for Europe and World War I is accurate, though exaggerated: "What *have* I ever done, except make one blunder after another?" When she is unmoved by his brutal self-critique, he continues, "Why didn't you keep me from making a fool of myself?" (345–46).

I am unsure of how Cather herself finally sees Claude. In "Miss Jewett," Cather offers two criteria she uses to judge successful and admirable country folks. "Miss Jewett," she comments, "wrote of everyday people who grew out of the soil, not about exceptional individuals at war with their environment" (1936, 851). A few paragraphs later, Cather notes Miss Jewett's belief that her "country friends . . . were the wisest of all, because they could never be fooled about fundamentals" (853). There is no doubt that Claude easily achieves, even exceeds, the growing-out-of-the-soil norm. But as to the second, while he may not have been fooled about fundamentals, he can be faulted, contra Miss Jewett, on the grounds that he did so little to war against an environment, specifically the mind-set of Nebraska's second- and third-generation farmers, that socially marginalized and emotionally paralyzed him.

NOTES

1. Younge says of Claude's parents, "His father is a bully, and his mother is her husband's submissive collaborator" (1990, 145). McComas argues that Claude's hatred of his father's abuse festers until it is finally allowed a legitimate outlet in combat that "transfigures a muted and thwarted young farmer into a military hero" (1997, 93).

2. Van Doren finds that Claude is not a member of the wrong generation of homesteaders but that he was born a century too late: "Claude, who has so much pioneer in his blood that he is bewildered by everything in the twentieth century except the war, in which he dies" (1931, 359).

3. On his voyage across the Atlantic on the *Anchises,* Claude overhears his fellow soldiers talking about their wives and sweethearts: "He listened for a moment and then moved away with *the happy feeling* that he was *the least married man* on the boat" (404, emphasis added). Early in their marriage, Claude finds that "the timber claim was his refuge . . . [for there] he felt unmarried and free" (284).

4. Schaefer also notes Mrs. Wheeler's preference for crafts and hand tools, commenting, "Neither of Cather's women [Mrs. Wheeler and Mahailey] can handle the milk separator or the mechanical dishwasher, but both contrive to supply hot water for baths, warm biscuits from the oven, preserves from the cellar" (1991, 140).

Cather herself expressed the same preference for handmade crafts versus massproduced commodities with reference to the old and new furnishings for the rural churches in New Mexico: "May I say here that within the last few years some of the newer priests down in that country have been taking away from those old churches their old homely images and decorations, which have a definite artistic and historical value, and replacing them by conventional, factory-made church furnishings from New York? It is a great pity" (1927, 959).

5. Mention of waste and prodigality reminds readers of Cather's powerfully apt wonder at how war could so easily empower "the watchfulness and devotion of so many men and machines . . . [resulting in such an] extravagant consumption of fuel and energy" (318). She echoes William James's "The Moral Equivalent of War" worry that the contagious attractiveness of the martial spirit makes it very difficult to eradicate. The Jamesian theme in Cather's reflections is not surprising—she was managing editor at *McClure's* when it published James's famous pacifism essay in 1910.

6. In her essay on Nebraska for the September 5, 1923, *Nation,* Cather is explicit on this issue:

> Of course, there is the other side of the medal, stamped with the ugly crest of materialism, which has set its seal upon all of most of our productive commonwealths. Too much prosperity, too many moving-picture shows, too much gaudy fiction have colored the taste and manners of so many of these Nebraskans of the future. There, as elsewhere, one finds the frenzy to be show[y]; farm boys who wish to be spenders before they are earners, girls who try to look the heroines of the cinema screen; *a coming generation which tries to cheat its aesthetic sense by buying things instead of making anything.* (1923, 260, emphasis added)

7. One would suppose that Acocella's widely noted and well-received 1995 *New Yorker* essay, "Cather and the Academy," had compellingly devastated gay-preoccupied critics of Cather so that, thereafter, they would be careful. Alas, Nealon is unable to resist his own agenda-driven commentary: "With a loving sadistic persistence Cather pushes Claude from scene to scene, from small humiliations of dress, carriage, and behavior in his early days to the more acute despairs of youth and love in the novel's middle. . . . *She has him submit to a college sweetheart's demands and pose nude for her drawing class*" (1997, 19, emphasis added). "College sweetheart" is a stretch; "demand" is a misread; and "pose nude," though it might do wonders to shore up Nealon's argument, does not appear in Cather's text.

8. On the Claude-Gladys paring, during last-minute wedding preparations at the Royce home, one of the girls "whispered to the others, 'Do you suppose Gladys will come out tonight with Bayliss Wheeler? I always thought she had a pretty warm spot in her heart for Claude, myself'" (252). And as for the Bayliss-Enid couple, after Claude and Enid are married, "Bayliss came out from town to spend evenings occasionally. Enid's vegetarian suppers suited him, and as she worked with him on the Prohibition campaign, they always had business to discuss" (283). The names Cather chose point the same way: Gladys is the feminine equivalent of Claudius (Claude); and, as Schwind notes, Enid is "Welsh for 'pure'" (1984, 64).

Works Cited

Acocella, Joan. 1995. "Cather and the Academy." *New Yorker* (November) 27:56–66, 68–71.

Arnold, Marylyn. 1986. *Willa Cather: A Reference Guide.* Boston: G. K. Hall.

Cather, Willa. 1922. *One of Ours.* Edited by Richard Harris, Frederick Link, and Kari Ronning. The Willa Cather Scholarly Edition. Lincoln: University of Nebraska Press, 2006.

———. 1923. "Nebraska: The End of the First Cycle." In *My Ántonia.* Edited by Joseph Urgo. Toronto: Broadview Literary Texts, 2001.

———. 1927. "On *Death Comes for the Archbishop.*" In *Willa Cather: Stories, Poems, and Other Writings.* New York: Library of America.

———. 1936. "Miss Jewett." In *Willa Cather: Stories, Poems, and Other Writings,* 849–58. New York: Library of America, 1992.

McComas, Dix. 1997. "Willa Cather's *One of Ours:* In Distant Effigy." *Legacy* 14:93–109.

Nealon, Christopher. 1997. "Affect-Genealogy: Feeling and Affiliation in Willa Cather." *American Literature* 69:5–37.

Schaefer, Josephine O'Brien. 1991. "The Great War and 'This Late Age of World's Experience' in Cather and Woolf." In *Virginia Woolf and War: Fiction, Reality, and Myth,* edited by Mark Hussey, 134–50. Syracuse, NY: Syracuse University Press.

Schwind, Jean. 1984. "The 'Beautiful' War in *One of Ours.*" *Modern Fiction Studies* 30:53–71.

Van Doren, Carl. 1931. "Willa Cather's New Chronicle of Virtue." *New York Herald Tribune Books,* August 2:1. Reprinted in *Willa Cather: The Contemporary Reviews,* edited by Margaret O'Connor, 358–60. New York: Cambridge University Press, 2001.

Younge, Patricia Lee. 1990. "For Better or Worse: At Home and at War in *One of Ours.*" In *Willa Cather: Family, Community, and History,* edited by John J. Murphy, 141–53. Provo: Brigham Young University Press.

16

Creating Community

Steinbeck's *The Grapes of Wrath* and Royce's Philosophy of Loyalty

> *"You sharin' with us, Muley Graves?" Casy asked.*
> *"If a fella's got somepin to eat an' another fella's hungry—*
> *why, the first fella ain't got no choice."*
> *—John Steinbeck*

Most of the chapters in this volume have brought the classical American pragmatic philosophers into conversation with the American literary realists and naturalists. Here I examine a remarkable overlap in the next generation of writers, both Californians: the philosopher Josiah Royce and the novelist John Steinbeck. Both authors were intrigued with the phenomenon of community building—its conditions, its catalysts, its benefits, and its dangers. What emerges is a striking interplay between Steinbeck's poignant (and efficient) narrative and Royce's abstract (and sophisticated) theory.

As a child, Josiah Royce followed his parents from town to town during the California gold rush. At a dinner given in his honor in 1915, less than a year before his death, Royce summed up his philosophical career:

> I was born in 1855 in California. My native town was a mining town in the Sierra Nevada—a place five or six years older than myself. My earliest recollections include a very frequent wonder as to what my elders meant when they said that this was a new community. I frequently looked at the vestiges left by the former diggings of miners, saw that

many pine logs were rotten, and that a miner's grave was to be found in a lonely place not far from my own house. Plainly men had lived and died hereabouts. I dimly reflected that this sort of life had apparently been going on ever since men dwelt on that land. The logs and the grave looked old. . . . What was there then in this place that ought to be called new . . . ? I wondered, and gradually came to feel that part of my life's business was to find out what all this wonder meant. (1916, 122–23)

Indeed, Royce's lifelong preoccupation was with an elucidation of the conditions of community life.[1] In addition, since loyalty is the fundamental value of community life, Royce sought principles to distinguish worthy loyalties from predatory ones.

What Royce struggled long and hard to articulate, John Steinbeck dramatically and economically captured in a single chapter (chapter 17) of *The Grapes of Wrath*. Therein, Steinbeck relates how the Okie migrants who happen to camp at the same place each night become a community. "In the evening a strange thing happened: the twenty families became one family, the children were the children of all . . . every night relationships that make a world, established; and every morning the world torn down like a circus" (1939, 264–65). Steinbeck's account dramatizes how wholesome relationships, or (to use Royce's terms) "worthy loyalties," emerged. After we take a look at Steinbeck's artful and penetrating account, we shall see how Royce's abstract and far-reaching theorizing provides both structure and insight into the phenomenon of community building.

Steinbeck's brilliant chapter begins with the nightly camp-making activities, moves through the process of twenty families becoming a camp unit of one family, and ends with new worlds in the making. His chapter begins and ends with a striking image: migrants as bug-people encased in cars. "In the daylight they scuttled like bugs to the westward; as the dark caught them they scuttled like bugs near to shelter and to water" (264). But the scene is quite different the next morning: "The tents came down. There was a rush to go. And when the sun arose, the camping place was vacant, only a little litter left by the people. And the camping place was ready for a new world in a new night. But along the highway the cars of the migrant people crawled out like bugs, and the narrow concrete miles stretched ahead" (273). Though we might expect that bugs would come out in the darkness, these bugs come out in the light, while people emerge in darkness. Steinbeck's bug-people nightly re-create new worlds. Though they were driven away from their failed farms, they do not despair. Still hopeful, they seek a "new country," "and because they were lonely and perplexed, because they had all come from a place of sadness and worry and defeat, and because they were all going to a new mysterious place, they huddled together; they talked together; they shared their lives, their food, and the things they hoped for in a new country" (264). These realistic, tough, but still forward-looking migrants epitomize the best in the American character. As they abandon (or are driven away from) their homes and farms, their slim reserves of energy, money, and food become focused on the future. "The loss of home became one loss, and the golden time in the West was one dream" (264). At first, the shocks of dislocation and an uncertain future make them fearful. But gradually they learn how to cope, and then they learn how to thrive: "At first the families were timid in the building and tumbling worlds, but gradually the technique of building worlds became their technique. Then leaders emerged, then laws were made, then codes came into being. And as the worlds moved westward they were more complete and better furnished, for their builders were more experienced in building them" (265).

The new nightly worlds they build adhere to a set of natural rights. There are rights to be embraced: "The right to privacy in the tent; the right to keep the past black hidden in the heart; the right to talk and to listen . . . the right of the hungry to be fed; the rights of the pregnant and the sick to transcend all other rights" (265). And there are monstrous rights to be destroyed: "The right to intrude upon privacy, the right to be noisy while the camp slept, the right of seduction or rape, the right of adultery and theft and murder. These rights were crushed, because the little worlds could not exist even for a night with such rights alive" (265).

Steinbeck's chronicling of this world building shows how rights become codified into rules and then those rules into laws. Such unwritten laws protect the weak: "A man might have a willing girl if he stayed with her, if he fathered her children and protected them. But a man might not have one girl one night and another the next, for this would endanger the worlds" (266). This code also deals with aggressors by "the punishments—there were only two—a quick and murderous fight or ostracism; and ostracism was the worst. For if one broke the laws his name and face went with him, and he had no place in any world, no matter where created" (266).

The nightly world building achieves stability, predictability, and order. "The families moved westward, and the technique of building worlds improved so that the people felt safe in their worlds; and the form was so fixed that a family acting in the rules knew it was safe in the rules" (266). In a word, "There grew up government in the worlds, with leaders, with elders" (266). The homes and farms that the bug-people left were ruined, their journey was perilous, their way was uncharted, and their errand into the wilderness had an uncertified goal. Still, on their way each night, a nurturing and protective community that released human potential and cultivated human solidarity was constructed. Beginning by addressing basic needs—fuel, food, water, and shelter—nightly communities soon responded to higher, more specifically human needs. Defensiveness and isolation were shattered; humanity and community were fostered: "And the worlds were built in the evening. The people moving in from the highways, made them with tents and *their hearts and brains. . . .* The families, which had been units of which the boundaries were a house at night, a farm by day changed their boundaries. In the long hot light, they were silent in the cars moving slowly westward; but at night they integrated with any group they found" (267, emphasis added). Steinbeck's optimism about the human spirit (and the pragmatic and resourceful American character) is clear in his moving and vivid depiction of democratic, self-regulating communities wherein reasonable customs, useful rules, and reliable government are unremarkable, matter-of-fact occurrences.

Josiah Royce's reflections on community as the catalyst and context for self-actualization, self-definition, and self-discovery spanned some thirty-six years, from *Fugitive Essays on Pessimism and Romanticism* (1880) to *The Hope of the Great Community* (1916), with eight volumes in between (as well as numerous other volumes on metaphysics, logic, and philosophy of religion). Royce's philosophical reflections range over a very wide area; indeed, his views on community and community building offer a fruitful framework for an account of the whole of *The Grapes of Wrath*—not just chapter 17. For example, Royce's account would highlight, in the Joads' journey, how their sense of solidarity expanded from family (plus Jim Casy) to the nightly world making just discussed to the near-cosmic loyalty to loyalty expressed in Tom's last conversation with Ma Joad:

> Tom laughed uneasily, "Well, maybe like Casy says, maybe a fella ain't got a soul of his own, but on'y a piece of a big one—an' then—"
> "Then what, Tom?"
> "Then it don' matter. Then I'll be aroun' in the dark. I'll be ever'where—wherever you look. Wherever they's a fight so hungry people can eat, I'll be there. Wherever they's a cop beatin' up a guy, I'll be there." (572)

Or in the last scene when Ma Joad thanks Mrs. Wainwright (with whom they share the boxcar home):

> "No need to thank. Ever'body's in the same wagon. S'pose we was down. You'd give us a han.'"
> "Yes," Ma said, "we would."
> "Or anybody."
> "Or anybody. Use'ta be the fambly was fust. It ain't so now. It's anybody. Worse off we get, the more we got to do it." (606)

In terms of Royce's analysis, the Joad family's loyalty to a widening circle of groups becomes the antidote to narrow self-assertiveness and cliquish divisiveness. Indeed, Royce has much to say about fidelity, decisiveness, sympathy, and compassion in community life. We will focus, however, on how Royce's thought can structure and clarify Steinbeck's dramatization of nightly world making and shared community life.

A variety of temporary gatherings—picnics, crowds at a game, or audiences at a play or concert—provide Royce with clues about the conditions for long-term, genuine communities worthy of a life-defining loyalty. This is a loyalty that "tends to unify life, to give it centre, fixity, stability" (1908, 12). At the very least, quasi communities are marked with a minimal level of shared experience, conscious awareness, cooperation, and communication. Richer senses of community require either a community of memory or a community of hope. Hence the Joads (and the other migrants on the way to the Promised Land of California) gradually shift from shared-memory to shared-hope communities. As Royce explains, "A community constituted by the fact that each of its members accepts as part of his individual life and self the same *past* events that each of his fellow-members accepts, may be called a *community of memory.* . . . A community constituted by the fact that each of its members accepts, as part of his own individual life and self, the same expected *future* events that each of his fellows accepts, may be called a *community of expectation* or upon occasion, a *community of hope*" (1913, 52).

Steinbeck and Royce agree that genuine communities of hope can be very quickly realized. Royce comments, "We see why long histories are needed in order to define the life of great communities. We also see that, if great new undertakings enter the lives of many men, a new community of hope, unified by the common relations of individual members to the same future events, may be, upon occasion, very rapidly constituted, even in the midst of great revolutions" (1913, 53). Steinbeck saw communities of hope emerging even in the midst of the Dirty Thirties and the Great Depression. Similarly, years earlier, Royce noticed that miners seemingly only intent on finding gold and then moving on had found themselves drawn into community life and social affairs: "Plainly the first business of a new placer mining community was not to save itself socially, since only fortune could detain even for a week its roving members, but to get gold in the most peaceful and rapid way possible. Yet this general absolution from arduous social duties could not be considered as continuing indefinitely. The time must come when, if the nature of the place permitted steady work, men must prepare to dwell together in numbers, and for a long period. Then began the genuine social problems" (1886, 278).

As already noted, throughout his career Royce sought to enumerate the conditions of the existence and well-being of a community. Initially, Royce found that there were three conditions needed for community life. First is the ability to extend one's sense of self: "The power of an individual self to extend his life, in ideal fashion, so as to regard it as including past and future events which lie far away in time, and which he does not now personally remember." Second, a plurality of selves must engage each other in communication: this is "the fact that there are in the social world a number of distinct selves capable of social communication, and, in general, engaged in communication." And third, an ongoing, experiential real-life grounding is needed: "The fact that the ideally extended past and future selves of the members include at least some events which are, for all these selves, identical. This third condition is the one which furnishes the most exact, the most widely variable, and the most important of the motives which warrant us calling a community a real unit " (1913, 253, 255–56).

In abstract language, the conditions requisite for community life are the ability to achieve the viewpoint of another and the gift of appreciating another's hopes and desires. For Royce, not only is shared interpretation the essential constituent of community; it is the very foundation of reality. That is, what is real in Royce's metaphysics are neither external, given realities nor private, conscious lives. Instead, he maintains that reality itself *is* publicly shared interpretations of experiences. Moreover, since such interpretations are in process, reality, too, is a living, evolving (or devolving) continuity that members of a community share and constitute. Royce puts it this way in "The Community and the Time-Process": "A true community is essentially a product of a time-process. A community has a past and will have a future. Its more or less conscious history, real or ideal, is a part of its very essence.

A community requires for its existence a history and is greatly aided in its consciousness by a memory" (1913, 35).

In the last section of *The Problem of Christianity*, Royce revisits and enriches his analysis of the conditions of community. This religious meditation recasts the question, asking what a community must do to become explicitly conscious of its own life.

Royce proposes that the conditions for community consciousness are (1) the ability of participating selves to extend themselves from a shared past and to an anticipated future, (2) communication that overcomes isolation and separation, and (3) the achievement of a common interpretation of shared events (past deeds and future hopes). The second and third conditions, communication and shared interpretation, enable mere members to become active, cooperative, and productive agents who foster the community's life. Thus enabled, each partner in a community has the right to claim that "my work and my life have become *our* work and *our* lives." Royce explains that for members of genuine community, "This activity which we perform together, this work of ours, its past, its future, its sequence, its order, its sense—all these enter into my life, and are the life of my own self writ large" (1913, 86).

In this enriched schema Royce captures the dynamic vitality of people energized by a devotion to a cause: each individual's understanding of her community's life and projects is secure and sound enough that she can identify, direct, and perform the community's deeds. Trusted members of a genuine community, though acting freely as autonomous agents, at the same time faithfully extend a community's projects. The eventual result is that love of and loyalty to the community sustain its well-being so that both individuals and their communities flourish.

Royce thereby stresses that in a genuine community, love of another is expanded into the love of the community itself, and loyalty to a cause is transformed into a loyalty to loyalty. Royce offers very concrete advice on this matter: "Find your own cause, your interesting, fascinating, personally engrossing cause; serve it with all your might and soul and strength; but so choose your cause, and so serve it, that thereby you show forth your loyalty to loyalty, so that because of your choice and service of your cause, there is a maximum of increase of loyalty amongst your fellow-men" (1908, 65). Steinbeck not only agrees but finds that the community worthiest of our loyal devotion is the human community, the whole human family. As Ma Joad puts it at the end of *The Grapes of Wrath* after the flood experience, a need to respond to anyone in need becomes a given.[2] This felt obligation is beautifully embodied in the unforgettable final scene in the novel in which Rose of Sharon breast-feeds a dying man, a man who is a stranger to both the Joads and the Wainrights.

Notes

This chapter is a slightly recast version of "Creating Community: John Steinbeck's *The Grapes of Wrath* and Josiah Royce's Philosophy of Community," *The Steinbeck Newsletter* 11.1 (Summer 1998): 4–7.

   1. See McDermott (1985) for an excellent introductory essay on Royce. For more on Royce's biography and philosophy, see Clendenning (1999).

   2. For more on Steinbeck's duty to share ethic, see my "John Steinbeck's lower-case utopia: Basic Human Needs, a Duty to Share, and the Good Life."

Works Cited

Clendenning, John. 1999. *The Life and Thought of Josiah Royce: Revised and Expanded Edition.* Nashville, TN: Vanderbilt University Press.

Dooley, Patrick K. 2005. "John Steinbeck's lower-case utopia: Basic Human Needs, a Duty to Share, and the Good Life." In *The Moral Philosophy of John Steinbeck.* Edited by Stephen K. George. 3–20. Lanham, MD: Scarecrow Press.

McDermott, John J. 1985. "Josiah Royce's Philosophy of Community." In *American Philosophy.* Edited by Marcus G. Singer. 153–76. Cambridge: Cambridge University Press.

Royce, Josiah. 1886. *California: A Study of American Character.* Boston: Houghton Mifflin.

———. 1908. *The Philosophy of Loyalty.* Nashville, TN: Vanderbilt University Press, 1995.

———. 1913. *The Problem of Christianity.* New York: Macmillan.

———. 1916. *The Hope of the Great Community.* New York: Books for Library Press. 1967.

Steinbeck, John. 1939. *The Grapes of Wrath.* New York: Penguin Books, 1992.

17

Human Dignity, the Need for Community, and "the Duty of the Writer to Lift Up"
Steinbeck's Philosophy of Work

> *I have finally found my pipes in the stuff that was sent out and they taste unbelievably good. They taste like work.*
> —*John Steinbeck to Webster Street*

When John Steinbeck's oeuvre is examined with an eye to his philosophy, three concerns emerge as central: the dignity of the person, the indispensability of human community, and the duty of the writer to inspire amelioration. Undergirding these three elements is Steinbeck's fundamental philosophical notion: work. No theme is more prevalent in the journals that he kept during the writing of *The Grapes of Wrath* (published as *Working Days: The Journal of The Grapes of Wrath*) and *East of Eden* (published as *Journal of a Novel: The East of Eden Letters*) and the nearly nine hundred letters published in *Steinbeck: A Life in Letters.* All his life, but especially during the one hundred days when he composed his masterpiece, Steinbeck was consumed by the discipline, the routine, the process, the rewards, and the value of work. All these elements are touched upon in two entries (from July to September 1940) on the writing of *The Grapes of Wrath:*

> In writing, habit seems to be a much stronger force than either willpower or inspiration. Consequently there must be some little quality of fierceness until the habit pattern of a certain number of words is established. . . . The forced work is sometimes better than the easy, but there is no

rule about it. Sometimes they come out better than other times and that is all one can say. . . . But one can never be sure, not even for a week. So I go on with my daily stint. . . . Oh! Lord, how good this paper feels under this pen. I can sit here writing and the words slipping out like grapes out of their skins and I feel so good doing it. . . . Here is a strange thing—almost like a secret. You start out putting words down and there are three things—you, the pen, and the page. Then gradually the three things merge until they are all one and you feel about the page as you do your arm. Only you love it more than you love your arm. (1990, 118–19, 121)

A half-dozen years earlier, he commented in a letter, "I work because I know it gives me pleasure to work. It is as simple as that and I don't require any other reasons. I am losing a sense of self to a marked degree and that is a pleasant thing. . . . I am happier simply to do the work and to take the reward at the end of the day that is given for a day of honest work" (1975, 87).

As a matter of fact, he often celebrated the pleasure of hard work: "Work is still fun and still work. It hasn't ever gotten any easier" (1975, 273). Then, too, he describes his own work as therapy, for "work is about the most things I do now. There's a fine safety in it. . . . Work saves me a lot" (223, 229). This is also seen with Doc working in his lab, when the narrator observes: "The making of the embryo series gave him pleasure. He had done it hundreds of times before, and he felt a safety in the known thing—no speculation here. He did certain things and certain other things followed. There is comfort in routine. . . . As he worked, a benign feeling came over him" (1954, 92). Similarly Steinbeck describes work as a palliative—"Hard work is the thing to kill sorrow" (1938, 87)—and as a gift—"One day Samuel strained his back lifting a bale of hay, and it hurt his feelings more than his back, for he could not imagine a life in which Sam Hamilton was not privileged to lift a bale of hay" (1952, 253). Steinbeck even remarks on the taste of work. While their house in New York was being renovated, Steinbeck moved his writing of *The Wayward Bus* to the basement. In all the moving back and forth to Webster Street, he wrote, "I finally found my pipes in the stuff that was sent out and they taste unbelievably delicious. They taste like work" (1975, 288).

Steinbeck's stance on work is many layered. Work, per se, has intrinsic value as an end in itself. Humans need work, for through it we impose our order on the material world. In *Pastures of Heaven*, Steinbeck writes of George Battle's beautiful farm. The trees in the orchard were trim and groomed, each on a counterpart of its fellows. "The vegetables grew crisp and green in their line-straight rows. George cared for his house and kept a flower garden in front of it. The upper story of the house had never been lived in. This farm was a poem by the inarticulate man" (1932, 6). (This is a striking recast of Emerson's rhetorical question in *Nature*: "What is a farm but a mute gospel?") Analogously, Steinbeck describes his literary work in terms of establishing order and creating patterns: "For a novelist is a rearranger of nature so that it makes an understandable pattern. . . . In the rearrangement of life called literature, the writer is the less valuable and interesting in direct relation to his goodness of taste. . . . His job then is to try to reassemble life into some kind of order" (1975, 554, 436, 592).

Secondly, still on the intrinsic level, humans need work, for it releases energy and expresses their vitality. In *The Grapes of Wrath*, Al, Tom, and Pa Joad's deep yearning to work could not be more tangible: "Oughta get some sleep. . . . But, hell, I can't keep my han's out of a tore-down car. Jus' got to git in. . . . They ain't nothin' I love like the guts of a engine," says Al (1939, 348). "Tom hefted the pick. 'Jumping Jesus! If she don't feel good!'. . . . 'Damn it,' he said, 'a pick is a nice tool (*umph*), if you don' fight it (*umph*). You an' the pick (*umph*) workin' together (*umph*)'" (405, 407). And later Pa says, "By God, I'd like to get my hands on some cotton! There's work, I un'erstan'" (551).

The sheer variety of workers—sharecroppers, hired hands, tractor drivers, car mechanics, junkyard boys, truckers, cooks, waitresses, fruit harvesters, pipeline layers—described in *The Grapes of Wrath* supports Steinbeck's generalization in chapter 14 that humans can be defined as workers: "The last clear definite function of man—muscles aching to work, minds aching to create beyond the single need—this is man. To build a wall, to build a house, a dam, and in the wall and house and dam to put something of Manself . . . to take hard muscles from the lifting, to take the clear lines and form from conceiving. For man, unlike any other thing organic or inorganic in the universe, grows beyond his work, walks up the stairs of his concepts, emerges ahead of his accomplishments" (204). Casy makes the same point more graphically: "These here folks want to live decent and bring up their kids decent. . . . They wanta eat an' get drunk and work. An' that's it—they wanta jus' fling their goddam muscles aroun' and get tired" (341).

Steinbeck was an incredibly hard worker, one who could see value in work even when its eventual result was uncertain. During his first year (1927) as a winter caretaker at Lake Tahoe, he worked daily (and at the end of each session even tallied the number of words he wrote) on the manuscript of his first novel, *Cup of Gold*. He also worked on drafts of short stories. In the span of a couple of months in 1938, he wrote a nearly 60,000-word draft of a satirical treatment of the plight of migrant workers, *L'Affair Lettuceberg*. He would destroy this and then start over with what was to be his finest novel, *The Grapes of Wrath*. In some cases, then, his hard work was mostly for its own sake. During the writing of *The Wayward Bus,* he wrote from Webster Street, "I don't have any other gifts but I can work and if it doesn't amount to a damn it was still hard work" (1975, 302). In this case, his suspicions about his current project were correct. Earlier, however, very hard at work and almost finished with *The Grapes of Wrath,* he mistakenly advised both his editor, Pascal Covici, and his agent, Elizabeth Otis, to arrange a small first edition, for "this will not be a popular book" (173).

Conversely, when humans are unable to work, their sense of self-worth, their self-respect, and their dignity quickly erode. Whenever Steinbeck was between books or temporarily could not work, he lapsed into depression. Not working, he explains, "was some of the hardest work I did, sitting still in a busy world, aching for nothingness or the meaning that could only grow out of non-participation" (1975, 625). Or, during a pause in the writing of *East of Eden,* he comments, "I am a little drained. But that's all right. One is never drained by work but only by idleness. Lack of work is the most enervating thing in the world" (1969, 115). After his heart attack, when he was advised to take it easy, he retorted, "That's not the way it is at all. That's the thing which makes invalids. It's not taking it easy that matters but taking it right and true. The mind does not tire from true work nor does the body moving efficiently" (1975, 657).

"True work" for Steinbeck often meant strenuous physical labor; even when it paid poorly, he still deemed it honorable. Early on he supported himself with manual labor as a ditch digger, surveyor, ranch hand, broncobuster, tree feller, wood splitter, and as a hod carrier and construction worker in the building of the original Madison Square Garden in New York City. Later when he was an established author, and still later after attaining best-seller celebrity, Steinbeck regularly returned to manual labor to recenter his life. Benson, commenting on Steinbeck's move back to California in 1948 after his separation from Gwyn, notes: "Steinbeck spent the first month and a half working to restore the house, cleaning and painting and doing repairs, and working in the garden, trimming all the overgrown and neglected shrubbery, mulching and fertilizing, and then planting. He did these things almost automatically, depending on the hard physical labor to help bring his life back into equilibrium. . . . But moving rocks around made his hands and arms ache, and that felt good, and checking his garden each day, noting the new buds and fighting off the pests, gave his mind occupation" (1984, 623). His direct and regular acquaintance with ordinary work equipped him to vividly and accurately portray the ordinary people who populate his works.

Beyond its intrinsic worth, of course, work has instrumental value as a means: if you don't work, you can't eat, and if you don't find work, you cannot provide for your family. This was the prime motive for the dust-bowl migration to California, "As time went on, there were fewer farms. The little farmers moved into town for a while and exhausted their credit, exhausted their friends, their relatives. And they too went on the highways. And the roads were crowded with men ravenous for work, murderous for work" (1939, 387). The first morning the Joads settle in the government camp, Tom is invited to eat with the Wallace family, who have found work. Wilkie says, "We been eatin' good for twelve days now. Never missed a meal in twelve days—none of us. Workin' an' getting' our pay an' eatin'" (397). After breakfast, they invite Tom to come along to see if he can find work, too. As they walk to the job, Tom asks about their car. Timothy says angrily, "No, we ain't got no car. We sol' our car. Had to. Run outa food, run outa ever'thing. Couldn' git no job" (400). Why, then, wonders Tom, are they sharing work? "'Why in hell you gonna get me on? I'll make it shorter. What you cuttin' your own throat for?' Timothy shook his head slowly, 'I dunno. Got no sense, I guess'" (401). Steinbeck's paradoxical pairing of the painful experience of knowing "you can't eat if you don't work" with the foolishly benevolent impulse of sharing scarce work neatly mirrors *The Grapes of Wrath*'s gritty depiction of a cruel, failed economic system alongside its unshaken trust in the goodwill, energy, and reflex generosity of ordinary people, "jus fellas." Ma Joad, however, sees no paradox here. When she shops at the company store at the peach orchard, she is short a dime for sugar. The company clerk gives her the sugar and takes a dime out of his own pocket. Leaving the store, she says, "I'm learnin' one thing good. . . . Learnin' it all a time, ever'day. If you're in trouble or hurt or need—go to poor people. They're the only ones that'll help—the only ones" (513–14).

As long as the poor can find some work and can share the little they have, they maintain dignity and self-worth. In chapter 2 of *The Harvest Gypsies*, Steinbeck chronicles the stages of the erosion of self-respect. He begins by describing a family, newly arrived to the squatters' camp, that has recently suffered severe reverses: "Five years ago this family had fifty acres of land and a thousand dollars in the bank. The wife belonged to a sewing circle and the man was a member of the grange. They raised chickens, pigs, pigeons and vegetables and fruit for their own use; and their land produced the tall corn of the middle west. Now they have nothing" (1936, 27). Still they are resilient, and at least initially their self-respect remains intact. "There is still pride in this family"—the children are put into schools, the mother tries to maintain a healthy diet, and the father works to provide decent housing and basic sanitation, "but he will only do things like that this year. He is a newcomer and his spirit and decency and his sense of his own dignity have not been quite wiped out. Next year he will be like his next door neighbor" (27). The decline of the next year will be brought on by scarce work and a progressively poorer diet (detailed in chapter 5): "This is what the man in the tent will be in six months; what the man in the paper house with its peaked roof will be in a year, after his house has washed down and his children have sickened or died, after the loss of dignity and spirit have cut him down to a kind of subhumanity" (30–31).

The other mainspring of human dignity in Steinbeck's philosophy requires opportunity for democratic participation. Migrant workers and, to an even greater extent, the dust-bowl refugees are disenfranchised: "And there is another difference between their old life and the new. They have come from the little farm districts where democracy was not only possible but inevitable, where popular government, whether practiced in the Grange, in church organization or in local government, was the responsibility of every man. And they have come into the country where, because of the movement necessary to make a living, they are not allowed any vote whatever, but are rather considered a properly unprivileged class" (1936, 23). Hence, the jobless and the communityless are robbed of human dignity. Steinbeck's position is clear and specific:

> In this series the word "dignity" has been used several times. It has been used not as some attitude of self-importance, but simply as a register of a man's responsibility to the community. A man herded about, surrounded by guards, starved and forced to live in filth loses his dignity; that is, he loses his valid position in regard to society, and consequently his whole ethics toward society. Nothing is a better example of this than the prison, where the men are reduced to no dignity and where crimes and infractions are constant.
>
> We regard this destruction of dignity, then, as one of the most regrettable results of the migrant's life, since it does reduce his responsibility and does make him a sullen outcast who will strike at our Government in any way that occurs to him. (39)

Given Steinbeck's philosophy of human dignity, his rehabilitation remedies—decent living conditions, work, and democratic participation—are predictable. The steps of his strategy, however, are somewhat surprising. Economic matters are not the first priority; psychological nostrums, encouragement, and reaffirmation are. The dispirited and the downtrodden—for example, *Of Mice and Men*'s dispossessed bindle stiffs, or *In Dubious Battle*'s marginalized, badly organized, exploited, and/or unemployed workers—first need to feel like persons who can hold their heads up. On the way to the government camp, Tom says, "Ma's going to like this place. She ain't been treated decent in a long time" (1939, 393). The first morning after the camp manager called on her at their family's tent, Ma recounts his visit to Rose of Sharon: "'He come an' set an' drank coffee, an' he says, 'Mrs. Joad' this, an' 'Mrs. Joad' that—an' 'How you getting' on, Mrs. Joad?' She stopped and sighed. 'Why, I feel like people again'" (420). A bath and, even more basically, food are the next steps in the recovery-of-humanity process. Jessie, head of the Ladies Committee, scolds a newcomer, Mrs. Joyce:

> "Now you hol' up your head," Jessie said. "That ain't no crime. You jes' waltz right over t' the Weedpatch store an' git you some groceries."
> "We ain't never took no charity," Mrs. Joyce said.
> "This ain't charity, an you know it," Jessie raged. "We had all that out. They ain't no charity in this here camp." (431)

What the Ladies Committee explains to all newcomers is that they are expected to become contributing members to camp life and camp upkeep. But, perhaps most significant and most telling from Steinbeck's vantage point, they need to become involved in establishing camp rules. Precisely on this point, before he began the government-camp chapter of *The Grapes of Wrath* (chapter 22), Steinbeck notes in *Working Days,* "Got to get [the Joads] out of Hooverville and into a federal camp for they must learn something of democratic procedure" (1990, 64).

Steinbeck's stress on democratic participation is remarkable. The first task of camp managers and member committees is to recover residents' sense of self-worth. He argues that getting newcomers meaningfully involved in self-government is the most effective and the quickest way for them to recover personhood: "From the first, the intent of the management has been to restore the dignity and decency that has been kicked out of the migrants by their intolerable mode of life" (1936, 39)

Steinbeck's rehabilitation prescription, then, follows distinct stages. The initial catalyst of self-restoration is becoming enfranchised. Second, restored persons help themselves via work. Third, shared work regenerates families and communities so that poverty and social dislocation can be ameliorated. Steinbeck's task as a writer is strikingly similar to "Hol' up your head," the already-discussed exhortation delivered by the Ladies Committee in *The Grapes of Wrath*: "It is the duty of the writer to lift up, to extend, to encourage. If the written word has contributed anything at all to our developing species and our half developed culture, it is this: Great writing has been a staff to lean on, a mother to consult, a wisdom to pick up stumbling folly, a strength in weakness and a courage to support sick cowardice" (1969, 115–16). The presentation address that preceded the award of the Nobel Prize to Steinbeck stated, "With your most distinctive works you have become a teacher of goodwill and charity, a defender of human values, which can well be said to correspond to the proper idea of the Nobel Prize" (Österling 1962, 919). In his acceptance speech, Steinbeck concurred: "The ancient commission of the writer has not changed. He is charged with exposing our many grievous faults and failures, with dredging up to the light our dark and dangerous dreams, *for the purpose of improvement.* . . . I hold that a writer who does not passionately believe *in the perfectibility of man* has no dedication nor any membership in literature" (1975, 898, emphasis added).

Steinbeck's melioristic and humanistic outlook philosophically maintains that the future of the world is neither optimistically nor pessimistically fated. Like William James, who coined the term "meliorism," Steinbeck casts his vote on the side of an improvable future. "I have too a conviction that a new world is growing under the old, the way a new finger nail grows under a bruised one" (1975, 194). Making the same point more abstractly, Steinbeck offers the following generalization about humans and their world: "Hope is a diagnostic human trait, and this simple cortex symptom seems to be a prime factor in our inspection of our universe. For hope implies a change from a present bad condition to a future better one. . . . For if ever any man were deeply and unconsciously sure that his future would be no better than his past, he might deeply wish to cease to live. And out of this therapeutic poultice we build our iron teleologies and twist the tide pools and stars into the pattern" (1941, 820). Again like James's, Steinbeck's philosophy is radically humanistic: future outcomes are in human hands. If we fail, humans suffer, but when we succeed, our victories improve, ameliorate, and enhance human dignity.

Steinbeck's philosophy of human dignity, then, revolves around work, decent living conditions, and social standing in a community. A close look at the opening pages of *The Wayward Bus* reveals how systematically Steinbeck had worked out the stages of personhood validation. Initially, Juan's hired helper Pimples gains a sense of self-worth working with Juan. But Pimples is no common laborer. As a skilled worker on equal work footing with the boss, he feels a sense of comradeship that enriches his enjoyment of work. Steinbeck writes, "The two men worked together well. Each understood what was to be done. Each did his piece. Pimples lay on his back too, tightening the housing nuts, and in the teamwork a good feeling came to him" (1947, 18). Readers of *The Grapes of Wrath* will remember similar instances of camaraderie born of a sense of shared work. This occurs, for example, when Tom and Casy replace the connecting rod of the Wilson's car in chapter 16, and when Tom and Al fix a flat tire in chapter 26.

For Steinbeck, the self-esteem gained from work and the sense of well-being that comes with fellowship are publicly sanctioned by way of name recognition. Recall that Ma Joad began to feel like a person again when the camp manager accepted her hospitality, shared a cup of coffee, and called her by name. In *The Wayward Bus,* the same sort of transformation is poignantly described in a conversation between Juan Chicoy and his helper as they repair the gearbox of the old bus:

> "Mr. Chicoy, could we fix it—I mean—could you fix it so you don't call me Pimples any more?"
> "What's your name?" he asked roughly.
> "Ed," said Pimples. "Ed Carson, distant relative of Kit Carson. Before I got these in grammar school, why, they used to call me Kit."

After a few more minutes of work on the bus, Juan says,

> "Kit, wipe your hands and see if Alice has got any coffee ready, will you?"
> Pimples went toward the lunchroom. . . . He stood there for a moment, holding his breath. He was shaking all over in a kind of a chill. (1947, 19–20)

It is through memorable scenes that Steinbeck impresses his humanistic philosophy of amelioration upon the minds and hearts of his readers. By way of conclusion, then, we can do no better than to revisit a scene early in *The Grapes of Wrath* that summarizes Steinbeck's views on human dignity, community, work, and democratic participation.

The night before the Joads begin their exodus to California, as soon as Pa, Uncle Connie, Rose of Sharon, Winfield, and Ruth return to the home place after selling the farm machinery they cannot take along, "Without any signal the family gathered by the truck, and the congress, the family government, went into session. . . . This was the new hearth, the living center of the family; half passenger car and half truck, high-sided and clumsy" (1939, 135–36). The men squat in a circle with the women and children standing behind them, and "only the preacher was not there. He, out of delicacy, was sitting on the ground behind the house. He was a good preacher and knew his people" (136). "Tom went on, 'I'd like to say—well, that preacher—he wants to go along'" (138). There is some debate about enough room, enough money, enough food, which Ma silences by saying, "It ain't kin we? It's will we?" (139).

> Pa looked at the face of each one for dissent, and then he said, "Want to call 'im over, Tommy? If he's goin', he ought ta be here." . . .
>
> "Callin me?" Casy asked.
>
> "Yeah. We think long as you're goin' with us, you ought to be over with us, helpin' to figger things out."
>
> Casy got to his feet. He knew the government of families, and he knew he had been taken into the family. Indeed his position was eminent, for Uncle John moved sideways, leaving a space between Pa and himself for the preacher. (140)

This scene so dramatically captures the essentials of Steinbeck's humanistic philosophy that no need exists to rehearse the claims or arguments of his outlook.

Notes

This chapter is a slightly recast version of "Human Dignity, Work, the Need for Community and 'The duty of the writer to lift up': John Steinbeck's Philosophy," *Steinbeck Studies* 15 (2002): 21–25.

WORKS CITED

Benson, Jackson. 1984. *The True Adventures of John Steinbeck, Writer.* New York: Viking.

Österling, Anders. 1962. "Nobel Prize Presentation Address to John Steinbeck." Quoted in Benson, *The True Adventures of John Steinbeck.*

Steinbeck, John. 1932. *The Pastures of Heaven.* In *John Steinbeck: Novels and Stories, 1932–1937.* New York: Library of America, 1994.

———. 1936. *The Harvest Gypsies: On the Road to The Grapes of Wrath.* Berkeley, CA: Heyday Books, 1988.

———. 1938. *The Long Valley.* New York: Penguin, 1995.

———. 1939. *The Grapes of Wrath.* New York: Penguin, 1976.

———. 1941. *The Log from the Sea of Cortez.* In *John Steinbeck: The Grapes of Wrath and Other Writings: 1936–1941.* New York: Library of America, 1996.

———. 1947. *The Wayward Bus.* New York: Penguin, 1979.

———. 1952. *East of Eden.* New York: Penguin, 1992.

———. 1954. *Sweet Tuesday.* New York: Penguin, 1996.

———. 1969. *Journal of A Novel: The East of Eden Letters.* New York: Penguin.

———. 1975. *Steinbeck: A Life in Letters.* Edited by Elaine Steinbeck and Robert Wallsten. New York: Viking, 1989.

———. 1990. *Working Days: The Journals of The Grapes of Wrath, 1938–1941.* Edited by Robert DeMott. New York: Penguin.

18

Work, Friendship, and Community in Maclean's *A River Runs Through It*

> *Working with hands is one of our deepest and most beautiful*
> *characteristics. I think the most beautiful parts of the human*
> *body are the hands of certain men and women. I can't keep my*
> *eyes off them. I was brought up to believe that hands were the*
> *instrument of the mind. Even doing simple things. I still look*
> *pretty good with an axe. My father was very stylish with any tool*
> *he worked with. Yeah, the fishing rod also. He was just beautiful,*
> *pick up a four-ounce rod and throw that line across the Blackfoot*
> *River. It was just something beautiful to behold.*
> —*Norman Maclean*

A River Runs Through It and Other Stories, Norman Maclean's slim fictional oeuvre—two novellas and a short story—has been increasingly read and commented upon by scholars in the last dozen years.[1] Still, beyond Maclean devotees, most people are probably only familiar with *A River Runs Through It,* either the 1976 novel or the 1992 film version directed by Robert Redford.[2] In this best known of Maclean's stories, three philosophical and theological concerns propel his narrative: queries about the presence and hiddenness of God, how humans can learn to appreciate the goodness and beauty of the natural world, and how we should align our lives to nature's patterns. Concretely, Maclean probes whether we can understand and help one another and whether we can love others while acknowledging faults, both ours and theirs. His repeated use of the words "beauty" and "grace," and especially "design" and "pattern," underscores his abiding belief that the natural furnishes the standard of excellence; furthermore, the natural environment we inhabit provides a rational, predictable, and coherent locus for human activity. While the growing body of secondary comment has focused on religious themes in Maclean's third story, *A River Runs Through It*,[3] his keen examination of the dynamics of humans working together and his astute exploration of the catalysts of community building in his first two works, "Logging, Pimping and 'Your Pal, Jim'" and *USFA 1919: The Ranger, the Cook and a Hole in the Sky*, have not been scrutinized. In what follows, after I analyze Maclean's views on work, friendship, and community, I show that when the California-born philosopher Josiah Royce's theorizing about community formation, with its resultant ethic of loyalty, is overlaid upon what Maclean has dramatized, a fruitful cross-fertilization of literature and philosophy results.

For Maclean, the obvious (and indeed the primary) community is a family who worships, works, and plays together. This so much the case that a family who prays and plays together is the leitmotif of *A River Runs Through It*. Anyone familiar with the wonderful and memorable opening line of that story knows, however, that separating playing from praying for the Maclean family involves making a distinction without a difference: "In our family, there was no clear line between religion and fly fishing" (1976, 1).

In the context of family life, Maclean's masterpiece explores fly-fishing and religion. The setting is decisive, given his argument that family membership is crucial to the personal flourishing and self-definition that culminates in an enriched shared living experience. Some years before, Maclean had laid the groundwork for his linkage of family, shared recreation, and religion. In his first two stories, he explored how working together can also be a catalyst for self-discovery and community building. In the Scholastic medieval view, grace builds on nature. This is a schema endorsed by the sequence of Maclean's stories. That is, group and self-identity based on work and shared interests in his first two stories are enriched by family ties and then elevated by religion in his third.

"Your Pal, Jim" follows the young Maclean in his struggle to survive a summer contest of wills with a sadistic sawing partner, his pal Jim, who does his level best to push Maclean beyond his breaking point. After his first summer of logging, Maclean agrees to work gyppo with Jim: "To gyppo, which wasn't meant to be a nice-sounding word and could be used as either a noun or a verb, was to be paid by the number of thousands of board feet you cut in a day. Naturally, you chose to gyppo only if you thought you could beat wages and the men who worked for wages. As I said, Jim had talked me into being his partner for the next summer, and we were going to gyppo and make big money" (107). Besides the money, the attraction for Maclean is personal, as "I suppose I was flattered by being asked to be the partner of the best sawyer in camp. It was a long way, though, from being all flattery. I also knew I was being challenged" (107). The challenge aspect of the partnership has sound footing based on Maclean's understanding of the value of work, his appreciation of fine tools, and his admiration for skilled labor. After only a few days, both partners agreed "it was good to be back at work" (110), and Maclean's estimate of his partner's stature was confirmed. "It didn't take long to find out that he was the best lumberjack in camp. He was probably the best with the saw and ax, and he worked with a kind of speed that was part ferocity" (106). As for appreciating craft and tools, Maclean gives a lengthy description of Jim's logging outfit, paying special attention to the boots that were essential to his work. Indeed, Maclean pauses to explain for the uninitiated how (and why) loggers' boots are fitted with "caulks, or 'corks' as the jacks called them; they were long and sharp enough to hold to a heavily barked log or, tougher still, to one that was dead and had no bark on it. . . . The design started with a row of blunt sturdy, hobnails around the edges . . . then inside came the battle-field of corks. . . . Actually, it was a beautiful if somewhat primitive design and had many uses" (109). Here and, as we shall see, in his second and third stories, Maclean is readily attuned to the beauty of and value in tools, noting that "the men worked mostly on two-man crosscut saws that were things of beauty, and the highest paid man in camp was the man who delicately filed and set them" (107).[4] Skilled artisans, especially when working together, also gain Maclean's aesthetic notice. Sawing, for instance, "is something beautiful when you are working rhythmically together—at times, you forget what you are doing and get lost in abstractions of motion and power" (113). Further, smooth teamwork does not just happen but has to be orchestrated through internalized, unspoken rules dealing with pace, joint tasks, and turn taking: "Sawyers have many little but nevertheless almost sacred rules of work in order to function as a team" (114).

Though Maclean takes satisfaction in keeping up with Jim's manic pace, and though he occasionally enjoys the work, inevitably the flattery component of his motivation to gyppo with Jim surfaces. They are not really a team; competition undermines their partnership and sabotages their friendship. In order to ward off Jim's killer pace, Maclean breaks the rules of work that sustain the rhythms that make their sawing pleasurable, fluent, and efficient:

"Most of the time I followed his stroke; I had to, but I would pick periods when I would not pull the saw to me at quite the speed or distance he was pulling it back to him. Just staying slightly off the beat, not being quite so noticeable that he would yell but still letting him know what I was doing. To make sure he knew, I would suddenly go back to his stroke. . . . Most of the time I took a lot of comfort from the feeling that some of this was getting to him" (113–14). The tension that develops between the two partners leads to a friendship-eroding silence. "Slowly we became silent, and silence itself is an enemy to friendship; when we came back to camp each went his own way, and within a week we weren't speaking to each other" (111). At the story's end, before Maclean returns to graduate school, he runs into Jim in town and they have a couple of drinks. When they go to meet Jim's new partners in his win- tertime pimping occupation, their conversation is stilted: "I was interested, too, in the way Jim pictured himself and me to his women—always as friendly working partners talking over some technical sawing problems. . . . I can tell you that outside of the first few days of the summer we didn't engage in any such friendly talk, and any sawyer can tell you that the technical stuff he had us saying about sawing may sound impressive to whores but doesn't make any sense to sawyers, and had to be invented by him" (121). Even after a whole summer, then, Jim is still not aware that theirs had not been a real friendship but only a work relationship. From the narrator's perspective, however, the "partner" in the "Dear partner" salutation and the "pal" in the "Your Pal" closing of Jim's off-season letters are clearly ironic.

Maclean's second story, *USFS 1919,* also pays attention to becoming skilled with special tools and working together. In this story, though, the forest service crew succeeds in forging genuine friendships through their summer work experiences. Maclean's story opens with a seventeen-year-old narrator Maclean beginning his summer job with the forest service. He is playing cribbage with his hero and mentor, Bill, who is good at almost everything but card playing, so the narrator tries to get the cook, Hawkins, to join in. The cook always refuses. "I never play cards against the men I work with" (132). Maclean's dislike of the cook eventually gets him exiled to a mountaintop as a solitary fire lookout. When Maclean rejoins "the regular crew," the cook has revealed that he is a cardsharp. The remainder of the story plays out a scheme to bankroll the cook. They are confident he will easily double their whole summer wages in a poker blowout at the Oxford saloon in the town of Hamilton, Montana, just before the crew disbands for the winter. The poker scheme, however, disintegrates into a barroom brawl, and each crew member's share of the wager (half a month's wages, about $30.00) comes to a disappointing $7.20 in winnings.

When the narrator Maclean initially joined the forest service summer crew, he became part of a working group that let him contribute to a larger reality and thereby gave him an identity. Maclean's linkage of self-identity, work, and community departs from the eighteenth-and nineteenth-century American transcendentalists' theory of personal identity that supposed a preexistent self waiting to be discovered in solitude, ideally in nature. Instead, Maclean's espousal of a contextual, public, process-oriented theory of human person-hood endorses the position of Maclean's University of Chicago colleague, the philosopher George Herbert Mead.[5] Mead argued that we achieve selfhood by interacting with and gaining definition from others. Moreover, Mead followed the lead of another one-time University of Chicago professor, John Dewey.[6] Dewey argued that our sense of uniqueness, identity, and, ironically, independence is based upon *shared* attributes. That is, a cluster of like-minded individuals who share our particular interests, skills, hobbies, and biographical and geographical backgrounds best accounts for personal individuality.

In terms of groups, interests, and activities, what individuates the young narrator of *USFS 1919* is that he likes the outdoors, works on a forest service crew, and has a "favorite indoor pastime of the woods" (131), playing cribbage. Though there are lots of cribbage and other card games in the story, and though the narrator paints an alluring picture of living in a bracing climate amid spectacular mountains and valleys, Maclean is emphatic that the key component that constitutes the narrator's summer experience is work. Not only does work provide young Maclean with self-esteem, but those he works with become the community that defines the person he has become. As we shall now see, Josiah Royce, a colleague of the founders of classical American pragmatism, C. S. Peirce and William James, took as his vocation the task of understanding the same dynamics of work and community building that Maclean's stories dramatize.

As already noted in chapter 16, there was a clear biographical basis for Royce's interest in community building as he followed his parents from one boomtown to the next in the 1849 California gold rush. Young Royce was puzzled that, though the town's location was not new—indeed the artifacts and relics of past occupants were still to be found—his elders spoke of the current resettlement as a "new community." He surmised, then, that nonphysical conceptual and spiritual factors must be the constitutive elements in community building. Further, he noticed that once a community's life is ongoing, loyalty to its enterprises becomes its members' fundamental value. However, since not all enterprises are wholesome, not all loyalties are admirable, so Royce's further theorizing sought to discover the characteristics that distinguish worthy loyalties from counterfeit ones. Likewise, the Maclean narrator of *USFS 1919* has to learn how to separate loyalty in service to genuine causes from a false fidelity to bogus ones. Maclean's first novelette, then, examines how a sense of group identity emerges through work and explores whether loyalty to the crew, intensified in crises such as fighting big forest fires, can be further galvanized by a crusade as they vow to "clean out the town" of Hamilton at summer's end.

Maclean's description adheres to Royce's prescription: shared tasks enable and enhance community life. At the beginning of the summer Maclean sees labor simplistically: "In the mountains you work to live" (128). But even at that stage, he admires his head ranger and mentor: "Bill was a major artist" (131). Bill Bell has earned near-universal adulation because he is skilled at so many kinds of work: "Bill was built to fit his hands. He was big all over. Primarily he was a horseman, and he needed an extra large horse. He was not a slender cowboy of the movies and the plains. He was a horseman of the mountains. He could swing an ax or pull a saw, run a transit and build trail, walk all day if he had to, put on climbing spurs and string number nine telephone wire, and he wasn't a bad cook" (128). Maclean's gradual appreciation of the value of work progresses to the point that he can see work as art. He is especially impressed with Bill's skill as a packer:

Every profession has a pinnacle to its art. In the hospital it is the brain or heart surgeon, and in the sawmill it is the sawyer who with squinting eyes makes the first major cut that turns a log into boards. In the early Forest Service, our major artist was the packer, as it usually had been in worlds where there are no roads. . . . After all, packing is the art of balancing packs and then seeing that they ride evenly—otherwise the animals will have saddle sores in a day or two and be out of business for all or most of the summer. . . . To take a pack string of nearly half a hundred across the Bitterroot Divide was to perform a masterpiece in that now almost lost art, and in 1919 I rode with Bill Bell and saw it done. . . . The unpacking was just as beautiful—one wet satin back after another without saddle or saddle sore, and not a spot of white wet flesh where hair and hide had been rubbed off. Perhaps one has to know something about keeping packs balanced on the backs of animals to think this beautiful, or to notice it at all, but to all who work come moments of beauty unseen by all the rest of the world. (128, 130, 131)

Maclean's comments on seeing artistry, grace, and beauty in well-done work perfectly capture John Dewey's contention that human activities, including end-of-task consummations, are the sort of generic traits of experience that warrant close inspection and deserve careful ethical and metaphysical analysis.

By midsummer, Maclean too can see beyond the unpleasant drudgery, the mundane, repetitive, and survival dimensions of labor, as he finds himself enjoying work and appreciating tools. Returning to the ranger station after his brief mountaintop exile as a fire lookout, he joins Bill at work:

> He wasn't building packs—he was just pulling things together at the end of the season. We didn't say much of anything to each other. . . . He was enjoying himself . . . [and] after a while we both got our minds on what we were doing and we both were enjoying ourselves. Maybe one of the chief reasons why you become a packer is that you like to handle groceries—and tools. By this time in the season . . . a lot of the tools have broken handles or need their points or edges sharpened, but that's all right. It's a good feeling to pick up an honest mattock that's lost its edge from chopping roots and rock while making a fire trench. (151)

Among other ways, the tools that are used define various work communities. The work groups most prized by Maclean are the ones that require hand-tool know-how. For the uninitiated reader, he provides precise descriptions and detailed explanations of all sorts of specialized tools and their uses; for example, he explicates the different kinds of tree- and pole-climbing spurs that are needed to string telephone wire between still-living and long-dead trees.[7]

By season's end, Maclean and his crew members have become adept with a variety of tools that they are able to use with efficiency and ease. Moreover, their work skills have won them both individual pride and group membership in, according to Bill, "a pretty damn good crew" (206): "Not one had ever seen the inside or outside of a school of forestry. But, as Bill said, we were a pretty good crew and did what we had to do and loved the woods without thinking we owned them, and each of us liked to do at least one thing especially well—liked to swing a jackhammer and feel the earth overpowered by dynamite, liked to fight, liked to heal the injuries of horses, liked to handle groceries and tools and tie knots. And nearly all of us liked to work. When you think about it, that's a lot to say about a bunch of men" (206).

The remainder of Maclean's story probes how the forest service crew fares in both crisis and crusade. The work-generated crew identity, won through the acquisition of individual skills that contribute to group success, also equips them to deal with emergencies and crises. Being able to calmly and competently handle stressful and dangerous situations further intensifies the group's sense of unity. For example, when outsiders are brought in to help fight fires, the insiders, "those of us who belonged to the regular crew" (141), assume supervisory roles. Since Bill Bell's crew understands fires and since they are equipped with the requisite tools and know-how—"both experience and gift" (142)—they become fire foremen. "For whatever reason, we had to spend as much time patrolling . . . [the] bums off the street . . . as we did [fighting] . . . the fire" (141).

Whether or not this group identity forged by work and tested in crises can be further elevated by a crusade—the quitting-time ritual of cleaning out the town—brings the story to its climax. The Maclean narrator, finishing his third summer in the forest service, knows that the dynamics of the group will progress through definite and predictable stages. First, group comradeship is forged by work; then group solidarity is tested by big fires; finally, a brotherhood bonds the crew as they leave the woods with their three months' wages: "Twice before I had gone through this autumn rite at quitting time. Twice before I had seen a catch-as-catch-can bunch of working stiffs transformed into blood brothers by the act of Cleaning Out the Town. Everybody got cleaned in this autumn rite of the early Forest Service—we cleaned up on the town and the town cleaned us out" (184). Maclean knows exactly what to anticipate: "At this time, I thought the Big Fire was no longer important, but before all this became a story I realized the Big Fire is the Summer Festival and Cleaning Out the Town is the way it all ends in the autumn. It's as simple as this—you never forget the guy who helped you fight the big fire or clean out the town" (184). Whatever Maclean's first two cleaning-out-the-town experiences were like, the expectation is that this go-around will go a step further. Though the crew had anticipated that their poker-game scheme would bring a deeper sense of group cohesion and prompt a higher sort of loyalty, the narrator (as will become evident) eventually realizes that the poker scheme brought only a bogus loyalty to a counterfeit community. Maclean's mock-heroic commentary says it best: "When the rite was completed, all of it thereafter could be *solemnized and capitalized*—the Crew, Quitting Time, and Cleaning Out the Town. Everything about us was bigger than before, except our cash" (184, emphasis added).

After the climactic rigged poker game, Bill breaks up the barroom brawl, dispatches the crooked cook, and reforms the crew:

> Bill rounded up his bunch and herded us out like sheep. . . . At the moment, in our hearts we felt indissoluble, although in our heads we knew that after tonight we might never see one another again. We were summer workers. We belonged to no union, no lodge, and most of us had no families and no church. In late spring, we had landed jobs in a new outfit called the United States Forest Service which we vaguely knew Teddy Roosevelt had helped get going and which somehow made us feel proud and tough and always looking for trouble of some sort, like fires, dynamite, and rattlesnakes on mountains too high to have any. Besides doing what we had to do, we did a few other things, like playing practical jokes and distilling dried apricots and having some troubles among ourselves. And at the end we banded together to clean out the town—*probably* something that also had to be done for us to become a crew. For most of us, this momentary social unit the crew was the only association we had ever belonged to, although somehow it must have been for more time than a moment. Here I am over a half a century later trying to tell you about it. (205, 206–7, emphasis added)

The next morning narrator Maclean reaffirms the validity of an identity based on work, honesty, and competence just as clearly as he realizes that group membership based on luck, dishonesty, and trickery is sham. (Note the word "probably" above.) Maclean's considered judgment, then, to use two of John Dewey's fundamental evaluative terms, finds the former to be genuine, and the latter spurious. Near the end of the story, the narrator Maclean talks to Bill, who is preparing to leave town for a winter of sheepherding.

> Bill asked, tossing the cinch to me under the horse, "What'r you going to do next summer?" Until I heard my answer tremble, I did not know how long I had been waiting for the question. "Nothing yet," I answered. "How would you like to work for me next summer?" he asked.
> I went looking for words like "privilege" and "honor" and ended up with, "It's a deal." (214)

"Honor" and "privilege" are fitting descriptions of his work-earned relationship with Bill—a genuine loyalty in Royce's scheme. At the other end of the spectrum, a specious fealty to the faux cause of cleaning out the town by cheating at poker is passed over without comment.[8] Earlier, however, Maclean had celebrated fighting the big fire as a "summer festival," just as he had cast ironic aspersions about cleaning out the town by branding the rite "solemnized" (184). While Maclean's *USFS 1919* vividly describes group-building dynamics along with differentiating worthy from predatory loyalties, Royce's philosophy of loyalty offers helpful structure and clarity about the processes of community building and the positive (and negative) energies that group identity releases.

Also as noted in chapter 16, Royce's investigations into community building begin with an examination of temporary gatherings like those of parade watchers and festival revelers and gradually move on to his investigations of more lasting and fulfilling communities. These genuine communities are bound together by a common memory and/or inspired by shared hopes for the future. By midsummer the forest service crew's work skills and big fire experience have provided the former, and they spend many hours anticipating the latter. Immediately after the cook reveals himself as a cardsharp: "With one movement he picked up the four hands, and we all started for bed. 'By the way,' Bill said as I went out the door, 'I have a scheme—I'll tell you about it tomorrow.' Before we went to sleep I had the scheme fairly well figured out" (154–55). Royce argues that beyond sharing a past and anticipating a future, the formation of a true community requires, in addition, a significant level of communication that can both eliminate isolation and generate a shared narrative of the meaning of the community's life and projects. Such communication enables individual members to act on behalf of each other. Each community member, so encouraged, begins to view his life and deeds as the life and deeds of the whole.

For Royce, then, members of a genuine community willingly transfer their allegiance to, concern for, and efforts on behalf of individuals into love and loyalty to the community itself. In the process, one's loyalty to individuals and to a cause is transformed into loyalty to loyalty. Of course, Royce's reflections on loyalty to loyalty involve community building far beyond Bill's "damn good" forest service summer crew's experiences. However, Royce's movement from a philosophy of loyalty to a theology of community accords well with the trajectory of Maclean's fiction. That is, Maclean's earlier narratives that explored the secular and pragmatic realities of work experience, work skills, and work friendships await the enriching experiences of family life and the consummation of the sacred that enliven *A River Runs Through It*.

Recall the memorable opening line of Maclean's best-known work: "In our family, there was no clear line between religion and fly fishing" (1); recall too the final words of his meditation on being his brother's keeper: "I am haunted by waters" (104). It is especially the waters in which his engaging, charismatic, yet deeply flawed brother Paul excelled as a fly caster that continue to haunt Maclean. Paul, as a first-class dry-fly specialist, had been one of the elite "fishermen who experience eternity compressed into a moment" (44). He had raised fly casting so far above the level of the skillful and artful that he had entered into the realm of the Graceful, and a sacred aura formed around him: "The mini-molecules of water left in the wake of his line made momentary loops of gossamer, disappearing so rapidly in the rising big-grained vapor that they had to be retained in memory to be visualized as loops. The spray emanating from him was finer-grained still and enclosed him in a halo of himself. The halo of himself was always there and always disappearing, as if he were candlelight flickering about three inches from himself" (20).

Interestingly, the later works of Royce, *The Hope of the Great Community* and *The Problem of Christianity,* and Maclean's third story, *A River Runs Through It,* both appeal to a religious community to ground personal identity. For both authors, family membership gives way to a religious community wherein group members receive and dispense grace. The sentences that follow the oft-noted opening line of *A River*—"In our family, there was no clear line between religion and fly fishing" (1)—explain how, in the Maclean narrator's family, fly-fishing leads to religion: "We lived at the junction of great trout rivers in western Montana, and our father was a Presbyterian minister and a fly fisherman who tied his own flies and taught others. He told us about Christ's disciples being fishermen, and we were left to assume, as my brother and I did, that all first-class fishermen on the Sea of Galilee were fly fishermen and that John, the favorite, was a dry-fly fisherman" (1). Note the careful ambiguity in the last clause of the first sentence, "and taught others"—taught them religion and/or fly-fishing? To further understand how, for Maclean, fly-fishing leads to grace, we need only recur to the above-noted Scholastic formula that grace builds on nature, noting that in Maclean's algorithm, grace completes nature by way of art: "My father was sure about certain matters pertaining to the universe. To him all good things—trout as well as eternal salvation—come by grace and grace comes by art and art does not come easy" (4).[9]

Why the troublesome, irresponsible, and immature Paul should be *graced* is a mystery; that he is favored, despite his faults, is not.[10] While Maclean's story grapples with why he did not or could not help his brother, it ends without a definitive resolution: "How can a question be answered that asks a lifetime of questions?" (103). Nonetheless, Norman Maclean's meditation on family and fly-fishing takes his readers with him to the point where "I sensed that ahead I would meet something that would never erode so there would be a sharp turn, deep circles, a deposit, and quietness" (63). Alternatively, Royce concludes that in a genuinely religious community, each of us can find his "own self writ large" (1913, 86). I suggest, then, that in Royce's "self writ large" and in Maclean's "deposit," philosophy and literature resonate, reinforce, and richly inform each other.

NOTES

This chapter is a slightly revised version of "Work, Friendship, and Community: Norman MacLean's *A River Runs through It and Other Stories* and Josiah Royce's *The Philosophy of Loyalty, Renascence* 53.4 (2001): 287–302.

1. Maclean's *A River Runs Through It and Other Stories* is the first and only work of original fiction published by the University of Chicago Press. The volume contains "Your Pal, Jim," a short story of about 7,000 words, a scant 19 pages in the edition; *USFS 1919,* a novella of about 34,000 words and 92 pages; and *A River Runs Through It,* a novella of about 38,000 words and 104 pages.

2. See Friedenberg (1992) for the screenplay adaptation as well as his interesting essay on the Maclean family, and also Redford's introduction (1992).

3. Especially helpful are the essays by Hesford (1980), Simonson (1982), and Weinberger (1997).

4. In his "Montana Memory: Talk to the Institute of the Rockies," Maclean explains that "the history in these stories [in *A River*], then, is a kind of history of hand craft, and the chief characters are experts with their hands—expert packers, expert sawyers and expert fishermen" (1977, 73).

Also in his brief autobiography, "Generations: First and Second," which originally appeared in the Studs Terkel–edited *American Dream: Lost and Found,* Maclean writes, "I was the first person in [my father's] family not to make his living with his hands. 'Maclean' means son of a carpenter. That's what my family had been. They were all carpenters. . . . He was a marvelous carpenter himself. He and I, way back in 1921, made this cabin out there that's still mine" (1980, 12)

5. Mead taught at the University of Chicago from 1894 to 1931, and Maclean from 1929 to 1973, so their tenures briefly overlapped.

6. Dewey taught at Chicago from 1884 to 1904, so Dewey was long gone before Maclean arrived at the university. Still, Dewey's influence upon his philosophy colleague George Herbert Mead and his teaming up with Jane Addams at Hull House ensured that Dewey's impact upon the intellectual climate of the University of Chicago lasted well beyond his twenty years on the faculty.

7. Also recall, for example, in "Your Pal, Jim," Maclean's detailed explanations

about when and how each sawyer handles the wedge and where it has to be inserted to keep a crosscut saw from binding. In *A River Runs Through It,* the numerous technical descriptions of different sorts of fly casts needed to succeed in varying wind and water conditions are discussed.

8. An apparent difficulty with a sharp separation between a bogus loyalty to Bill's scheme and a genuine loyalty to the work-constituted group is Bill's complexity in the former. However, when Maclean's account of the scheme is carefully examined, it is clear that there always had been two schemes: the rigged poker game and "cleaning out the town." The second, also repeatedly described as "looking for trouble" (183), was to be accomplished through fistfights, which would assert the group's dominance. The narrator notes that as he tries to grab the poker pot, "All of a sudden things fell apart. I say 'all of a sudden,' but for a long time I had only been pretending not to know that I was going to take a hell of a beating when I reached across the table to pick up the money. I always suspected that Bill was looking for trouble more than for the money. . . . I had not fully realized how I was doomed until I had seen that the oldest men on the crew, Mr. Smith and Mr. McBride, were counting on a fight just as much as Bill was and, independently, had worked out an almost identical plan" (183). Maclean's deft treatment of both elements of the scheme, and his stress upon Bill's real interest in cleaning out the town by way of fistfights (and not cardsharping), means that the Maclean narrator's loyalty to Bill's work crew is well founded and deserves to be called genuine. (I thank Ed Block for raising this issue to me.)

9. Stegner expertly glosses Maclean's formula: "But fishing with a dry fly, which is the skill that gives both meaning and form to 'A River Runs Through It,' is not labor but an art, not an occupation but a passion, not a mere skill but a mystery, a symbolic reflection of life" (1988, 157).

10. Though beyond the scope of my analysis here, as far as I could discover, no one had explored the parable of the Prodigal Son (Luke 15:11–32) as an exemplar for Paul, in particular his position as the younger son, and his father's (and mother's) willingness to look beyond his dissolute and dangerous lifestyle, so I did. See my "The Prodigal Son Parable and Maclean's *A River Runs Through It.*"

WORKS CITED

Dooley, Patrick K. 2005. "The Prodigal Son Parable and Maclean's *A River Runs Through It.*" *Renascence* 58:165–75.

Friedenberg, Richard. 1992. *"A River Runs Through It": Bringing a Classic to the Screen.* Livingston, MT: Clark City Press.

Hesford, Walter. 1980. "Fishing for the Words of Life: Norman Maclean's 'A River Runs Through It.'" *Rocky Mountain Review* 34:34–45.

Maclean, Norman. 1976. *A River Runs Through It and Other Stories.* Chicago: University of Chicago Press.

————. 1980. "Generations: First and Second." In *American Dreams: Lost and Found,* edited by Studs Terkel, 112–14. New York: Pantheon Books. Reprinted in McFarland and Nichols, *Norman Maclean,* 11–13.

————. 1977. "Montana Memory: Talk at the Institute of the Rockies." In McFarland and Nichols, *Norman Maclean,* 68–74.

McFarland, Ron, and Hugh Nichols, eds. 1988. *Norman Maclean.* Lewiston, ID: Confluence Press.

Redford, Robert. 1992. Introduction to Friedenberg, *A River Runs Through It,* 1–2.

Royce, Josiah. 1886. *California: A Study of American Character.* Boston: Houghton Mifflin.

————. 1908. *The Philosophy of Loyalty.* Nashville, TN: Vanderbilt University Press, 1995.

————. 1913. *The Problems of Christianity.* New York: Macmillan.

————. 1916. *The Hope of the Great Community.* New York: Books for Library Press, 1967.

Simonson, Harold. P. 1982. "Norman Maclean's Two-Hearted River." *Western American Literature* 17:149–55.

Stegner, Wallace. 1988. "Haunted by Waters." In McFarland and Nichols, *Norman Maclean,* 153–60.

Weinberger, Theodore. 1997. "Religion and Fly Fishing: Taking Norman Maclean Seriously." *Renascence* 49:281–89.

Appendix

Suggestions for Further Reading and
American Philosophy Critical Edition Projects

A good place to begin reading about pragmatism is a short survey article by Louis Menand, "The Return of Pragmatism" (*American Heritage,* October 1997, 48–63). Beyond the big three (Peirce, James, and Dewey) and Rorty, Menand has a nice section on the impact of pragmatism on the jurist Oliver Wendell Holmes. Menand's longer study, *The Metaphysical Club: A Story of Ideas in America,* (New York: Farrar, Straus and Giroux, 2001) has been well received by general readers, though some philosophers have been critical: see, for example Bruce Wilshire's "But Where Are the Metaphysics?" (*Times Literary Supplement,* July 26, 2002, 28–29.) The five good book-length resources on American philosophy (pragmatic and other) are *American Philosophy,* edited by Marcus Singer (Cambridge: Cambridge University Press, 1985), *Classical American Philosophy: Essential Readings and Interpretative Essays,* edited by John Stuhr, 2nd edition (New York: Oxford University Press, 2002), *Classical American Pragmatism: Philosophy: Its Contemporary Vitality,* edited by Sandra Rosenthal, Carl Hausman, and Douglas Anderson (Champaign: University of Illinois Press, 1999), *Classical American Philosophy,* edited by Max Fish (New York: Appleton-Century Crofts, 1951), and John McDermott's *Streams of Experience: Reflections on the History and Philosophy of American Culture* (Amherst: University of Massachusetts Press, 1986). Singer's volume contains four articles on general issues and eleven others devoted to individual thinkers. Stuhr recruited experts to write introductory essays on Peirce, James, Royce, Santayana, Dewey, and Mead and then had each of them select fairly lengthy excerpts from the major works of his or her author. Both Singer and Stuhr offer helpful bibliographies. Concentrating on the classical period of American philosophy, each essay in the Stuhr volume concludes with a generous "Suggestions for Further Reading" bibliography that lists "anthologies" and "essential works" on and by each author. The

Rosenthal volume offers four valuable essays on each of four figures: Peirce, James, Dewey, and Mead. Each thinker is examined for his position on "the centrality of practice," "the significance of social life," "quality, value, and normative conditions," and "creativity, experience and the world." The Fish volume, a mainstay since the early 1950s, now reissued with a preface by Nathan Houser (New York: Fordham University Press, 1996), contains ample selections from not only Peirce, James, Dewey, and Royce, but also Whitehead and Santayana. Valuable introductory essays are provided on all six authors. Finally, McDermott's volume offers fourteen essays that situate the classical American thinkers in their historical and cultural context.

Definitive, critical editions of the works of the classical American philosophers are complete, ongoing, or in the planning stages:

C. S. Peirce (1839–1914): Though only a couple dozen of Peirce's essays were published during his lifetime, he wrote continuously and voluminously "to erect a philosophical edifice that shall outlast the vicissitudes of time" (1887, 1). Between 1935 and 1958, first Charles Hartshorne and Paul Weiss and then Arthur Burks selected, arranged, and published *The Collected Papers of Charles Sanders Peirce* in eight volumes (Cambridge: Harvard University Press). The relative incompleteness and topical arrangement of the Harvard edition made it difficult for scholars to explore the patterns of development in Peirce's thought. Accordingly, in 1976 the Peirce Edition Project was begun at Indiana University. This comprehensive and critical edition, *Writings of Charles S. Peirce: A Chronological Edition,* edited first by Edward C. Moore, then Christian Kloesel and, since 2000, by Nathan Houser (Bloomington: Indiana University Press) brought out the first volume, which covered Peirce's writings from 1857 to 1866, in 1982. Thus far, five more volumes carrying the edition to 1890 have appeared; three more volumes are scheduled for 2007–2008; in all, thirty volumes are projected.

William James (1842–1909): Between 1975 and 1988 a nineteen-volume definitive, critical edition, *The Work of William James,* was edited by Frederick Burkhardt, Fredson Bowers, and Ignas Skrupskelis (Cambridge: Harvard University Press). The introductions to these volumes are an invaluable resource. In addition, the publication of *The Correspondence of William James,* edited by Ignas Skrupskelis and Elizabeth Berkeley (Charlottesville: University Press of Virgina), is now complete. The first three volumes, which contain the correspondence between Henry and William, appeared between 1992 and 1994. Since then, nine additional volumes covering William's correspondence from 1856 to 1910 have been published.

Josiah Royce (1855–1916): A group of Royce scholars is at work securing funding and textual experts to launch a critical edition. In the meantime, Royce's most popular book, *The Philosophy of Loyalty* (1908) has been reissued in paperback (Vanderbilt: Vanderbilt University Press, 1996). Most of Royce's important essays are available in *The Basic Writings of Josiah Royce*, (two volumes) edited by John McDermott (Chicago: University of Chicago Press, 1969).

John Dewey (1859–1952): The standard reference to Dewey's works is to the critical edition, *The Collected Works of John Dewey, 1882–1953*, edited by Jo Ann Boydston and published as *The Early Works: 1882–1898* (five volumes), *The Middle Works: 1899–1924* (fifteen volumes), and *The Later Works: 1925–1953* (seventeen volumes) (Carbondale: Southern Illinois University Press).

George Herbert Mead (1863–1931): Mead was not a prolific writer; indeed, none of his works appeared in book form during his lifetime. His most influential work, *Mind, Self and Society: From the Standpoint of a Social Behaviorist*, edited by Charles W. Morris (Chicago: University of Chicago Press) appeared in 1934 shortly after his death. Another standard resource is *The Individual and the Social Self: Unpublished Works of George Herbert Mead*, edited David L. Miller (Chicago: University of Chicago Press, 1982).

George Santayana (1863–1952): Santayana was a philosopher, cultural critic, poet, and novelist. The ambitious Santayana Edition, housed at Indiana University—Purdue University–Indianapolis is well under way. The critical edition volumes are published by MIT Press; so far four of Santayana's books, including his best known works, *The Sense of Beauty* and *The Last Puritan*, along with eight volumes containing more than three thousand letters he wrote to over 365 recipients, have appeared. Work on his influential *The Life of Reason* (in five books) continues apace.

WORKS CITED

Peirce, C. S. 1887. "A Guess at a Riddle," *The Collected Papers of Charles Sanders Peirce,* Edited by Charles Hartshorne and Paul Wiess. Cambridge: Harvard University Press. 1935:1–14.

Index